SECRETS OF
POWER
PERSUASION

ALSO BY ROGER DAWSON

Books

> *You Can Get Anything You Want—*
>   *The Secrets of Power Negotiation*
> *Confident Decision Making*

Audio Cassette Programs

> *Secrets of Power Persuasion*
> *Secrets of Power Negotiating*
> *Secrets of Power Performance*
> *Confident Decision Making*

Video Training Programs

> *Guide to Everyday Negotiating*
> *Guide to Business Negotiating*

SECRETS OF POWER PERSUASION

Roger Dawson

PRENTICE HALL
Englewood Cliffs, New Jersey 07632

Prentice-Hall International, Inc., *London*
Prentice-Hall of Australia, Pty. Ltd., *Sydney*
Prentice-Hall of Canada, Inc., *Toronto*
Prentice-Hall Hispanoamericana, S.A., *Mexico*
Prentice-Hall of India Private Ltd., *New Dehli*
Prentice-Hall of Japan, Inc. *Tokyo*
Prentice-Hall of Southeast Asia Pte., Ltd., *Singapore*
Editora Prentice-Hall do Brasil Ltda., *Rio de Janeiro*

10 9 8 7 6 5 4 3 2

Library of Congress Catatoging-in-Publication Data

Dawson, Roger.
    Secrets of power persuasion : everthing you'll ever need to get anything you'll
ever want / by Roger Dawson.
        p. cm.
    Includes index.
    ISBN 0-13-799354-4 -- ISBN 0-13-799362-5 (pbk.)
    1. Selling. 2. Persuasion (Psychology) 3. Influence (Psychology)
I. Title
HF5438.25D393   1992
658.85--dc20
                                                                    92-16777
                                                                    CIP

ISBN 0-13-799354-4

ISBN 0-13-799362-5 (PBK)

PRENTICE HALL
Professional Publishing
Englewood Cliffs, NJ 07632
Simon & Schuster. A Paramount Communications Company

PRINTED IN THE UNITED STATES OF AMERICA

■

DEDICATION

To my three children: Julia, Dwight, and John.
Sure, you made it all necessary, but you also made it all worthwhile.
And to Goody: you were always on my mind.

ABOUT THE AUTHOR

Roger Dawson was born in England, emigrated to California in 1962, and became a U.S. citizen in 1974. Formerly the president of one of California's largest real estate companies, he became a full-time author and professional speaker in 1982.

His Nightingale-Conant cassette program *Secrets of Power Negotiating* is the largest-selling business cassette program ever published.

Companies throughout North America call on him for his expertise in negotiation and persuasion. His seminar company Roger Dawson Productions, P.O. Box 3326, La Habra, California 90632 (Tel 800 YDAWSON) conducts seminars on Power Negotiating, Power Persuasion, and Confident Decision Making throughout the world.

He lives in La Habra Heights, California.

■

CONTENTS

■ **CHAPTER TWO**
FIFTEEN MAGIC KEYS THAT MAKE PEOPLE BELIEVE YOU 15

■ **CHAPTER THREE**
HOW TO MAKE THEM WANT TO DIE FOR YOU 38

■ **CHAPTER FOUR**
HOW SCARCITY DRIVES PEOPLE WILD **56**

Even smart people can fall for the scarcity yo-yo.

Scarcity drives value and prices sky high.

My aunt had one of those but she threw it away!

Using scarcity to get real estate bargains.

■ **CHAPTER FIVE**
BRINGING THEM TO THEIR KNEES WITH TIME PRESSURE **61**

The faster you can persuade the other person to decide, the
 more likely you are to get what you want.

The longer you give them to think about it, the less chance
 you have of getting what you want.

How children use time pressure like a pro.

Moving people with the power of time pressure.

Secrets from inside a time share closing room.

■ **CHAPTER SIX**
THE ZEN-LIKE ART OF SHARING SECRETS **68**

The magical three-step formula for getting cooperation from
 the other person.

Why forbidding aggravates family problems.

Why censored information seems more valuable.

■ **CHAPTER SEVEN**
THE POWER OF ASSOCIATION: TYING YOUR PERSUASION
TO SOMETHING GOOD **73**

It's hard for our mind to break associations.

Utilizing the value of celebrity spokespeople.

How to get people to react more favorably to a proposal.

Pacing the mention of your product or service to the high
 points of a business lunch.

Painting pictures that tie your product to pleasurable
 experiences.

■ **CHAPTER EIGHT**
THE POWER OF CONSISTENCY: IT'S MORE IMPORTANT
TO DO IT OFTEN THAN TO DO IT RIGHT   78

Using the power of consistency.
Why it's better to be a tyrant than a wimp.
Why we're suspicious of inconsistent behavior.
Using consistency to move the merchandise.
Why Carter's downfall was Reagan's windfall.

■ **CHAPTER NINE**
WHY CONSISTENT BEHAVIOR KICKS YOUR
PERFORMANCE INTO HIGH GEAR   86

The personal value blueprint.
Life is sweeter with a value blueprint.
Trying to live with the golden rule.
Straight up. It's a way to climb a mountain, a way to pour a
    drink, and a really fine way to live a life.

■ **CHAPTER TEN**
BONDING—THE MAGIC KEY TO PERSUASION   91

How to sell up a storm using the principle of bonding.
How people bond to their mental investments.
Experimenting with bonding in your personal life.
How interrogators use the power of commitment.
The essay contest phenomenon.
Making commitments to yourself.

■ **CHAPTER ELEVEN**
PERSUASIVE SPEECHES   100

Knowing what caused your audience to be there.
Knowing whether to put your strongest argument at the
    beginning or at the end.
If several speakers will present, knowing whether to go first
    or last.

How to pose the question when asking the audience to vote.

A simple and effective way to get the audience on your side.

Knowing whether to use emotion or logic to persuade.

Improving your ability to persuade an audience.

Using constructive distractions to improve your ability to persuade.

Using of humor as a persuader.

When to present both sides of the argument, or only one.

Avoiding the overstatement trap.

The art of getting the most effective introduction.

The number one thing you can do to persuade from the platform.

■ **CHAPTER TWELVE**
EIGHT VERBAL PERSUASION PLOYS TO CONTROL THE OTHER PERSON

Diffusion.

Yes, I take it personally.

Being Nixonesque.

"I'm not offended."

"Easy to deny."

"I'm not suggesting."

Give the other person options.

"Why would you want to do that?"

■ **CHAPTER THIRTEEN**
EXPOSING AND DESTROYING THEIR NEGATIVE EMOTIONS

Suspicion—they don't appear to trust you.

Anger—they're upset with something that happened.

Greed—you appear vulnerable, and they want to take advantage of it .

Hurt—they're upset and want revenge.

■ **CHAPTER SEVENTEEN**
WHAT MOTIVATES THE OTHER PERSON

Possibility versus necessity.
Self-centered versus externally centered.
Moving toward pleasure, or away from pain.
Field dependent or field independent.

■ **CHAPTER EIGHTEEN**
HOW THE OTHER PERSON DECIDES

Assertive versus unassertive.
Emotional versus unemotional.
Open or close minded.
Conscious or unconscious thought processors.
Visuals, auditories, and kinestetics.

■ **PART THREE**
HOW TO BECOME A POWER PERSUADER

■ **CHAPTER NINETEEN**
DEVELOPING CHARISMA: HOW TO MAKE THEM
LOVE YOU!

A very special quality.
Charisma—the nonverbal persuasion power.
Auras in darkest Africa.
To understand charisma, imagine the opposite.

■ **CHAPTER TWENTY**
TWELVE WAYS TO PROJECT AN AWESOME CHARISMA

Treating everyone you meet as if they're the most important
  person you'll meet that day.
Developing a sensational handshake.
Noticing the color of their eyes as you shake hands.

The key to remembering faces.

An exercise in memory discipline.

How important is it to remember names?

Using the other person's name at the beginning or the end of a sentence.

Making your request.

Tilt your head and smile as you say it.

Why the magic formula works.

How to use the formula.

Stage 1—Establishing objectives.

Case study one: the unhappy employee.

Case study two: the problem teenager.

Case study three: the alcoholic husband.

Stage 2—Finding out what they want.

Stage 3—Identifying the pressure points.

Stage 4—Looking for compromise.

Are you the target?

A magic expression.

Restating the objection.

That hasn't been my experience.

Handling the showman.

■ INTRODUCTION

WHAT THIS BOOK CAN DO FOR YOU

Do you know someone who has an incredible ability to influence people? A power persuader?

Perhaps you work in a corporation, and there's this guy down the hall who doesn't seem to have any of the problems you have. He never has to cajole people into working overtime—all his people seem happy to do it for him. He doesn't have to threaten to fire the people in his department to get them to get to work on time. What's more, he doesn't spend half the time you do preparing proposals for the president of your company. He breezes into company meetings, shoots from the hip, and always seems to get what he wants.

Perhaps you're an area sales manager, and you're in a competitive, price-conscious industry. You sweat buckets getting a new account to open up for you. However, the person who works the territory in the next state ever seems to have that kind of trouble. At every sales meeting he's up there getting an award for the most new accounts. To rub salt into the wound, you bet he doesn't work half as hard as you do.

Or perhaps you are a parent, and keeping tabs on three young kids is about as much as you can handle. You love 'em, but they're driving you up the wall. They never come home when they promised to, and they won't clean up their rooms unless you threaten to dump everything in the garbage. You actually had to do that once to convince them you were serious. It wouldn't be so frustrating if other parents had the same problems—but they don't seem to. Take the woman down the street.

You were there once when her children got home from school. They were so polite. They went straight to their rooms, which looked like a page out of *Better Homes and Gardens*, for heaven's sake. They wanted to go out to play, but their mother quietly said, "No, you must finish your homework first." And, miracle of miracles, they didn't even argue!

What do these people know that you don't?

That's what this book is all about. Because, like it or not, we all live in a world where we need to be good persuaders. We need to know how to get other people to see it our way—without threats, without bribes, and without manipulation.

■ THERE'S A DIFFERENCE BETWEEN NEGOTIATION AND PERSUASION

If you've read my book *You Can Get Anything You Want—The Secrets of Power Negotiating*, you may be saying "OK, Roger, so you know about negotiating—but what's the difference between negotiating and persuasion. Where does one end and the other begin?"

The two are very close, and the skills in each area will apply to the other, but for the purpose of this book, let's make this distinction.

Negotiating involves reaching an agreement on price, or on the specific terms of an agreement. We negotiate the price of an automobile, or we negotiate an increase in pay. There's very clearly a monetary amount involved. But we also negotiate when there is no money involved. For example, we negotiate the terms of a nuclear arms cutback agreement, or we negotiate to get a kidnapper to release a hostage. In those instances, no money is involved, but there is a give and take in the specifics of the agreement.

Persuasion, on the other hand, is the art of getting people to go along with your point of view, to see it your way. Of course, you need negotiating skills to be a good persuader, and you need persuasion skills to be a good negotiator, but this definition will give us a blueprint for what we're going to talk about here.

So that's what I'll teach you in this book—the skills to get people to see things your way.

We're doing this all the time, aren't we? Anytime we interact with another human being, there's an element of persuasion. Not only in our business lives, where we may be very aware we're using persuasion skills, but also in our social and personal lives, where the application of the skills may be much more subtle.

■ FORCE WON'T WORK ANYMORE, SO HANG IT UP!

First, let's accept that force is no longer an effective persuasion tool. If you long for the "good old days" when you could count on employees always to show up to work and always put in a long, hard day because they were scared of getting fired, forget it.

Do you yearn for a world where you could count on everyone doing exactly what they said they were going to do? When your car always got fixed on time, and you never had to wait in anyone's office because people always kept their word on appointments? A world in which your customers never dreamed of going to your competition? Where nobody ever shopped a bid? If that's what you're waiting for, hang it up!

Let's face it, the world has changed. The days are over when you could say "jump" to employees and expect them to ask, "How high?" The world where we could take a product into the marketplace and name our price, because there wasn't any credible competition, will never be seen again. The world in which our children would willingly do the chores before heading off for school exists only in Norman Rockwell paintings.

We can't solve problems with force any more. It just won't work. It won't work in corporations, it won't work in selling, and it won't work with our family and friends. We must learn to solve our problems by sitting down with the other person and persuading him or her to our point of view.

■ THE DYNAMITE STUFF YOU'LL LEARN IN THIS BOOK

The ability to persuade, comes from a combination of skills, and I'll cover all of them in this book.

The first skill is the ability to use psychological pressure points that cause one person to be influenced by another. There are always underlying factors that affect the way people are going to react to you. When we know about these hidden persuaders, and have learned to use them, we not only become better persuaders, but we know how to protect ourselves when people use these factors against us.

Then I'll teach you about credibility. Nobody will be persuaded by you unless he or she believes you. Some people are as sincere as they can be and yet have trouble getting people to trust them. Others are outrageous con artists who should never be believed and yet always seem able to persuade. I'll show you why—and how you can build your credibility.

Next I'll teach you the subliminal factors that cause one person to be persuaded by another. You'll be fascinated when you read them, and you'll probably realize that all your life you've been persuaded by them, without perceiving what was going on.

Then I'll teach you specific verbal techniques that can be used to persuade. You'll learn a series of techniques that you can use word for word that will get the other person to see it your way. You'll develop the ability to say what you want to say in such a manner that it has irresistible appeal to other people.

The next skill is to learn and use the personal characteristics that cause the other person to want to be influenced by us. I'm sure you've had the experience of meeting a truly charismatic person, someone who has an uncanny ability to draw people to him or her. I used to envy people like that because I assumed they were born with this magical gift. It was something they had and I didn't. Then I figured out that there really wasn't any magic involved—they were really using learned people skills. I'll teach you some specific ways to improve your charisma and to develop the two key skills that charismatic people find so essential: the ability to remember names and faces and the development of a sense of humor.

Next I'll teach you the four stages of persuasion and how to follow them to get what you want. Although persuasive people may seem to be winging it, and getting their point across with sheer personal charm and ingenuity, they're really working to a strict formula for success.

Then I'll talk about what to do when things go wrong. How to persuade the difficult person. I'll teach you how to deal with the person who's so angry with you, he or she can't see straight, and also that perennial persuasion challenge—the clam. The person who just won't open up and talk to you.

Finally, we'll talk about leadership and the Power Persuader. Wouldn't it be grand, just once before we die, to lead a great nation into battle as did Eisenhower and Churchill? Or to save a company from the brink of extinction as Lee Iacocca did with Chrysler? I'll show you just how great leaders like this use Power Persuasion to get people to want to die for them.

The power of persuasion! How much it means to success and happiness in our lives. And I can teach it to you. Really! If you'll stay with me, I promise you that by the time you lay down this book, you'll have acquired a new power that's so important to you, you'll wonder how you ever got along without it!

The book is divided into four parts:

In Part One you'll learn how to play the persuasion game—what to say, what to do.

In Part Two you'll learn how to analyze the other person—how to reach inside his or her mind and know exactly what will turn him or her on.

In Part Three you'll learn to develop the characteristics of a Power Persuader—an irresistible charisma, a dynamite sense of humor, and an uncanny ability to remember names—the things that will make the other person putty in your hands!

In Part Four you'll learn some magical persuasion techniques—how to move the persuasion through four distinct stages, how to deal with impossible people, and how to use your new persuasion skills to become a dynamic leader of people.

I promise you that by the time you finish this book, you'll have everything you'll ever need, to get anything you'll ever want!

Roger Dawson
La Habra Heights, California

■ PART ONE

HOW TO PLAY THE PERSUASION GAME

Anytime we do anything, it's because someone played the persuasion game with us. Now that sounds like an overstatement, doesn't it? But it's true. Anytime we're doing anything, it's because somebody persuaded us to do it. We get up in the morning because our parents persuaded us, at an early age, that it was the thing to do. We live where we live because somebody persuaded us to buy or rent a home there. As we move through our day, we abide by the laws of the land because we were persuaded to do so. We don't lie, cheat, or steal because somebody persuaded us to adopt a set of moral and ethical standards.

We're surrounded by things people persuaded us to buy. The ability to persuade is the complex web upon which our whole world is suspended. Since our entire world is composed of the results of our ability to persuade others, or their ability to persuade us, doesn't it make sense that we take the time to learn how to play the persuasion game?

In the first part of this book, I'll teach you how to play the persuasion game.

1

■ CHAPTER ONE

EIGHT MAGIC KEYS THAT CONTROL PEOPLE

We spend the first few moments of our life hanging stark naked in a room full of strangers with a doctor in a mask and cloth bootees paddling our backside.

The battle lines are drawn! We will either spend our life being influenced like this, or we'll get control of our world by learning how to influence other people.

Let's lay the foundation for Power Persuasion by looking at what influences people. There are underlying forces at work in our life that cause us to control other people or be controlled by them. Although we spend our lives controlling or being controlled, very few of us have ever stopped to identify those underlying forces. What are the magic keys to persuading the other person?

MAGIC CONTROL KEY NUMBER ONE
People can be persuaded if they think you can reward them.

The first control key is obvious. People can be persuaded to do something if they feel they'll be rewarded. You can even get children to eat lima beans if you promise them ice cream afterward!

Your young son strikes a deal with his mother that he'll go to bed if she lets him first watch half an hour of television. One of your salespeople works extra hard to win a trip to Puerto Rico. You can persuade one of your regional managers to accept a transfer to a problem region if you can convince her it would put her in line for a vice presidency.

At an international level, we saw President Assad moving Syria away from Soviet influence and aligning with the United States, because the rewards for his country were clear, or East Germans risking their lives to break away from the Soviet Bloc because they saw the rewards of reunification with West Germany.

So reward power is always present in any persuasion situation. Do you realize that four people out of five spend most of their waking lives doing something they don't want to do, simply because reward power is working on them! Now here's a pathetic statistic! Surveys show that 80 percent of people in this country would quit their jobs if they weren't paid. Isn't that sad?

Reward power is the fastest way to persuade.
It's also the most expensive way, and the law of diminishing returns quickly takes over.

Sure you can persuade people by offering to reward them. That's simple enough, isn't it? So why don't we quit worrying about persuasion skills and just bribe people to do what we want them to do. The problem is that it's the most expensive way of getting anything done. Also, the law of diminishing returns quickly takes over. Every time you reward someone, the value of the reward diminishes. You have to keep increasing the amount of the reward to get the same effect.

We can get things done a lot cheaper with persuasion skills. And have a lot more fun, too.

Superstar salespeople never take the approach that customers reward them by giving them an order. Their attitude is always that they are rewarding their customers, when they're willing to serve them. Now you have to be careful how you get this across. It can't be done with arrogance. "Hey, buddy, if you don't buy from me, it's your loss, not mine," just doesn't cut it. Nor does it mean that you fail to show appreciation for the business. However, the top people in every profession have learned the art of projecting that they're so good at what they do, the customer or client is being rewarded, not them.

I once spoke at a convention where Wayne Dyer, the author of *Erroneous Zones* and *You'll See It When You Believe It*, was also on the program. At dinner the program chairman was bragging about how he'd been able to persuade Wayne to come and speak at the program, even though initially he didn't want to do it. Isn't that amazing? There are three thousand speakers out there who are frantically trying to sell their services, and here's a meeting planner bragging about how he could get Wayne Dyer. Wayne is so incredibly good on the platform that people compete to get him.

That's how Tom Watson positioned IBM—as so good at what it did that the company was rewarding anybody who was smart enough to do business with IBM. During the 1930s and 1940s IBM almost monopolized the business machine industry worldwide.

Top attorneys can also position themselves like this—to the point where people see them as being so good at what they do that the attorney is rewarding the client by being willing to represent them. After only eight months of marriage to heavyweight boxing champion Mike Tyson, Robin Givens headed out to California to hire a divorce attorney. She probably wasn't thinking that she would be rewarding Marvin Mitchelson by giving him the case. No! She was probably thinking, "If I can get Marvin Mitchelson to represent me, that would be terrific! He's the best in the business."

In many respects, reward power is subjective, not objective. It's in the mind. A great example of that was Nelson Mandela. He was in jail for twenty-seven years, and he had the nerve to negotiate the terms of his release with the President F. W. de Klerk of South Africa! But I can even top that story! One day I went to have lunch with my parents at the retirement home where they lived. They weren't in the dining room at noon, so I went up to their apartment. Mom was sitting there in her wheelchair. Since her cancer operation when she was 85, she needs Dad to push her around. "Where's Dad?" I asked her.

"We've separated," she told me.

"Excuse me," I said, "what do you mean you've separated? You've been married for sixty-four years. You need Dad to push you down to meals. How can you separate now?"

She told me, "He said some things I didn't like, so I told him it was best if we separated." I took her down to lunch, while Dad was out somewhere blowing off steam. Two hours later, he was back, full of apologies, and as loving as ever. As I said, power is subjective, not objective. Power is in the mind—it's not a real thing.

How does that apply to your business? If your salespeople think your customers are rewarding them by giving them the order, they're probably communicating just that.

How does the salesperson move away from that? In two ways.

The first is by understanding that selling is a numbers game, that if she's out there prospecting for business as hard as she should be, there always will be a high percentage of people who will turn her down. There's no reason to feel personal rejection because they don't all buy.

The numbers philosophy can be helpful in other areas too. I once watched an employee get a royal chewing out from his boss, and it didn't seem to bother him at all, which surprised me. "Roger," he told me, "I've worked here for twenty-six years—for a dozen different bosses. I've seen them come, and I've seen them go. Some of them liked me, and some of them didn't. What's there to get upset about?" How's that for common sense ?

The second way the salesperson changes his perception that the customer is rewarding him by placing an order is to move away from what the product will do for the customer and toward what he'll do for the customer. Joe Girard, the world's top car salesperson, says "They don't buy Chevrolets. They buy me."

The more you can convince the customer how hard you're going to work for him or her, the less the customer can project that he or she is rewarding the salesperson by giving the person the order.

MAGIC CONTROL KEY NUMBER TWO
People can be persuaded if they think you can punish them.

The next control is punishment power, which is so very powerful, because it triggers the most primal of instincts, fear.

We're in sales and we're persuaded to give that big account what they want, because we fear losing the account. That's an obvious emotional reaction, but what's really going on? Are we really so afraid of losing that account? Not really. What's really going on is that our mind is racing ahead. Faster than the speed of light, our mind races through a sequence of compounding tragedies. If I lose the account I might get fired and be unable to find another job. If I can't find another job, I'll lose my house. I won't have money for food, so I might starve to death. And the fear of dying is a primal fear.

Abraham Maslow's *pyramid of human needs* clearly shows us that the fear of dying is the most powerful persuasion force. As human beings, we must survive. It's our most basic urge; we'll do almost anything to survive.

Fear is without question the most intense persuasion factor. If someone is holding a gun to your head, you suddenly feel a strong desire to give him your wallet. Or at least you readily perceive that it's in your best interests to do so.

An interesting dimension is added, when the fear of dying is removed. The Christians in the coliseum were not afraid of dying, so the threat of feeding them to the lions wasn't an effective enough motivator for them to renounce their faith. In the Iraq/Iran war, the Iraqis found the fundamentalism Moslem Iranians didn't fear death, they welcomed it. They saw dying as a martyr in the war as a rare privilege. Later, when we went to war with Iraq, we found out that they didn't share this fundamentalism belief with their Moslem brothers. They surrendered by the thousands rather than face death.

However, you don't have to be threatened with death to be motivated by fear. Many of our fears are far more subtle. The fear of embarrassment is a very powerful motivating force. The great actor Sir Laurence Olivier lived his life terrified of stage fright. Even after decades of performing in front of audiences, he insisted on a friend standing in the wings, where he could see him from the corner of his eye. If stage fright overcame him, he knew that the friendly face of his friend would distract him enough to pull him through.

Glenda Jackson: "The important thing in acting is to be able to laugh and cry. If I have to cry, I think of my sex life. If I have to laugh, I think of my sex life."

The fear of ridicule can stop us from accomplishing many of the things we'd like to accomplish with our lives. Many years ago, when I was learning to ski, I was skiing at Mammoth Mountain in California with friends who skied much better than I. They said, "Roger, we're going to take you up to the cornice today."

I said, "I don't think I'm ready for the cornice yet."

And they said, "Oh, come on, Roger, you can make it. Let's go."

So we rode the gondola up to the top of the mountain, which is about 12,000 feet above sea level. I can still feel the tension in that tiny gondola as we drifted silently up the snow-covered face of this almost vertical cliff. It's such a daunting run that not even the most experienced skiers talk as they approach the top. They sit there in silence, deep in their private thoughts, forcing themselves to overcome the fear of what lies ahead. Finally, we slid into the terminal and stepped outside, into the icy wind. I nervously put on my skis, and skied down a few hundred yards with my friends, until we were standing at the top of the cornice. A cornice is an overhang of snow blown over the corner of the cliff by the wind. The skiers had cut a V shape through this cornice, out onto the cliff. I would have to shoot down this V shape chute, on to the face of the cliff, which is almost vertical. If I made just one slip, I'd go down the next fifteen hundred feet on my head.

Spanish proverb: "If I die, I forgive you; if I live, we'll see."

I stood there, looking down through this chute, and as I saw it, I had two options. Option number one was to hike back up to the gondola and ride down. But, if I did that, my friends would laugh at me. Option number two was to die! I chose to die rather than be ridiculed. That's how strong that type of fear of punishment can be!

Recently, I skied the cornice again with my children, and now they have a sign at the top that says, "When your friends say go—don't be afraid to say no!"

The fear of failure causes a salesperson to give away things that may not be necessary to get the sale. All across the country, every day, this is costing corporations billions of dollars of bottom-line profits.

The fear of loneliness causes many people to stay in failing relationships long after true love and affection have gone. The same fear of loneliness causes parents to spoil their children. I know a man who still supports his 30-year-old son. The son would be much better off if the father had cut him off years ago, but the father is afraid to do that—because he's afraid of being lonely without the son around. Isn't that sad?

Because of the negative aspects, fear is not a very good motivator, but there's no denying what a powerful persuasion force it is.

MAGIC CONTROL KEY NUMBER THREE
Apply the dual pressures of reward and punishment.

Let's look at how Power Persuaders make reward and punishment work together as a persuasion force. Parents use reward and punishment with their children. "If you go to bed now I'll read you a story. If you don't eat your carrots, you can't watch television."

Salespeople stress benefits to their customers to persuade them to buy and try gently to imply the dangers of not investing. "Making this investment will do wonders for your bottom line. Do it now before the competition gets the jump on you."

Managers use the carrot and stick approach to motivate their employees. "Do a good job on this one, and it'll really make you look good. Joe, watch my lips. Don't mess up on this one."

And politicians use it to maintain the balance of world peace. "Maintain a democratic government and we'll give you favored nation status. Mess with us and we've got ten thousand nuclear warheads ready to take off on 15 seconds' notice."

In any persuasion situation, the elements of reward and punishment are always present. Let's say that your car is in the shop. They're telling you it won't be ready until tomorrow, but you must have it tonight. You let them know how you feel in no uncertain terms.

What's going on in the repair shop manager's mind as he listens to you? If he goes along with your request, you'll reward him with your gratitude and a nice warm environment. If he doesn't, he's apprehensive that things will turn nasty. Power Persuaders understand these two elements and know how skillfully to apply both of them.

People who don't understand Power Persuasion use one, but not the other. They threaten punishment, but don't understand it can be much more powerful when coupled with reward power. You've seen people make this mistake, I'm sure. When the car isn't ready, poor persuaders get angry and try to force the other person to give in against their wishes. "If my car isn't ready by five o'clock, I'm going to sue you for everything you've got. I'll own this place!" Applying fear tactics is an effective persuader, but it's done so crudely that it often backfires. Then, if the other side does cave in, they often gloat: "Well, I guess I showed you," is their response.

The Power Persuader knows the subtle application of both punishment and reward power is much more effective. They imply that things will get unpleasant if they don't get what they want. But then, when the other side looks as though they're going to give in, they quickly switch to reward power by showing their gratitude. "That's great, I really appreciate it. You're very nice."

MAGIC CONTROL KEY NUMBER FOUR
People will buy what you're saying, if they think you can both reward and punish them.

Let's look at how reward and punishment power affects people in sales and marketing.

New salespeople are not as effective as they could be because they're overly influenced by reward and punishment. They think that every customer can reward them by giving them an order, or punish them by turning them down, or worse yet ridiculing them for what they've proposed. Years ago, when I ran a large real estate company, we had a terrible time getting people to "farm." Farming means to select an area of five hundred homes and knock on doors in your farm regularly, until people get to know you as the real estate expert for the area. When I looked into the problem, I realized the salespeople weren't farming because they were afraid of people ridiculing them when they knocked on the door. Furthermore, their office managers weren't teaching them how to farm because they were afraid also. And the regional managers weren't training the office managers to farm because they were afraid of ridicule. So I went out with every one of our twenty-eight office managers, and the three regional managers, one at a time, and knocked on doors with them. Once they found out that there was nothing of which to be afraid, the whole company started farming, and the number of listings we were taking soared.

```
┌─────────────────────────────────────────────┐
│         MAGIC CONTROL KEY NUMBER FIVE         │
│  People can be persuaded if you have bonded with them. │
└─────────────────────────────────────────────┘
```

Power Persuaders know that people are also motivated to follow the needs of people with whom they've bonded. Bonding is a term that psychologists use to describe the change that takes place when a mother first touches her newborn baby. A bonding takes place between the two that never goes away.

So bonding is almost a given with our children, our parents, and our brothers and sisters. Power Persuaders know how bonding with people in the marketplace inspires tremendous loyalty.

H. Ross Perot, the Texas billionaire who founded E.D.S., is a leader at this. He has such deep concern and love for his employees that they're fiercely devoted to him. Remember what happened when some of his employees were trapped inside Iran as the Ayatollah Khomeini's revolution swept through the country? He risked his life by personally going into the country to get them out. Ken Follett brilliantly described the escapade in his best-selling book *Wings of Eagles*. Later, when General Motors bought E.D.S. and Perot was forced out, the company lost its momentum.

We bond with other people simply because very few of us want to be hermits. We derive great joy and satisfaction from our relationships with other human beings, and it motivates us to sustain those relationships.

```
┌─────────────────────────────────────────────┐
│          MAGIC CONTROL KEY NUMBER SIX         │
│  People can be persuaded if the situation limits their options. │
└─────────────────────────────────────────────┘
```

The next influencing factor can be situation power. In certain situations we know that regardless of what we do, we're going to lose this one. In the end, we'll become the persuadee, not the persuador.

If you're walking down a side street in Manhattan and somebody puts a hammerlock on you and sticks a knife up against your throat, you're well advised to give them your money. Companies train their cashiers not to argue with a person who has a gun, to stay calm and give them what they're asking for.

But we also run into situation power in many less threatening situations. If we're in business and we've sold one of our best customers a piece of equipment that hasn't performed as we promised, we're probably going to have to replace it. But what if it's their fault it didn't work right, and you can't persuade them it's their fault? Perhaps you sold them a lightweight chain saw, and they started using it for a major tree clearing project. Within a month the chain saw is shot. It's obviously their fault, but they're such a good customer, you can't afford to upset them. They've got situation power on you. If you expect to get any more of their business, you'd better replace it—whether it's fair or whether it isn't.

The key here is the way that you replace it. If they've got enough situation power on you that you're going to lose this one, you might as well make the concession as gracefully as you possibly can. It doesn't make any sense to get all upset about it, lose the goodwill of the customer, and still have to make the concession.

It doesn't make any sense. However, look how often we have gone into a strange bank to see if they'd cash a check for us or into a store to get a refund on something. And finally they're saying to us, "Well all right. We'll do it this one time. But it isn't our normal policy." What sense does that make? If they're going to give us what we want eventually, they'd be better off to do it quickly and gracefully, maintaining our goodwill. What sense does it make to get us all upset and still have to make the concession? If we've got enough situation power on them that they're going to lose it anyway, they might as well make the concession as gracefully as they possibly can.

As an employer you very often have situation power over people. Without it being said, they know that they're going to have to follow your instructions, because if they don't they're going to get fired. If this is the case, there's no point in pouring on the persuasion power. They're probably frustrated enough, knowing they don't have any options, without you rubbing it in. This is the time to be courteous and polite. You've got everything to gain, and nothing to lose, when you say, "Would you mind doing this for me?" or "Do you have time to do this?"

Save your powers of persuasion for when you need them.

MAGIC CONTROL KEY NUMBER SEVEN
People can be persuaded if they think you have more
expertise than they do.

The next influencing factor is expertise. If you can convince the other person that you know more about something than he or she does, you can use that as a very effective influencing factor.

Remember when you first got into your profession? You learned all the technicalities of it, but you still weren't yet comfortable with what you knew. Then you ran into somebody who appeared to know more about it than you did. Remember how intimidating that was?

Always stay one step ahead of your employees so that you can influence them with your expertise power. If you have people within your organization who have exceptional expertise in an area, keep them segmented. Don't give them broad-based power.

Doctors and attorneys project expertise power by developing a specialized language that you can't understand. Why else would doctors write prescriptions in Latin? Why else would they write *post cibum* when they mean "after meals"? Why specify Q.I.D. when "four times a day" means the same thing? Why write P.R.N. instead of "as needed"? Because if we think the other person has a specialized knowledge that we don't, we tend to be influenced by them.

Attorneys develop a whole new language that we can't understand, in order to project expertise power.

MAGIC CONTROL KEY NUMBER EIGHT
People can be persuaded if you act consistently.

So what's the most powerful influencing factor of all? Is it monetary reward? Is it recognition? Is it fear? No. It's none of those. The most powerful influencing factor of all is one that you may never have thought of before.

The most powerful influencing factor of all is consistency. Being able to project successfully that you have a consistent set of standards, and that you'll never deviate from them, has an awesome effect on people. I'll explain why later, in Chapter Eight, but let me just point out for now why it's more powerful than the obvious influencing factors of reward and punishment. While those two may have an immediate and dramatic effect on people, they cannot be sustained because they eventually tend to backfire on you.

The parent who's always persuading her child by offering him rewards quickly finds out the child learns to expect those rewards and will rebel if he doesn't get them.

You can pay a corporate executive $20 million a year, and in the early stages it will be a tremendous motivating factor. He'll do anything to assure the continuation of that reward. But year by year the value of that reward starts to diminish.

You can motivate someone with punishment power—by threatening to fire her, for example. However, it always backfires if you keep it up too long. When you keep on threatening, she'll either find a way to get out from under the pressure, or she'll learn to live with it.

Yet consistency power just grows and grows. The longer you project that you have a consistent set of standards from which you'll never deviate, the more people learn to trust you. From that trust grows a tremendous ability to persuade. This is such an important part of Power Persuasion that I'll devote all of Chapter Eight to it.

However, before we can learn how to use trust as a Power Persuasion factor, we must learn how to make people believe us. In the next chapter, I'll teach you about credibility—the factors that cause others to believe you—and how you can build on them to become a Power Persuader.

■ KEY POINTS IN THIS CHAPTER

1. People can be persuaded if they think you can reward them.

2. Instead of believing that your customers are rewarding you by giving you business, do this: get so good at what you do that you are rewarding them when you accept them as a customer.

3. People can be persuaded if they think you can punish them.

4. Power Persuaders know how to apply the dual pressures of reward and punishment.

5. People can be persuaded if you have bonded with them. The closer you become to the other person, the more you can influence them.

6. People can be persuaded if the situation limits their options. If you have situation power over the other person, use it gently. If they have it over you, accept it gracefully.

7. The most important power of all is the power of consistency, which you'll learn about in Chapter Eight.

■ CHAPTER TWO

FIFTEEN MAGIC KEYS THAT MAKE PEOPLE BELIEVE YOU

The cornerstone of your ability to persuade—what it all rests upon—is the level of credibility you have with the other person. When you speak, do they believe you? Unless they do, there is no possibility that you can get them to do what you want them to do.

People will listen to you, but they won't act—until they believe you. Let me stress that one more time. People won't act unless they believe you.

So if you're a salesperson trying to get an order, you should always be thinking, "Do they believe me?" Because if you haven't built enough credibility, they won't place the order.

If you're a manager, and you're trying to get your people to accept a new program, you should always be thinking, "Do they believe me?" Because if you haven't built enough credibility, they'll give lip service to your program, but they won't enthusiastically support it.

If you're a parent, does your son believe you when you say, "Don't do it son, I tried it once and lived to regret it"? Or does he feel you're trying to manipulate him and are being less than truthful?

Fortunately, you can build credibility with a few simple techniques. Let me teach you fifteen tips to raise your level of credibility with other people.

CREDIBILITY TIP NUMBER ONE
Never assume they believe you.

Power Persuaders have three "never assumes" that are uppermost in their thoughts at all times.

1. Never assume poverty—that the prospect can't afford what you're selling.

2. Never assume that the prospect understands you.

3. Never assume that the prospect believes you.

Until she left to go into business for herself, my daughter Julia was a stockbroker with Dean Witter in Beverly Hills. Here's how she learned that you should never assume poverty. One day a young man walked into her office dressed in scruffy clothes and hiking boots and toting an old backpack. He said he had some bonds, and he'd like to open an account because his bank was charging too much to clip the coupons. He said he didn't know how much he had, but they could figure it out. Then he upended his backpack on the desk and poured out over $2 million worth of bonds!

Of course not all scruffy people are wealthy. One day Julia had an equally decrepit looking man come in who looked as though he'd been sleeping in the park. He said he was Howard Hughes's son and he'd come for his inheritance. Julia asked her manager what to tell him. The manager happened to be stewing about a top salesperson who'd just left to work for the E. F. Hutton office across the street.

"Tell him his inheritance is at E. F. Hutton," he said. "Be sure he asks for Joe."

She dutifully relayed this to "Howard Hughes, Jr.," and he skipped off happily to claim his billions. Later she learned that E. F. Hutton had assured him that Merrill Lynch had his money.

The next "never assume" is never assume that people understand you. If you're a salesperson trying to close a sale, you've got everything to lose and nothing to gain if you fail to verify that people completely understand what you've told them.

The problem is, they're probably embarrassed to tell you that you've lost them. People never like to admit that something is too complicated for them to understand. However, a confused mind will always say "no."

Your secretary may be too intimidated to let you know that she didn't fully understand what you wanted done. The result? Wasted time while she's down the hall asking someone else if they know what you mean, or doing a job that wasn't what you wanted. Everybody wins when you take the time to say, "OK, before you start, tell me what it is you heard me asking you to do."

The last "never assume" is the one I want to talk about in this chapter. Never assume that people believe you.

Let's face it. We get downright offended if someone questions our credibility. We hate it when a bartender cards us or when a bank teller asks us for identification. So when we're persuading people, we don't like to admit that the other person is sitting there thinking "prove it to me."

If you're a salesperson, you can present a glorious list of benefits that will descend upon the buyer when they have the common sense to make an investment. It isn't even illegal to exaggerate your claims. Lawmakers call it "puffing." You can say you've got the greatest copy machine the world has ever known, even when you know it isn't, and you won't get into trouble. Just avoid any specifics and you're all right in the eyes of the laws. Still, it doesn't mean a thing until we've built the credibility needed to make them believe it.

You may be a manager whose persuasion challenge is to talk a key employee out of quitting. You can talk until you're blue in the face about the wonderful future that awaits him just around the corner if he stays with your company. But it won't mean a thing until you've convinced him that you're sincere and that you really do have the power to make it happen.

Don't be offended by people's natural unwillingness to believe you. Remember that we live in a world where a thousand advertising messages are screaming at us everyday. We can't possibly believe everything we hear. To take everything at face value in today's world would be a shortcut to disaster.

So Power Persuaders learn instinctively to build credibility into their presentations. Never assume they believe you.

CREDIBILITY TIP NUMBER TWO
Tell them only as much as they'll believe.

I was visiting my son John when he was a student at Menlo College in Atherton, California. He'd just completed a final and another student asked him how he did on it. "I think I may have aced it," John told him. "All right!" the other boy said, and gave him a high five. A few moments later another boy came by and asked John how he did on the test. "It was tough," John said, "but I hope to get a B."

"What's going on here," I asked John, "you told the first boy that you got an A and the second that you got a B."

"The first guy was the best student on campus, so he'd believe I got an A. The second guy would never believe it. Haven't you learned that you should never tell anyone more than you think they'll believe?" Now that's smart!

James Brady: "We can see California coming, and we're scared."

I don't think a thousand psychologists with an unlimited research budget could come up with a greater truth than that. Even if you're telling the truth, if the other person begins to doubt it, your chances of persuading them are falling like a rock.

Many years ago I was the merchandise manager for a large department store. We were heavily promotional, which means that our business went up dramatically when we advertised a sale and business died when we didn't. So we'd run a big Sunday, Monday, Tuesday sale, and then come back with a Thursday, Friday, Saturday sale. The problem was, how could we run the biggest sale of the year, twice a week, year 'round? Soon, we'd lost all credibility with our customers. The salespeople would try to close a sale by saying, "Get it now, while it's on sale," only to have the customer respond, "Yes, but you'll have another sale next week."

You'll recall that Sears ran into the same problem—and eventually made the switch to year-round low pricing.

There's a law of diminishing returns that's directly tied to diminishing credibility. Of course you have to be excited and enthusiastic in making your case, but the moment your claims pass the point of credibility, your chances of persuading them drop off abruptly.

The principle of "never tell them more than you think they'll believe" is supported by a lot of sound research. For example, for decades, psychologists have conducted studies to determine the effectiveness of fear as a persuasion tool. To their surprise, early studies indicated that people were just as persuaded by mild threats as they were by powerful threats. Curious, they continued to conduct studies that nearly always produced the same conclusion. Finally they realized that fear is a powerful persuader, only up to the point where people feel genuinely threatened by it. The moment they begin to doubt that the threat is as great as it is being made out to be, the power of fear as a persuader diminishes.

So a fundamental rule for building credibility is, "Never tell them more than you think they'll believe." You may genuinely have a product or service that will far exceed their expectations. However, if you can't make them believe it, you're better off to temper your claims.

CREDIBILITY TIP NUMBER THREE
Tell the truth, even if it hurts.

Some brilliant advertising people have taken advantage of this. Remember the old Volkswagen sedan, the round top one that had no design change in twenty years or so? It was one of the ugliest cars ever made. And it had no extra features about which an advertising person could brag. Only in later years did it even have a gas gauge: you could get so many miles per gallon of gas that you simply drove it until it ran out. Then you switched to a small reserve tank, which was more than enough to get you to the next gas station.

When the Doyle, Dane, Bernbach Advertising Agency won this account, it must have groaned! What could they say about the car? It only had two features. It was cheap to run and it was reliable—but everybody knew that. What more could be said? Then the agency had a flash of inspiration.

The copywriters decided to tell the truth!

I can imagine every advertising person in America bolting out of their chairs and saying, "You're going to what!!??" Doyle, Dane ran a whole series of ads that said,

"This car is ugly, it looks like a bug—a beetle."

"This car is slow—you'll be lucky if you ever get a ticket."

The results were phenomenal. People loved the campaign, and sales shot up. The truth, the simple pristine truth, is an astounding force.

Doyle, Dane went on to use the same principle with Avis rental cars. In a world where everyone was scrambling for some excuse to say they were the biggest and the best, the new Avis campaign proudly shouted "We're number two!" And followed it up with the line, "So we try harder."

It had an interesting effect on the employees of Avis and the number one company, Hertz. A survey showed that the Avis employees really were trying harder, but the Hertz people were taking it easy on Avis. Even they were sympathetic to Avis's underdog positioning!

These two campaigns revolutionized American advertising. They were startling in their impact. Everybody was running around Madison Avenue saying, "Why don't we try a Doyle, Dane ad," meaning, "Why don't we try telling the truth?" Nobody had ever pointed out the disadvantages of the product before. Nobody had ever paid millions to let the public know that the competition was more successful. Telling the truth, even when it hurts, is an astounding force.

CREDIBILITY TIP NUMBER FOUR
Point out the disadvantages.

Many years ago, Benson and Hedges came out with a campaign for its new long cigarettes that bluntly stated, "Oh, the disadvantages!" Mary Wells, at the ad agency, didn't go as far as saying, "These things are going to kill you!" But she did show scenes of people smoking in elevators and getting their cigarette caught in the door and other tongue-in-cheek situations where a long cigarette would be a disadvantage.

These advertising people had touched on a very important key to persuasion. If you point out the disadvantages, it makes everything else you say much more believable.

Research has shown that there are four sound reasons for also presenting the other side of the argument:

1. It makes the other side believe that you have objectivity.

2. It flatters the listener that you believe that he or she is intelligent enough to be aware of the disadvantages and still be persuaded in favor of your proposal.

3. It forces you to anticipate objections and rehearse counterarguments.

4. It gives credibility to everything else you say.

Consider the retail chain that had structured its line of appliances so the salesperson could sell down, off the most expensive one? The chain had really structured the profit margins so it made more profit on the middle of the line than it did on the high end. Not only was it making more money that way, it was building a powerful plus. The salespeople gained so much credibility doing it that when they recommended the service contract—one of their most profitable items—they met with very little resistance.

CREDIBILITY TIP NUMBER FIVE
Use precise numbers.

People believe precise numbers more than they believe rounded numbers. The Ivory Soap people figured this out decades ago when they started claiming that "Ivory Soap is 99 and 44/100ths percent pure." Obviously we wouldn't challenge them if they told us that Ivory Soap was 100 percent pure, but the precise figure is subliminally more believable. We assume that somebody had gone to a lot of work to figure out that the soap wasn't 99 and 43/100ths percent pure, or 99 and 45/100ths percent pure.

Why bother to say that Taster's Choice decaffeinated coffee is "99.7%" caffeine free. The company could probably get away with simply saying, "Caffeine free." The reason is that we believe specific numbers far more than we believe rounded numbers.

We can use the believability of the odd-figure syndrome as a persuasion technique. Let's say you're buying a piece of property. They're asking $250,000. If you offer $200,000, it doesn't sound as firm as if you say this: "We've done a thorough research on the property, and after running all the numbers, we feel that a fair price would be $198,700."

Studies have shown that when you take that approach, the seller will respond with a counteroffer that is, on average, $4,722 less than if you start at $200,000. No! I have no idea what the real number is, but it sure sounds more believable, doesn't it?

I once bought a hundred acres of land in the state of Washington. They were asking $185,000 for the land, and I asked Marge Winebrenner, the real estate agent, to make an offer at $115,050. She said, "Roger, what's this fifty dollars? Where did that come from?"

"Marge," I told her, "I've just been buying land for so long now that I have a formula that I use. I punched in the numbers and that's what came out." In fact I knew that I was less likely to get a counteroffer from a specific number like that. Marge did a terrific job of presenting the offer and the seller accepted it.

So to build credibility, use precise numbers. Strangely enough, you're better off to claim that your new word processing machine will increase the productivity of a secretary by 87 percent than to claim it will double his or her productivity.

CREDIBILITY TIP NUMBER SIX
Let them know if you're not on commission.

Until it closed after over seventy years at the same location, my favorite furniture store was Angelus Furniture in East Los Angeles. It's right in the heart of the Mexican barrio. That's the area that inspired the song, "Born in East L.A.," where Cheech is outraged because he's stopped by a police officer who automatically asks to see his green card, just because he looks Mexican.

It's also a part of Los Angeles where gang warfare is a way of life, and drive-by shootings are commonplace. So the store was in a terrible location. It had been there since the 1920s and used to be a furniture factory. The inside was like an ugly old barn. So why did I like it so much?

A big reason was because the salespeople weren't on commission, and I feel I can trust the advice of the salespeople better if they don't have anything to gain.

Isn't that strange? A more logical approach would be to think: commissioned salespeople make more money. Higher-paid people must be better at what they do. Therefore they'd know more. Therefore their advice would be sounder.

However, as Power Persuaders, we have to accept that the other person is probably sitting there thinking, "Oh sure, of course you'd tell me that—you're on commission." Or that in some other way you benefit from persuading them.

So here's the rule: if you're not on commission, let them know. Don't make a big deal out of it, but find a place to slide this into the conversation.

The first selling job I ever had was set up like that. I was selling televisions and kitchen appliances in a resort town in Southern England. Instead of each individual salesperson getting paid a commission, they paid a bonus at the end of the month, based on our combined sales. I liked that. We were happy to help the other salesperson's customer if they came back, because it didn't matter which one of us wrote up the sale. We were just as aggressive in getting the business, but we were working with each other instead of against each other. Since we worked on a bonus system, not commission, we could say to people, "We don't work on commission, so our only interest is in finding exactly the right appliance for your needs."

Today many high-tech sales organizations are beginning to see the advantage of a team bonus rather than individual incentives. As I travel around the country giving speeches to corporations in many different industries, I find that computer companies are the most advanced in their selling skills. Both hardware manufacturers and software vendors seem to be on the cutting edge of sales technology. For several reasons, I suppose. First, they are comparatively new industries, so they don't have a lot of old-time salespeople who cling to the old way of selling—the "that guy's got my money in his pocket, and I'm going to get it from him if I have to stay here all day" brigade. Second, computers are so sophisticated that they call for above-average intelligence salespeople. And, third, computers call for a long-term relationship between vendor and client, so the selling is more needs based. In plain language that means you sell the customer what they need rather than what you want to sell them.

So I run into many computer companies that reward their salespeople for team accomplishment rather than individual sales performance. Yet I always wonder if the salespeople are being sure to let their customers know that they're not on commission. They should, because it's a big credibility builder.

So if you're not on commission, let the customer know that. Also, don't assume it's obvious that you don't work on commission. It may be obvious to you, but customers may still have a question about it, and they don't feel comfortable asking you.

For example, have you ever wondered whether your doctor gets a kickback if he or she refers you to a specialist? I wondered enough to check it out, and the answer is—probably not. However, if you end up having an operation, your doctor could well benefit because he or she will probably "assist" in the operating room and charge a hefty fee for doing it.

Don't be offended if people suspect your motives. Just let them know you're not on commission.

```
CREDIBILITY TIP NUMBER SEVEN
Downplay any benefits to you.
```

If you are on commission, how can you overcome the problem of the other person feeling that you'd say anything to make the sale? The key is to downplay any benefit to you.

When monetary benefit isn't an issue, it may take a little more finesse to get the point across. Let's say that you're a manager and you have the job of persuading one of your people to leave Massachusetts and take over a dog territory in Amarillo, Texas.

You say, "Bob, I'd like nothing better than for you to stay here with me. You've made me a hero—I'll never find another person as good as you. But I'm prepared to make the sacrifice because I know what a great thing this is going to be for your career." Bob may be well aware that you're soft soaping him, but it's a lot better than the opposite approach of "Do it or you're fired."

The office equipment salesperson says, "John, I'm asking you to make an additional $500 investment to get the top of the line because it's best for you, not us. We've been in business for twenty-eight years. We do over $300 million a year. We're not going to jeopardize our reputation for one sale. We have to be absolutely convinced that every time we see you in the future, you'll thank us for getting you to invest in the best."

In my La Habra, California, company, Roger Dawson Productions, that books me for speaking engagements, I've taught our people to deemphasize the importance of a potential booking by saying,

"Please understand that Mr. Dawson turns down many more invitations to speak than he could possibly fulfill. Fortunately he's still available for that date. Of course, if he's not speaking for you on that day, he'll be speaking for somebody else. He just happens to be excited about working for you because he really feels he can make a big difference to your bottom-line profits."

This way, we let the meeting planner know that there's no particular financial gain to us in getting this booking, while still letting them know that we're excited about it. It also gives us an opportunity to reemphasize the benefits to them. Also, we've cut short any thoughts they may have about asking for a reduced fee.

That's why the sell-down close is so effective. The salesperson advises you to save money by buying the less expensive model. Implied in that is that they're putting your interests above theirs because they'll be making less commission. Never mind that this may not be true. The lower-priced model may have a "spiff" on it—a special bonus payment to the salesperson—that makes selling the cheaper model better for them also.

There is endless research to prove that the ability to persuade goes down dramatically if the other person thinks you have something to gain. Would you believe that a criminal could be more persuasive than a district attorney? It's true. A study published by researchers Walster, Aronson, and Abrahams had a criminal and a district attorney talk to the same audience. Both the district attorney and the criminal argued in favor of more power for district attorneys. The criminal was found to be far more persuasive—because he appeared to be talking against his own best interests: he had nothing to gain.

Then they did the experiment again, with both of the speakers arguing for less power for district attorneys. Here the district attorney was found to be far more persuasive because he appeared to have nothing to gain.

It's a key point: if you want them to believe you, let them know you have nothing to gain.

CREDIBILITY TIP NUMBER EIGHT
Dress the part of a successful person.

There's another, subliminal, way in which you downplay the importance. Dress the part of someone who's above doing things for personal gain. Have you ever been in a restaurant and gotten the feeling the waiter is pushing expensive dishes to increase his tip? What if the owner of the restaurant came over and said, "So nice to see you again! You really must try the quail and lobster appetizer this evening. I know you'll love it."

We're less inclined to think the owner is hustling food than if the waiter were to say the same thing. Yet that's strange, isn't it? The owner has more to gain than the waiter. The waiter will make the 15 percent tip on the sale, while the owner will make 70 percent or more depending on how well he has controlled his food cost.

We tend to trust the owner, and be more easily persuaded by him or her, because our perception is that such people are above hustling food. So by our manner and the way we dress, we project the image of Mr. Success or Ms. Success—a person who's far above recommending something merely for monetary reward.

Questions I get asked a lot by salespeople are, "How should I dress?" and "What image should I project?" The answer is that you should dress well enough that you don't appear to need the sale to survive but not so well that they can't relate to you. That's where top-quality clothing comes in. It has a quiet elegance about it. It doesn't shout how much it costs. Take a $500 sports coat, for example. People who wear $50 sports coats probably would have no idea how much it cost, but they know it looks good. People who wear $200 sports coats would know that you were wearing a top-of-the-line coat, although it wouldn't be so ostentatious that they'd think that you were a drug dealer. People who wear $500 sports coats would simply admire your good taste. Of course, people who wear $1,000 sports coats will think it's a potato sack! However, you won't run into too many of those.

There's no question that we are more easily persuaded by people who dress better than we do. Researchers Freed, Chandler, Mouton, and Blake conducted a now-famous experiment on how easy it would be to encourage people to ignore a "Don't Walk" sign at a city intersection. When a well-dressed individual ignored the sign, 14 percent of the people who had been waiting for the light to change followed him across. When the same person repeated the experiment the next day, now dressed in sloppy clothes, only 4 percent of the people followed him across. Clearly, we are more easily persuaded by people who dress better than we do.

CREDIBILITY TIP NUMBER NINE
If you do have something to gain, let them know.

The other way to handle the problem of diminished credibility because of the personal gain factor is my favorite. Confront the problem head on.

Let's say you're a commercial real estate broker. Your customer is undecided about making an investment in a new office building. You say, "Mr. Jones, I want to be up front with you. I work on commission. If you don't invest in this building, I lose money. However, the problem is, you lose too, because the potential profits in this building are enormous. So we both lose. But do you know what really bothers me, Mr. Jones? It's that I know to the penny what I'm going to lose if you don't invest. What really bothers me is that I don't know how much you're going to lose. It could be hundreds of thousands of dollars. Mr. Jones, if you went ahead, would you take title in your name or in your corporation's?"

CREDIBILITY TIP NUMBER TEN
Confront problems head on.

We'll talk more about confronting the problem in a later chapter on persuading difficult people, but we often let problems fester simply because we're afraid to talk about them.

If something is bothering you, or bothering the other person, you're much better off to get it out in the open and deal with it. It'll make you a better persuader.

For example, you're meeting with your boss, trying to get your pet project approved, but it's obvious he's not listening to you. The body language isn't right. His head is vertical and his eyes never move from your eyes. If he were listening his head would be slightly inclined, and his eyes would be active, reacting to what you're saying. Instead of plowing ahead with what will be a lost cause, have the courage to confront the problem. "I can see you're preoccupied. Do you have a problem with which I can help you?"

His eyes jump back into focus. "Oh, I'm sorry," he says, "I just got some bad news and it was distracting me, but this is important too. Let's go ahead and make a decision."

Perhaps you're a salesperson trying to get an appointment with a business executive. He's being rude to you, saying, "I'm just too busy to waste my time with another salesperson."

Have the courage to confront the problem. "I can tell by the tone of your voice," you say, "that you've had a bad experience with a salesperson in the past. However, I promise you this is important to you, and if it takes more than 15 minutes, it's because you asked me to stay. Fair enough? Would 10 or 11 o'clock be better for you?"

If something is bothering you or the other person, it's better to get it out in the open, it'll make you a better Power Persuader.

CREDIBILITY TIP NUMBER ELEVEN
Use the power of the printed word.

One of the surest ways to build credibility is to use the power of the printed word. If you've had some neurolinguistic training, you'll know that human beings do not give equal weight to their five senses of sight, hearing, touch, smell, and taste. We're all oriented to respond most to our primary sense. The two key ones are sight and hearing: visual and auditory. More people are visual than are auditory. Most people believe more what they see in writing than they do when they just hear it. They are visual people rather than auditory.

To figure out your primary orientation, think of some friends you visited who lived in another town. Are you remembering what you saw? That means you're a visual. Or are you remembering what you heard when you were there? That means you're an auditory. You probably said what you saw. That's because most of us are visuals. Most of us remember what we saw much more easily than we can remember what was said.

Not everybody, though. I have a friend who's a psychotherapist, and he can remember every word of a conversation but has trouble remembering what he saw. That's because he's an auditory person.

Visuals remember better what they see and most people are visual. That's why most people believe more what they see, than what they hear.

Once I was getting dressed in the men's locker room after a swim at a community pool. There was a man getting dressed on the other side of the room. I glanced at him and then did a double take. He was putting on women's clothes. He pulled women's frilly panties and a brassiere out of his bag and put them on. Then he put on shirt and pants (or should I say blouse and slacks?), got his stuff together, and walked out.

My first reaction was, "Roger, you've been working too hard." I was going through that weird process of not believing what I know I just saw. Then I noticed that all the other men in the locker room were similarly in a state of stunned silence.

Now why didn't any one of us say to this guy, "Hey, no dressing in women's clothes!"? A dozen times before in that locker room I'd seen people point up at the No Smoking sign and ask people to put out a cigarette. They weren't bashful about letting people know their feelings. Then I realized he had gone unchallenged only because there wasn't a sign on the wall that said "No dressing in women's clothes."

The written word validates our beliefs. It gives us tremendous credibility. This presumably is rooted in our civilization ever since Moses came down from Mount Sinai forty-nine hundred years ago with the Ten Commandments written on stone tablets.

We simply tend to believe more what we see in writing than we do when we just hear it.

One of my favorite "Candid Camera" stunts involved the posting of a Stop sign on a Manhattan sidewalk. Although there was obviously no danger, and no reason to stop, people would obediently stand there waiting for something to happen. On another occasion Allen Funt posted a sign on a road next to a golf course in Delaware. The sign read, "Delaware Closed," and Allen Funt stood by the sign in a trooper's uniform. What happened was amazing. People were coming to a screeching halt and saying things like, "How long is it going to be closed for? My family's inside!" One man started to argue with Funt, and Funt finally agreed that as soon as one car left the state, he would let this man in! People believe what they see in writing when they won't if they just hear it.

A few years ago, I was in Australia on a speaking tour, when I got a call that there had been a fire at my home. Nobody was hurt, but the fire gutted a room on the second floor. When I returned I got three contractors to give me estimates to repair the damage. Two were around $24,000, the other for $49,000. I submitted all of them to the insurance company and got them to accept the higher bid. Why did the larger bid have more credibility? The contractor had presented a computer generated proposal, which looked very professional, that computed the cost of each item based on the square footage. The others had merely scribbled out proposals. If I were in any type of business that required written estimates, I'd run, not walk, to the store and pay what it took to get a computer and laser printer. The equipment would pay for itself in the first week.

Many types of businesses use presentation binders in presenting their goods or services. They're a great help to new salespeople because they don't have to memorize all the details. They can follow along and read with the customer. If you're in sales, you remember your presentation binder, don't you? It was the book your sales manager made you put together when you first joined the company. You used it for a week or two and then decided that your presentation was so good that you didn't need the crutch of a presentation binder anymore. Dig it out and start using it again! People believe what they see in writing! Don't wait until you get into a sales slump and your sales manager has to lecture you about getting back to the basics.

People tend to believe what they see in writing even when they know that you just came from the print shop with it. They might not believe the same thing when they just hear it. The power of the printed word is a key element in building credibility.

CREDIBILITY TIP NUMBER TWELVE
Let them know who else says so.

Here's a key idea that Power Persuaders use to build credibility. When you're sitting across from someone else, imagine she has a sign on her forehead that says, "And who else says so?" The person knows that you think your product or service is good, but believes that you're paid to say that! Who else says so?

Without a doubt, the key element in building credibility is to let people know that somebody else, besides you, thinks that you've got the greatest product or service in the world.

Several years ago, a seminar promoter hired me to teach negotiating skills to a group of real estate investors. There were three speakers earlier in the day, and I was the wrap-up speaker. I went down to the ballroom of the hotel to hear the last 15 minutes of one of the other speakers.

There was a table set up in the back of the room, where his sets of cassette tapes were for sale at $395. I took a seat to hear what he had to say. I was amazed to see that people were getting up and heading for the back of the room even though he was still talking.

At first I thought they were leaving in protest. But no! They were heading back to buy his cassette tapes. As a crowd formed at the table, others in the audience were getting up and hurrying back, evidently afraid he would sell out before they got a chance to buy. Half his audience was back there, and he was still conducting the seminar!

I was fascinated to find out what on earth would cause this kind of hysteria. Later I found out it wasn't unusual for him to sell $50,000 worth of these cassette tapes at a seminar. Since we were going to repeat the program in Los Angeles the following day, I made a point of being at his session to hear his entire presentation.

He was promoting a get-rich-quick scheme that involved using government money to rehabilitate slum property. My years as a real estate broker told me that the scheme was unworkable in the real world, even if it was legal—which I seriously doubted. I promptly refused to speak on any more programs if he'd be one of the other speakers. Later I heard that he was indicted for defrauding the government.

How could he be so persuasive when there was no substance to what he was selling? One reason was that he was using the power of the printed word by throwing up on the screen pictures of huge checks that he claimed he had earned with his methods. However, his audience was still very skeptical until a particular point in his presentation. This was when a member of the audience put up his hand as if to ask a question. "I just want to say that what you're telling us really works. I bought your tapes, and I've made over $92,000 in the last sixty days."

The reaction was stunning. An audience that a moment ago was very skeptical now was sold completely. That's the power of the third-party endorsement. I later found out that the same person would pop up at this speaker's seminars all over the country. You can draw your own conclusions.

Of course I'm not advocating that you do this, but I am saying that if we study how unethical people can convince others to do something that's not in their best interest, we can learn to become Power Persuaders and use that power for the good of our businesses, our society, and our world.

CREDIBILITY TIP NUMBER THIRTEEN
Build and use a portfolio of testimonials.

If you're marketing a product or service, you should maintain a display binder of letters from happy customers. Be sure the letters are current, with the writer's telephone number so they can be called for verification.

How do you accumulate these letters? Some of them will come to you because your customers are so thrilled about what you did for them that they write you about it. But very often you have to ask for the testimonials.

When my house caught fire it was only about six months after I'd bought the only really comprehensive fire insurance policy I'd ever owned. My thinking was that I'd owned houses for twenty-five years and had never had a fire. Nor did I even know anybody who'd had their home burn, so the risk couldn't be too great. The lender required a policy in the amount of the loan to protect their mortgage, and if that were optional, I'd have said no to that. But my insurance salesperson, Gary Bressick, was a good one, and he convinced me I needed every coverage known to man. Because he cared enough to persist until I took the full coverage, it saved me over $30,000 when disaster struck.

I wrote Gary a great thank you letter, knowing that he'd use it in his presentation binder. Still, don't count on people doing that for you. You have to ask them for the letter!

Whenever somebody compliments you on what you've done for them, simply ask, "Would you mind putting that in writing for my presentation binder?"

If you promise not to tell anybody, I'll share a little trade secret with you. Sometimes they'll say to you, "Well, I wouldn't know exactly what to say." What a great opportunity for you! You should say, "I can imagine how busy you are. Would you like me to draft a letter for you—that you can approve and have your secretary type up?"

Since this is going to save them the work of having to think about it, they usually say, "That'd be fine." Now you can let your creative juices flow, as you prepare a dynamite reference letter. Type it on blank paper, with a cover note. As long as you don't go too far into fantasy land, your client will chuckle when she sees it and send it on for her secretary to type on her letterhead.

CREDIBILITY TIP NUMBER FOURTEEN
Get endorsements from people they'd know.

Since we're sharing trade secrets, here's a dynamite way to get a key endorsement. If you're in a business where you prepare a brochure about your services, which would include almost any self-employed person or independent contractor, this technique will do wonders for you. How would you like to have a famous person give you a great endorsement? It might be a celebrity or a top business leader in your industry. Write the person a polite letter and ask for his or her endorsement of what you do.

To save the person time, offer three different options: three different sentences endorsing you. Ask the person to initial his or her approval on one of them and mail it back to you in the enclosed stamped addressed envelope. Here's how you get the endorsement you really want. The first endorsement should be outrageous, something to which nobody would ever lend his or her name, for example, "Joe Smith is the greatest life insurance salesman in the world." The second endorsement is a strong one, and the one that you hope to get. It might say, "Listen to Joe Smith. I did, and I'll never regret it." The third endorsement might say, "Joe Smith appears to be a very qualified life insurance salesperson."

When the recipient gets the letter, he'll glance at the three suggestions. He'll quickly eliminate choice one as too strong. Choice two is more than he'd like to say, but choice three is far too weak. So he comes back to choice two, initials it, and mails it back to you. And you get exactly the testimonial you want.

In selecting the person you want to endorse you, don't pick a person who can market his or her endorsements. Even if Jay Leno wanted to help you out, he has a business manager who would expect to get a piece of the action and would veto it. Unless, of course, you're asking him to endorse a charity or a political candidate, which isn't an endorsement for which he could get paid.

And look for people who have given endorsements before. Some people are very willing to help, others don't like to do it.

CREDIBILITY TIP NUMBER FIFTEEN
Use "If they can do it, I can do it."

Now that we understand how important third-party endorsements are to your credibility, the next question would have to be, "just how credible does the third party have to be—the one who's endorsing you?" The answer may surprise you. An obvious response would have to be: "As credible as possible." Someone who's so famous, or so successful, he or she wouldn't possibly receive any personal gain from endorsing you.

I buy my dress shirts from Turnbull & Asser on Jermyn Street in London. They proudly proclaim: "By appointment to His Royal Highness, The Prince of Wales—Shirtmakers." Would the future king of England let them say that, simply because they slip him a few pounds under the table? Probably not.

Here's something that may surprise you. There is one type of endorsement where the less credible the person, the more effective it becomes.

I used to be president of a large real estate company. We were expanding rapidly and had a constant need for new sales associates. To fill this need we'd hold career nights. People would get to hear about the company and also hear a motivational talk about the advantages of a career in real estate.

At the end of the evening, we'd give them an opportunity to enroll in our licensing school at a specially reduced rate. As many as one hundred people would sign up on a successful evening. It was all very much above board, and many people picked up the challenge and became very successful in their new careers.

The highlight of the evening was always when we'd bring on one of our own sales associates to speak to them. We had some very sophisticated, articulate associates, but we'd never call on them. We'd pick on somebody who came into real estate from a minimum wage job—someone who was successful even though he wasn't the most stylish or outgoing person around. One fellow would come on wearing a pale green polyester leisure suit. The white stitching in the suit coordinated with his white belt and shoes. He'd talk about his first days in real estate. "I couldn't believe how much money I was making," he'd say. "I used to meet my wife at the coffee shop in the evening, and we'd sit there figuring out on a napkin how much money we'd made that day. We were drunk with success. The first year I'd made more money than the governor of the state. I started buying real estate and now I own over a million dollars' worth."

The effect on the audience was galvanizing. They were all sitting there with their mouths slightly open, thinking exactly the same thing: "My goodness, if he can do it, I can do it." There's a tremendous appeal to this. Be aware of it if your persuasion challenge is to recruit people, or convince them to sign up for training, or even sell exercise programs or diet pills.

A friend of mine got involved in a multilevel marketing program and persuaded me to attend one evening when they were recruiting new distributors. The evening ended with a kind of "parade of stars," an almost continuous line of successful distributors who would come across the stage, pausing at the microphone to say a few words about their success.

Without exception they were very ordinary looking people. They all seemed scared to death of being in front of a group. Many of them had trouble speaking English. Everyone in the audience was getting the same message: "My goodness, if they can do it, I can do it."

That's the right way to do it. Compare that to a speed reading program demonstration I attended whose sponsors made a very effective presentation but based their credibility on a performance by a former student.

From a stack of books, an audience member chose one the student hadn't seen before. The student then sat there and read the entire book in front of our astonished eyes. Pages were flapping as if he was standing in a hurricane. Then an audience member took the book and started asking him questions about what he'd just read. The comprehension level was nothing short of sensational.

Woody Allen: "I took a course in speed reading once and was able to read War and Peace in twenty minutes. It's about Russia."

It was a brilliant demonstration, except for one thing. The former student was clearly a smack. He dressed like the absentminded professor and wore superthick glasses taped up with Band-Aids. He was the kind of person who graduates from college at 14 and then gets a doctorate in nuclear physics when he's 16. If he doesn't have a Nobel Prize by the time he's 30, he thinks he's a failure.

Sure, he could do it, but how about us normal folks?

I've sat in countless motivational seminars over the years where the speaker looked like a Greek god. And I've thought, "Well sure, if I had his looks I'd be happy all the time too." Then he or she would say how poor they used to be and how rich they are now, and I'd think "Oh sure, if I lived in a mansion and drove a Ferrari F40, I'd be excited too."

Then they tell you how they used be fat and now they compete in marathons. "Oh sure, if I had the discipline to run 26 miles, I'd be energetic too."

One day I'm going to put on a seminar for ordinary people like me. I think I'll call it "How to Stay Motivated When It's a Hassle to Get Out of Bed in the Morning, You're Twenty Pounds Overweight, and You Have to Hang Pork Chops Around Your Neck to Get the Dog to Play With You."

Can you relate to that?

■ KEY POINTS IN THIS CHAPTER

So a key part of Power Persuasion is making them believe what you're telling them. You can do that if you'll remember these key points:

1. Never assume they believe you.
2. Tell them only as much as they'll believe.
3. Tell the truth, even if it hurts.
4. Point out the disadvantages.
5. Use precise numbers.
6. Let them know if you're not on commission.
7. Downplay any benefits to you.
8. Dress the part of a successful person.
9. If you do have something to gain, let them know.
10. Confront problems head on.
11. Use the power of the printed word.
12. Let them know who else says so.
13. Build and use a portfolio of testimonials.

14. Get endorsements from people they'd know.

15. Use "If they can do it, I can do it."

So credibility—"Do they believe you?"—is the cornerstone of Power Persuasion. Work with and analyze the key points of credibility introduced in this chapter, and you'll experience a transformation in your ability to persuade.

CHAPTER THREE

HOW TO MAKE THEM WANT TO DIE FOR YOU

In this chapter I'll teach you a magical way to create desire in other people—a desire to give you exactly what you want! It's powerful enough to make them want to die for you!

It's the art of creating an obligation in the mind of the other person. It such a powerful persuasion tool that it's almost like creating a vacuum—a vacuum that causes what you want, to flow to you.

It works because, in this country, we have an enormous sense of fair play. In our minds we have a set of mental scales, like the scales of justice. If we don't think the scales are fairly balanced, we tend to want to do something about it. That's why, in this country, "What do you think would be fair?" is a devastating persuasion technique! Let me tell you a story that will illustrate the high degree of "fair play" thinking that exists in this country.

I was returning from New Delhi after having spent four weeks in India and Nepal. In India, *backsheesh* is a way of life. *Backsheesh*, a term that stems from Britain's colonial rule of India, refers to a tip paid to a guide or a helper all the way up to an outright bribe of a rajah. Anybody who helps you expects to get paid. You don't have to tip very much, but you tip little and often.

For example, at New Delhi airport, natives appear at your side as you stand in line to check in. They don't say anything, but they silently start moving your bags forward for you as the line moves. People who try to shoo away the unwelcome helpers, find out what a mistake they've made when they start to go through customs. The unofficial porters have evidently worked out a little kickback to the customs inspectors. The passengers with porters go through quickly. The others are liable to be searched.

The flight home to California was a nightmare. We were delayed for hours in Tehran, sitting on a sweltering runway. At Frankfurt, they couldn't find a passenger to match a piece of luggage someone had checked onto the plane. Fearing a bomb, they emptied the plane of passengers and luggage and had us reidentify our luggage on the runway.

London airport was completely fogged in and no planes were leaving. Heathrow is among the world's busiest international airports, and the distances in Europe are so short that any delay in London causes chaos throughout the continent. It was very close to Christmas, and everyone was trying to do the same thing I was doing—get home for the holidays.

It reminded me of the final scene in the movie *Casablanca*, where everybody is frantic to get on a plane to anywhere. Sleeping people, who looked as though they'd been there for days, covered the entire terminal. At every ticket counter there were lines of hostile people, most of them screaming at the airline employees. I took the opposite approach: I stayed calm and complimented the counter supervisor for the great job he was doing. He rewarded me with the last seat on the only flight to New York.

David Letterman: "New York now leads the world's great cities in the number of people around whom you shouldn't make a sudden move."

At JFK airport, there was a plane leaving for Los Angeles, but the gate was in the next terminal, and the plane left in 30 minutes. The cab driver refused to take me on such a short trip, but I bribed him with a $20 bill. When I got to the gate they were announcing the final boarding call, but I had one more thing to do.

I needed to call California to let my assistant know I was back in the country, so that he could meet me at the airport. In those days, phones didn't work without a coin, and I didn't have any American coins. So I approached a large family group, waived a dollar bill at them and asked for a quarter. They produced a quarter, but insisted I get a full dollar's worth of coins. I told them it didn't matter and tried to break free. They wouldn't let me go! They followed me through the airport, with all of them going through their pockets and purses, trying to scrape up the 75 cents change.

The irony of it all! Here I was after spending a month in an environment where bribery, corruption, and payoffs were a way of life, and I was about to miss my plane because these Americans couldn't bear to take a 75 cent advantage of me!

The great sense of fair play we have in this country explains why creating an obligation is such a powerful persuasion technique.

METHOD NUMBER ONE TO CREATE AN OBLIGATION
Ask for more than you expect to get.

There are many ways that Power Persuaders create an obligation in the other person's mind. A key way to do this is to ask for more than you expect to get. Then when you scale back your demand you have tilted the scale in your favor. Your concession in reducing your demand, creates an obligation on the part of the other person to make a reciprocal concession. Unfortunately, most inexperienced persuaders are too intimidated to do this. They're so unsure of their ability to be persuasive that they actually reduce their demands before they start.

Let's put ourselves in an actual situation where the ability to persuade may be critical, and I'll tell you what I mean by this.

Let's say that Tom is a program designer for a software developer in the Santa Clara Valley and he's getting ready to ask the boss for a raise. It took Tom months to work up the courage to do it, but in 15 minutes he meets with the president of his company to ask for more money.

He's rehearsed the conversation in his mind dozens of times. Three months ago he started thinking, "I wonder if it's too soon to ask for more money." Two months ago he moved to thinking, "I've got a good track record with these people. Of course they'll give me an increase." A month ago he was saying to himself, "If they don't give me an increase when I ask for it, I'm going to look for something else." An hour ago he was downright hostile about it. "Why should I have to ask them for more money? After all the things I've done for them, they should be coming to me!"

By now he's in such a state of agitation that his self-confidence is beginning to drain away. He thinks, "If they don't give me what I want, I'll really give them a piece of my mind. I'll quit on the spot. But where would I go? What would I do? There must be hundreds of people out there who would jump at the chance of getting my job."

Tom has become like the farmer whose generator breaks down, and he needs it to run the milking machine. He thinks, "No problem, my neighbor Joe will lend me his." As he's driving over to his neighbor's ranch, his self-talk is running like this: "I wonder if Joe will lend it to me? Maybe he'll be mad at me for asking. He shouldn't be; I've done lots of favors for him, but he probably won't care about that. You just can't rely on people these days. Always taking from you, but never giving back. Who needs neighbors like that anyway?"

He pulls into his neighbor's yard, and Joe comes out of the barn, saying "How are you this morning Harry? What can I do for you?"

And Harry yells at him, "You can keep your stinking generator, that's what you can do!"

Don't we all tend to engage in that defeating kind of self-talk? Under pressure we conjure up and answer a thousand questions that will never be asked. Under pressure our minds invent and handle a thousand imaginary crises. Under pressure we mentally experience a hundred disasters we'll never have to face.

James Thurber: "It is better to know some of the questions than all of the answers."

Have you ever stopped to think how many bad things have really happened to you in your lifetime. How often has your house been broken into? How often have you really been mugged? How many times has your home caught fire? How many people have really struck you in a lifetime? How many of your bags have the airlines really lost?

Now think about the time that you've wasted worrying about these bad things! Isn't it ridiculous that we worry ourselves to death over imaginary fears when we could be using the time to enrich our lives?

■ HOW ASKING FOR MORE GETS TOM HIS RAISE

Back to Tom. Unless we're absolutely sure that we're entitled to what we want, asking for something very often strikes fear in our hearts. Then, even before we even meet with the other person, we've scaled back our demands.

Power Persuaders know that it's not enough to have the courage to expect and confidently request what we want. We must be willing to have the courage to ask for more than we expect to get. Then when we scale back our request, it will create an obligation in the mind of the other person.

Whether you're asking for an increase in pay, or you're trying to close a sale, or get a promotion at your company, asking for more than you expect is a key persuasion technique. If Tom is hoping for a 10 percent increase in pay, he should be asking for 20 percent.

Number one, he might just get it. But more important, when they settle at 10 percent, it's Tom that will have made the concession of "lowering" his expectations. With the high degree of fairness that exists in this country, any concession that's made creates an obligation on the part of the other person to make a reciprocal concession.

So Tom should start out like this: "Boss, I'm here to get a raise in pay from you, but don't worry, it isn't anything you can't afford, and I'm going to show you exactly why it's justified."

In this way, Tom has reassured the boss that his demands aren't going to be unreasonable, and he's also forestalled the possibility of the boss trying to cut him off before he even starts.

Some managers, when they hear the word raise, tend to panic and jump in with, "Tom, we'd love to give you an increase, but we just don't have a dime in the budget right now."

However, Tom's been smart enough to short-stop that before it can occur. Tom continues: "Let's look at what's happened in the three years since I took over the division. Sales have increased 50 percent, but more important profits have doubled."

Note Tom's use of a technique that I call the "Time Value of Assertions." A 50 percent increase compounded over three years is really less than 15 percent a year, but it sounds like more.

Salespeople use this in reverse don't they? They call it breaking it down to the ridiculous. The real estate salesperson says, "But we're only talking $5 a day here. Surely you're not going to let $5 a day stand between you and your dream home, are you?" What he's not saying is that $5 a day over the life of a 30-year loan contract is $54,750 more they'll pay for the house.

Tom lays out his supporting data in writing, because as we talked about in Chapter Two, the written word is always more believable than the spoken word. He continues: "So with me bringing in double the profit, you'd think I'd be making double the money I was three years ago, but I'm not. Now I realize that this isn't your fault. I should have come to you a long time ago about this."

Tom has now planted in the boss's mind the idea that he's going to ask for a 100 percent increase in pay. He notices the boss's complexion is turning green. Tom talks on for a few more minutes, letting this impression settle in a little deeper.

Finally, the boss begins to sputter. "Tom, you're not asking me to double your pay, are you? That's ridiculous! Why, you'd be making more money than I!"

Tom replies calmly, "That may be so, but in fact what I'm asking for is much less than that. All I'm asking you to OK is a 20 percent increase and an upgraded automobile."

There's not a thing wrong with Tom's car, and getting a different one isn't important to him, but he's still asking for more than he expects to get. After 15 more minutes of discussion, Tom finally agrees to a scaled-down request of a 10 percent increase with no new car. He got his boss to see it his way, and yet the boss feels he did a brilliant job persuading Tom to settle for less than he wanted.

He may even brag later that "I got him to settle for only 10 percent and made him feel glad he got that much."

In reality, Tom got everything he wanted, but because he has made all the concessions up to this point, he can still take advantage of the obligation he has created. So he uses it to get another important concession.

"Boss, if I settle for only 10 percent now, how quickly could we review this again? In three months?"

"Three months? No way. Maybe in six months we'll take another look at it."

■ HOW CHILDREN NAIL YOU TO THE WALL—AND MAKE YOU LOVE IT!

To see how truly effective asking for more than you expect to get can be, let's consider the group of people in the world who almost always get what they want. They're legendary for their incredible persuasion skills. Wise men have written volumes about their mystical ability to get what they want under the most challenging conditions. Their talents are so unique that thousands of scientists devote their careers to studying them. I'm talking about your children!

How naturally they slip into the technique of asking for more than they expect to get, instinctively knowing it creates an obligation.

For the last fourteen years I've lived in La Habra Heights, a little town about 10 miles north of Disneyland in California. During that time I've raised three children. Which means umpteen trips to the Magic Kingdom.

If you're going to let your children go to Disneyland, you expect to pay about $30.00 per person for admission and lunch. When they ask for a trip to Disneyland, and then back off and settle for a movie and popcorn, you think you've died and gone to heaven.

> Gloria Swanson: "All creative people should be required to leave California for three months every year."

A while back, when my daughter Julia was working for Dean Witter in Beverly Hills, she called to ask if I'd like to go to lunch. My youngest son John, who was home from college, had a summer job at her office and she thought it would be great if we could all go to lunch together.

That's fine, except that Beverly Hills is an hour and a half drive for me, and it was already 1 o'clock. It would mean taking an entire afternoon away from a book I was writing, to say nothing of the fact that lunch to Julia means the Polo Lounge and a $120 check.

I told her, "I'd really love to, Julia, but I just can't spare the time."

"Then would you mind if I took John to lunch?"

Relieved, I replied, "Oh, sure, that's fine, and I'll reimburse you." When I'd hung up, I thought, "She's done it to me again. I fall for that every time. She had no intention of having me join them for lunch. She was just asking for more that she expected to get."

More recently my older son Dwight asked me if he could borrow my Corvette for the evening. I told him that I needed it, but he could borrow the minivan if he wanted to. Half an hour later, I glanced through the window, and there he was, loading all his musical equipment into the minivan. He was evidently going off to play somewhere with his group. No way could he have put all that equipment in the Corvette!

He'd been very smart. If he'd have asked to borrow the minivan in the first place, I might have said no. Since he had to have it to move his equipment, an argument might have followed. Once people have made a decision on something, they hate to back down, and I'm no exception. We all tend to dig in to our positions. By asking for the Corvette, he knew that he could always back down to the minivan, and I would feel that I'd had things my way. I'd feel that I'd won. How smart!

There are three reasons for asking for more than you expect to get:
1. You might just get it.
2. It gives you room to negotiate.
3. It lets the other person have a win.

A classic example of asking for more than you expect to get was the divorce of Johnny Carson from his third wife, Joanna. At issue was the amount of money that Joanna should get to maintain her life-style, until the divorce could be settled. Johnny's lawyers offered $15,000 a month. Joanna's attorneys produced papers to show it would take $220,000 a month for her to maintain her life-style! Did he expect her to settle for $15,000? No way! Did she expect to get $220,000 a month? Of course not!

You ask for more than you expect to get because it creates an environment where the other person can feel that he or she is the recipient of a concession and that a reciprocal concession is due.

■ HOW THIS TECHNIQUE BROUGHT SADDAM HUSSEIN TO HIS KNEES

When Saddam Hussein invaded Kuwait in the summer of 1990, we demanded three things of him: (1) get out of Kuwait, (2) restore the legitimate government of Kuwait—no puppet governments, and (3) make reparation for the damage he'd done.

Fine, except that those three demands were also the least we were prepared to accept. We didn't ask for more than we expected to get. Because we asked for our minimum demands, the negotiations had to deadlock, because we didn't allow Saddam Hussein room to win. You can say, with a great amount of justification, that Saddam Hussein is not high on your list of people to whom you want to give a win! I agree with you, but it's simply poor negotiating.

Had we have asked that he and all his cronies be exiled, that a non-Arab neutral government be installed in Bagdad, and that U.N. supervision of the destruction of all military capability be included, plus our three original demands, we could have let Saddam Hussein have a win and still got what we wanted.

When you look back on this scenario, you can draw one of two conclusions. Conclusion number one: the negotiators at our State Department are blithering idiots. That's a possibility, isn't it? Conclusion number two: we wanted the negotiations to deadlock. We had no intention of settling for Saddam merely getting out of Kuwait, restoring the legitimate government, and making reparations. We wanted the negotiations to deadlock, so that we'd have a reason to invade Iraq and settle the larger problem of Saddam's military belligerence. Otherwise, we'd have to be back there, a couple of years later, to care of the problem again.

What I'm concerned about is that you inadvertently create deadlocks by not asking for more than you expect to get.

■ HOW UNIONS AND MANAGEMENT GET EACH OTHER'S GOAT

Here's how asking for more than you expect to get works in business negotiations. Many years ago I helped negotiate a renewal of a union contract at a retail store. During the prior contract period, the union pay raises hadn't even kept up with the increases in the federal minimum wage. Management genuinely felt the union was doing a disservice to its members—their employees.

The union's initial demand was absolutely outrageous. Its proposal was to put store clerks' pay on a par with that of the Teamsters in Alameda County, California. We had trouble even figuring out why they'd picked Alameda County, which was over 100 miles away. But it wasn't that complicated, when we analyzed it. The Teamsters in that county simply had the best contract in the state.

I thought that proposal was outrageous enough, but it was timid compared to the company's first proposal—that union membership become voluntary. With the union's dismal track record of obtaining benefits for the employees, it was a proposal that would destroy the union at that location.

To a layperson's eye it would seem that we'd never be able to get together, but both sides were experienced negotiators. We worked our way in toward the middle and reached an agreeable solution.

Why had they asked for so much, knowing they'd never get it? Why had we asked for an open shop, knowing that we'd never get it? Because both sides wanted the other side to feel they'd won. Really, the perception of thinking they'd won may have been far more important than the reality of the settlement. Both sides had to report on the results of the agreement: the union to the members and the corporate attorneys to the company management. The other side did them a favor by asking for so much and then conceding most of it. The union negotiators could say to the members, "We didn't get you a huge increase, but they were insisting on an open shop, which would have left you without any protection at all. We forced them to give up on that idea."

The corporate attorneys could say, "Sure we had to concede an increase in pay that was larger than we hoped for. But you should have heard their initial demand."

■ SOMETIMES THEY GIVE YOU WHAT YOU WANT ANYWAY

When I first began to understand the idea of always asking for more, I decided to experiment with the owner of the company at which I worked. Abandoning any sense of reason, I worked on a list of demands and then kept expanding them.

When I met with the owner, I thought that I'd be lucky if he agreed to any of my demands. But to my amazement, an hour later I walked out with a substantial promotion, a 60 percent increase in base pay, a bonus program, a new suite of offices, and permission to hire an assistant for my secretary.

■ UNETHICAL WAYS TO USE THIS CONCEPT

Remember the department store chain I mentioned in Chapter Two— the one that had trained its salespeople to sell down—off the top of the line? It had devised a completely unethical scheme for marketing major appliances that worked like this.

For each type of product, such as televisions, ranges, and washing machines, it developed a good, a better, and a best: a low-end product, a middle of the line, and a top of the line. It'd advertise the low-end product at a very attractive price, and then, through salesmanship and creative display work, sell the customer on the more expensive model when they came into the store.

Bait and switch is serious enough, but besides that, the store developed an interesting new wrinkle. It structured the line so the maximum profit wasn't on the most expensive model but the middle of the line.

The store trained the salesperson to sell up to the top of the line, but then in a confidential whisper, tell the customer he didn't think the extra money was worth it. That if he were them, he'd buy the less expensive middle-of-the-line model, which was, unknown to the customer, the model on which the store made the most profit and the model on which the salesperson made the biggest bonus.

Of course this is completely unethical, and the chain deserved to be brought to task. Which it was, by the Federal Trade Commission.

Of course, you shouldn't do things like this, but as a Power Persuader you must understand these techniques so you won't be vulnerable to other people's efforts to exploit you.

Yet, in this example we see why asking for more than you expect to get is a powerful technique. When you back away a little bit from the initial demand, you actually create an obligation in the mind of the other person. You've made a concession to the other side, and therefore they should make a reciprocal concession to you.

When the salesperson went ahead to suggest the customer use some of their "savings" to invest in a service contract on the appliance, the acceptance rate was remarkably high. They probably would've got away with it for a long time if they hadn't been so outrageously successful. The incredibly high percentage of business the firm was doing on the middle-of-the-line products drew the attention of consumer activists and subsequently a federal action that ended the practice.

■ THE OLIVER TWIST SYNDROME

There's a big danger to be aware of when asking for more than you expect. Oliver Twist, the Charles Dickens character who grew up in the poor house, and had the nerve to ask for more food, might put it this way: "Asking for more is one thing, demanding more is another."

Remember that this is a persuasion technique. If you up your demands to beyond what's reasonable and then convince yourself you're going to get them all, you may be heading for trouble.

When you ask for more, be sure it doesn't come across as a demand. Imply some flexibility. You've got plenty of room to give a little. Let the other side know that you think the request is reasonable, but that you have their interests at heart too. If need be, you're willing to listen to a counterproposal.

METHOD NUMBER TWO TO CREATE AN OBLIGATION
Volunteer concessions—but only those that won't hurt you.

If you can help the other side without it taking away from your position, why not? Power Persuaders look for concessions they can make—as long as it doesn't hurt their position.

Years ago, during the cold war, Interior Secretary Stewart Udall visited Odessa in the Soviet Union and asked Premier Khrushchev to pose for a picture with him. "Certainly," said Khrushchev, "and if it would help you, you can shake your finger in my face."

Khrushchev may have just been displaying his wit, but he knew he had nothing to lose by making the concession, since he had total control of the press in his country.

One of the most powerful thoughts when you are trying to persuade people is not, "How can I get them to give me what I want?" It's "What can I give them that wouldn't take away from my position?" Giving something that's of value to them creates an obligation in their mind. If you give people what they want, they'll give you what you want.

When we get into trouble, it's because we've assumed that the other person wants the same thing that we want. Stewart Udall wouldn't want a picture taken of Khrushchev shaking a finger in his face, so he assumed Khrushchev felt the same way. It didn't occur to him that Khrushchev could care less, because he controlled the press anyway.

When Tom was negotiating his increase in pay, he may have assumed the company didn't want to upgrade his car because it would cost money. He didn't stop to think that the company may have wanted him driving a better car, to improve its image. Or perhaps his sales manager wanted to get a better car, and he'd trade his Buick with Tom, so that he could justify getting a Cadillac.

METHOD NUMBER THREE TO CREATE AN OBLIGATION
Give a small gift.

Another way to create an obligation is to give a small gift to the other person. Remember the scene in the Robert Redford movie *Jeremiah Johnson*, where Redford had killed some Crow Indians and was now a hero with the rival tribe, the Flatheads? As they brought him in triumph to meet the chief of the Flatheads, he thought it would be appropriate to give the chief a small gift. His more experienced friend and guide tried to stop him.

"Don't do that, you'll get us all killed!" he yelled. "Now he's obligated to give you a gift, and he doesn't have anything good enough for a hero like you."

It was a tense situation until the chief came up with a way to fulfill the obligation, which was to let his daughter marry Redford. It was the last thing Redford wanted to do, but to refuse would've insulted the chief and put their lives in danger. Soon we see Redford leaving the Indian village with his new bride, together with a young boy he had inherited when he did a favor for someone else earlier in the movie.

Robert Orben: "Illegal aliens have always been a problem in the United States. Ask any Indian."

The fact that giving a small gift creates an obligation is why Fuller Brush and Avon salespeople have been so successful. Even if the free sample at the door is something we don't particularly want, we feel obligated enough to let them into our homes and allow them to present their wares.

The Hare Krishna Society took ruthless advantage of this with their collecting techniques at airports. The Hare Krishna is a Hindu sect founded in a small town about half way between New Delhi and Agra, in India. In the 1960s, the devotees of this sect could be seen in New York City, Hollywood, and other exotic parts of this country: with shaven heads and long robes, they'd usually be seen pounding on small drums and dancing up and down like Indians doing a rain dance.

During the turbulent years of the Vietnam war, they attracted some fairly affluent followers. I was curious enough about them to travel to the shrine in the Indian town in which their sect got its start. Frankly it was a big disappointment. I found nothing mystical there.

During the 1980s, the sect started having trouble raising money. The world had changed from rebellion to respectable conformity, the hippies of the 1960s became the yuppies of the 1980s, and the Hare Krishnas had turned into a weird blight on society.

Then they hit upon a brilliant scheme to collect money. Using members dressed in more conventional clothing, they set up shop in the major airports. There, they would approach someone, stick a small flower into his or her lapel, and then ask for a contribution. The results were phenomenal and enabled the sect to fund over a hundred temples and centers around the world.

It turned out that very few people could resist the obligation that was created with even so small a gift as an unwanted flower. To underscore the power of creating an obligation for persuasion further, remember that if the public could resist it, the problem of airport solicitation would quickly have gone away. Airports wouldn't have been a profitable place to solicit funds.

METHOD NUMBER FOUR TO CREATE AN OBLIGATION
Use the magic in a gift of flowers.

Power Persuaders know there's magic in the gift of flowers. I remember my business manager working on a sale of my services that would eventually lead to over $200,000 worth of income to us. She'd had an encouraging meeting with the man who would take our proposal to his executive committee for consideration. I told her to send a dozen roses to the man, to be delivered on the morning of the meeting. She didn't think it was such a great idea. She felt foolish and was concerned that it might be seen as manipulative. However, she went ahead, and we got the contract. Later she told the executive that she hoped he hadn't seen the roses as a bribe. He laughed and said of course he did, but he was touched anyway.

Remember that it's the personal touch that makes this effective. Flowers have the personal touch because the perception is that somebody selected them, and they come with a handwritten message, even though the recipient knows the sender dictated the message to the florist over the phone. Florists know it would be a big mistake to type out that message. It would lose its personal touch.

How would you feel if you'd attended a wedding and received a printed card thanking you for your gift, without a signature? It's probably worse than getting no thank you at all.

So a nonpersonalized gift, such as a paperweight or a letter opener, doesn't create the personal obligation, because people perceive it as coming from the company, not the individual.

I had learned how effective this can be when I bought a four-unit apartment building a couple of years before. A developer had purchased a whole street of these rental units and had subdivided them so they could be sold individually.

The developer ran a small ad in the Sunday paper, and I drove by to look at the units. When I got there, the place was in an uproar. It was a very hot real estate market in California at the time, and hundreds of investors were there to check these units out. Frantic buyers crowded the sales room.

Over the heads of the crowd, I yelled to the salesperson, "Do you have any left?"

"Only one," he yelled back "It's $129,000 with 20 percent down."

"I'll take it!" I screamed back.

And he started tacking up a "sold out" sign. Sure, I was taking a risk buying a building I hadn't even seen. Yet if they'd sold that many in the first couple of hours after putting them on the market, it couldn't be too bad a buy. There was a remote possibility that they'd loaded the sales room with phony buyers. But since it was a Sunday, I always had the option of putting a stop payment on my deposit check, and backing out, if they'd been deceptive.

The next morning I was having an acute attack of buyer's remorse at this rash purchase when a florist delivered a bouquet of flowers. There was a handwritten note attached that said "Congratulations on your wise investment." It was signed by the salesperson with whom I'd dealt.

Suddenly I forgot all thoughts of backing out. As does everybody, I like to think of myself as a person who keeps his commitments. This salesperson was working on commission and was depending on me. He could have sold it to somebody else if I hadn't jumped in. What a brilliant move by the developer! For $20 or so, they'd locked in a $129,000 sale. And I was much better off for being persuaded. Three years later I sold the building for $190,000.

METHOD NUMBER FIVE TO CREATE AN OBLIGATION
Give the gift of thoughtfulness.

The gift doesn't have to cost anything. The gift of thoughtfulness creates a powerful obligation.

One salesperson I heard of developed a strong bond with a key client simply by finding out that the man's grandson collected foreign stamps. Whenever he came by, he'd be sure to have a few new stamps with him. This powerful executive, known to chew up salespeople and spit them out, was so impressed with the man's thoughtfulness that he'd get his calls held and enthusiastically go over the new arrivals every time the salesperson came in.

Another more subtle gift is the cheerful willingness to stick around if the person you're waiting to see is delayed, rescheduling the appointment if necessary. This inconvenience can be one of the best things to happen to you, as long as you handle it well. You create an obligation.

And don't think that you can act irritated and annoyed in front of the person's secretary and charming and compliant in front of the boss and get away with it. Most bosses trust their secretaries and value their opinions. Many a big sale has gone down the tubes because the secretary whispered to the boss, "That salesperson is a real pain. You can't believe what a nuisance he's been."

And many a relationship blossomed because the secretary reported, "He's so nice, he's been sitting there for hours and hasn't complained once."

METHOD NUMBER SIX TO CREATE AN OBLIGATION
Make it win-win.

At this point, I'm sure you're thinking that all this is very manipulative and, therefore, unethical.

Remember that how you do something doesn't decide whether it's ethical or not, it's what you accomplish, the end result, that counts. If your heart is in the right place, if you're absolutely sure that you're acting in the best interests of the other person, I say that you have an obligation to understand and apply the principles of Power Persuasion.

That would apply if your persuasion challenge is to get your child to stay in college or if you're a doctor persuading a patient to have a desperately needed operation.

The art of creating an obligation is a key Power Persuasion factor for us to understand. That obligation creates a vacuum that causes what you want to flow to you.

■ KEY POINTS IN THIS CHAPTER

Knowing how to create an obligation subtly in the mind of the other person is a powerful persuasion tool. It creates a vacuum that draws what you want to you. The key ways to do this are to

1. Ask for more than you expect to get: you might just get it. Also, it gives you room to negotiate, and it makes the other person feel obligated when you back down. Don't fall into the trap of turning the request into a demand—you must imply flexibility.

2. Volunteer concessions that don't take away from your position. When you give people what they want, they'll give you what you want.

3. Give a small gift. In our society, even the smallest gift demands a reciprocal concession.

4. Use the magic in a gift of flowers. Because they have such a personal touch, a small gift of flowers can put together, or confirm, a huge transaction.

5. Give the gift of thoughtfulness. Don't get irritated when people make you wait or in other ways break a commitment. Recognize that by responding with thoughtfulness, you can create an obligation.

6. Make it win-win. If you genuinely have the other person's interests at heart, you needn't feel guilty about manipulating them. You're acting in their best interests.

■ CHAPTER FOUR

HOW SCARCITY DRIVES PEOPLE WILD

In this chapter, I'll teach you how to use a powerful pressure point that persuades people to act: the perception of scarcity. Putting a limit on what you're offering gives you the power to persuade them. It creates a sense of urgency, which makes them move quickly to seize the opportunity. It drives people wild!

Whenever I think about this principle, I'm reminded of a visit to the Soviet Union during the early days of Gorbachev's reforms. Standing on a second floor balcony, I was watching an incredible scene take place below: a new phenomenon in Soviet life. The recent policy of *perestroika*, or restructuring, was permitting a very small amount of entrepreneurial activity. Before *perestroika*, all sources of supply were government controlled; now a few people could buy and sell goods and keep the profits.

Below me a man had just opened up a cardboard box and was selling the contents. They appeared to be very poor quality wristwatches. In seconds, the word spread of something new for sale, and a panic started. People mobbed the man, fighting their way through the crowd to thrust rubles at him. Then they'd fight their way back out through the crowd to unwrap the packages and find out what they'd just bought.

It made me think of a trip I'd made into the upper reaches of the Amazon. One day we stopped to catch and fry some piranha for lunch. I've never been an Ernest Hemingway when it comes to fishing, but even I can catch piranha. All you need is a hook on the end of a piece of string. The minute you toss it in, the water boils with frenzied activity, as the piranhas attack the bare hook. That's the kind of frenzy I was watching in Moscow that day.

It was a graphic demonstration of the power of scarcity. The man may have had access to many more watches, but he was smart enough to bring in only one box. The implication that there is a limited supply, and that the buyer must act quickly before it's too late, is a powerful persuasion force.

■ EVEN SMART PEOPLE CAN FALL FOR THE SCARCITY YO-YO

Don't think for a moment that only unsophisticated people are panicked into buying in times of scarcity. I once taught negotiating skills to a company that manufactures bearings for aircraft engines. The normal lead time for producing a bearing is about 10 weeks. However, there had been rumors that there would be a shortage of a raw material needed to manufacture the bearings, and the aircraft manufacturers weren't about to stop production on a $30 million jet because they couldn't get a relatively inexpensive bearing.

Despite the company's assurances of supplies, the aircraft manufacturers started increasing their orders in order to build up an inventory. As word got out about what one manufacturer was doing, the others jumped on the bandwagon. Soon the orders far exceeded the bearing company's ability to produce them. So it started telling its customers that deliveries would be delayed, which only increased the panic. Soon it was having to quote delivery dates almost two years out!

Imagine the havoc that this created with this small bearing company, especially since it knew the pendulum would have to swing the other way soon. When the aircraft manufacturers began to realize the panic wasn't justified, they had ten times their normal inventory on hand. Then would come many months when the bearing company had no orders at all.

■ SCARCITY DRIVES VALUE AND PRICES SKY HIGH

Scarcity increases the value and makes you want to act quickly. Let's say you're shopping for a refrigerator in an appliance store and you can't bring yourself to spend all that money on a new refrigerator. The salesperson's getting impatient, and finally, he says, "Look, before we go any further, I'd better be sure that we've got one of those left in the warehouse. They've been going like hot cakes."

He calls out to his manager, "Charlie, do we have any more 7256s left?"

The manager calls back, "I just checked on that because I've got a customer who's interested. There's only one left. You better grab it now if you want it. I really goofed pricing those things so low."

And you yell, "I'll take it, I'll take it!"

Now, you might think you're too sophisticated to fall for this, but appliance salespeople are a breed apart when it comes to persuading customers. I used to be a merchandise manager in a large department store, so I know what I'm talking about.

I'll always remember a hot summer's day in Bakersfield, California when we were having a sidewalk sale. It was 100 degrees at 9 o'clock in the morning, and the temperature was heading for 110. Bob White, my appliance manager, was manhandling slightly damaged appliances out to the sidewalk and taping sale price tags to them. Sweat was pouring off him.

"How much is that refrigerator" asked an early bird customer.

"The store's not open yet."

The customer ignored this and persisted, "Yes, but how much is it?"

"It's exactly what it says on the sign. One of a kind—$399."

The customer responded hopefully, "Could you knock a little more off?" The heat and the frustration finally got to Bob. He reached into his tool box, pulled out a hammer, and whacked the side of the refrigerator, chipping off a piece of the porcelain finish.

"There," he said, "I knocked some off. Do you want me to knock some more off?"

"No, no!" screamed the customer, "I'll take it, I'll take it!"

■ MY AUNT HAD ONE OF THOSE—BUT SHE THREW IT AWAY!

Nowhere is the value of scarcity more clearly illustrated than in an antique store. We've all walked into an antique store at one time or another, and said: "My aunt (or my mother or my grandmother) had one of those, but she threw it away!" In fact there really is an antique store called: "My Aunt Had One of Those, But She Threw It Away."

Why did your aunt throw that umbrella stand or tasseled lamp away? Because it was ugly and impractical, and for those reasons it was worthless. Now, have tastes changed so much that now it's beautiful and practical? No, not at all. It became valuable simply because there are so few around.

When George McGovern had to drop Thomas Eagleton from the ticket in 1972, the price of McGovern/Eagleton campaign buttons went from $3 to $100. In 1988, when it was even rumored that George Bush might not hang in with Dan Quayle, Bush/Quayle buttons were selling for $50 at the Republican convention in New Orleans. Both of these, of course, were contrived shortages. At any time, the button manufacturer could have cranked out thousands more buttons.

■ USING SCARCITY TO GET REAL ESTATE BARGAINS

Let's look at how we can use the power of scarcity to persuade someone to accept a proposal they otherwise wouldn't.

A few years ago, I bought 100 acres of land, which was listed for $185,000, near Mount Rainier in the state of Washington. Because of the superb location, on a hill with sweeping views from Mount Rainier in the East to the Olympic Peninsula in the West, I knew it would be a terrific buy at $150,000. My opening offer was $115,050, using the Ivory Soap odd number principle I described earlier, in our chapter on credibility. When you use a precise number, people believe you have really analyzed this thing and have made them your very best offer.

In negotiating, I teach that if you're going in so low that the first offer is liable to offend the other person, it's better to imply some flexibility. Otherwise, you may not even get the negotiations started: they'll be so insulted, they won't even counter.

However, in this instance I decided to go for broke. I told the agent that if she couldn't get this offer accepted exactly as written, I would go ahead and make an offer on a much smaller 20-acre parcel that she'd shown me earlier. This parcel was listed at $69,000.

This wasn't true—I was willing to go up in price, but I didn't want to let the real estate agent know this. After all, she wasn't working for me, she was working for the seller. Which is almost always true in a real estate transaction. The seller is paying the agents, so even if they are working for you, the buyer, they still have a primary responsibility to the seller who is paying them.

When she relayed this piece of information to the seller as she presented my offer, she was sending a clear signal: there's only going to be one offer on this property. Take this exactly as proposed, or there may never be another. That's scarcity!

To my delight and surprise, they accepted the offer exactly as I'd presented it!

So scarcity is a powerful persuasion tool. Never give the other person the open-ended opportunity to take advantage of your proposal. Let them know that an opportunity such as the one you're proposing only comes along once in a blue moon, and they should seize that opportunity now. Whenever you're trying to persuade someone, always imply that if they don't accept your proposal, there's a scarcity of options available to them. It'll give you control!

■ KEY POINTS IN THIS CHAPTER:

1. Scarcity is a key pressure point in persuasion. If you can convince the other person that the opportunity you're offering is limited, you can persuade him or her to act quickly.

2. Scarcity increases value. People will pay more for something they perceive to be in short supply. This is an obvious principle that can be validated by a visit to any antique store. However, we rarely understand how, by subtly implying scarcity, we can raise the value of a product or service in the buyer's mind.

■ CHAPTER FIVE

BRINGING THEM TO THEIR KNEES WITH TIME PRESSURE

In this chapter you'll learn about the power of time pressure. The faster you can persuade the other person to decide, the more likely you are to get what you want. The longer you give the person to think about it, the less chance you have of getting what you want.

It amazes me that it has become the custom in the real estate industry to give the seller two or three days to "think about" the buyer's offer. The longer you give someone to think about a proposal, the less chance you have of it being what you want.

> The faster you can persuade the other person to decide, the more likely you are to get what you want. The longer you give the person to think about it, the less chance you have of getting what you want.

If we lived in a world of trained negotiators, with both sides genuinely interested in seeking creative solutions that also benefit the

61

other side, there would be an advantage to giving the other person time to think about it. This is so because if they truly have your interest at heart, they may think of a benefit they could give you, one that doesn't detract from their position. Unfortunately, we don't live in a world like that. The reality of the situation is that if you give the other side time to think of a change to your proposal, it will probably be a change that benefits them and detracts from your position.

The faster you can get people to decide, the more chance you have of getting what you want. The longer you give them to think about it, the less chance you have of getting what you want.

■ HOW A CHILD USES TIME PRESSURE LIKE A PRO

Don't your children use time pressure on you all the time? When do they ask you for something? Just as you're leaving, or just as they're rushing out of the house, right? Once, when my youngest son was home from college, he drove me across town to Los Angeles airport for a speaking tour. We didn't talk about anything of consequence on the way over. We were curbside, and the skycap had my luggage on his cart. John said to me, "Dad, I'm sorry, I forgot. I need $50 to fix the muffler on my car."

I said, "John, don't do this to me—I teach this stuff! How come this didn't come up before? Why are you waiting until now?"

"I'm sorry, Dad, but I got a fix-it ticket, and it has to be done before you get back from your trip. Let me have the money and I'll explain it when you get back. OK?"

They're not really that manipulative. It's just that, over the years, they've instinctively learned that they stand a better chance of getting what they want under time pressure.

■ MOVING PEOPLE WITH THE POWER OF TIME PRESSURE

So the question becomes, "Does the person you're trying to persuade feel he must act quickly, to seize the opportunity while he still can?"

If you're applying for a job, have you let them know that, while they're your first choice, you have three other offers to choose from?

That's time pressure, isn't it? Because you won't be in the job market very long.

If you're an employer trying to get an employee to accept a transfer, have you put it like this?

"Bob, I hate to put any pressure on you . . . ." I call that a preparer: you've just prepared Bob for pressure—you've given yourself permission to put pressure on him. "Bob, I hate to put any pressure on you, but the president is insisting I fill this spot right away. Of course, you're my first choice, but if I can't convince you that this move to Guam is great for you, I'm just going to have to go with my second choice. I don't want to do that, Bob. So where are we, on a scale of one to ten?"

That's time pressure, isn't it? You're letting Bob know that this opportunity won't be around for long.

■ SECRETS FROM INSIDE A TIME SHARE CLOSING ROOM

If you really want to experience what a powerful persuader time pressure can be, take a tour of a time share real estate development.

On the face of it, time sharing is very much a win-win idea. It takes the condominium concept one step farther. The condo concept says that sometimes you're better off not owning the entire piece of real estate. That if you only own the portion of the building you occupy, the cost of the portions that have mutual benefit for all the owners—such as recreational facilities—can be shared. Time sharing says that for a second home, you don't have to own all the building, all the time. That if you just owned it for the weeks when you'd be using it, you'd be better off. Unfortunately, the idea got into the hands of some unscrupulous promoters, and what could have been an outstanding concept got a bad reputation.

I was once privy to the inside workings of a Florida time share operation. Let's face it, time share people eat their young! They just don't take any hostages. They know how to take unsuspecting people off the street and have them make a $20,000 investment before their free breakfast hits their stomachs.

Here's how they do it. The hook is an offer of free tickets to DisneyWorld. You can't buy gas, or go to a store or restaurant in Orange County, Florida, without being approached with this offer. To a vacationer on a budget that's almost irresistible: at 8 in the morning, you can get a free breakfast, take a quick tour of the time share project, say no, and pick up $50 worth of tickets. By 9 o'clock you'll be walking down Main Street, feeling good that you've beaten the system.

Not exactly. The free breakfast puts you under an obligation to listen, just as I taught you in Chapter Three, and the salesperson who escorts you isn't the kind of person you expected at all. You had braced yourself to resist a high-pressure sales pitch, but this isn't high pressure at all. She's just the sweetest person in the world and reminds you of your favorite aunt.

She explains the time share concept over breakfast and deliberately understates the appearance of the unit you're to see. Remember what we talked about in Chapter Two, on credibility? Never tell a person more than you think they'll believe. Here, they've done even better than that—the image the sales agent has created in your mind is that the unit's a good value but nothing to get excited about.

Then you're taken over to see the model. And, wow! Is this thing ever fantastic! It looks like the Taj Mahal. It has a sunken whirlpool bath, mirrors all over the place, and all the latest appliances. By now you're excited. Maybe this is something you should think about.

You go back to the closing room to get your free tickets. There are twenty other families crowded into a small room, seated at tiny cocktail tables. You tell them you'd like to think about it. They drop the price, for a today only special. They're applying the potent effect of time pressure. If you could buy it today, for $5,000 off the regular price, would you wait to think about it and then be willing to pay the full price three days from now? Of course not.

Their whole presentation is dependent on the credibility of this one issue. That there are no "be backs" in the time share industry. Unless they can persuade you the offer to sell at $20,000 is no good tomorrow, they're sunk.

You're still resisting. Now you're dealing with a T.O. person, as they're known in the trade, literally, a turnover person. If the first salesperson can't close you, you're turned over to a hard closer. Nobody gets their free tickets until they've dealt with the T.O. person, and they'll do anything to get you to buy.

I once asked a time share sales manager what was the hardest close he'd condone at his operation. I expected him to say, "Nothing stronger than the salesperson turning to the husband and saying 'You mean to tell me that this beautiful lady has loved you and cared for you for twenty-two years, and she wants to do this, and you won't spend the money?'"

But this sales manager responded with a straight face, "Roger, I don't approve of physical violence in the closing room. Anything short of that is OK."

At the next table a T.O. man is praying with his customers for the right decision. They've linked hands around the table and their heads are down, waiting for guidance. Finally he says, "I feel the Good Lord talking to me. Yes I do! He's telling me that you should make this investment! Glory be!" You're shaking your head in disbelief. This has to be "Candid Camera"!

Now a different persuasion factor is taking over in the closing room. Other couples have made the decision to invest. They're being introduced to the group as the "proud owners of week forty-four." Everyone's applauding. There's an ether in the room that's intoxicating people. The new factor is peer group pressure. It's devastatingly powerful.

Swept up in all the excitement, the feelings of obligation, and the time pressure, it isn't long before you're the proud owner of a time share week also. A $20,000 investment that you hadn't even been considering three hours before.

But wait a minute. Hasn't Florida, along with many other states, passed rescission laws to protect the public against these high-pressure tactics? Oh sure, in Florida you can call back days later and tell them that you've changed your mind, and they must refund your deposit. But a very small percentage of people do that.

Why? Because the time share people have perfected another persuasion technique called "bringing them back off the mountain." Just as a mountain guide knows that getting his clients to the top of the mountain is only half the battle, the time share salesperson must bring you back from the heights of giddy excitement. They must get you to confirm your decision in a more rational mood. They do this with all the care of an anesthesiologist bringing you off ether.

They'll prestate every one of your possible reasons for wanting to rescind. "You'll probably think that you made a rash decision in the heat of the moment. You'll probably wake up in the middle of the night wondering if you've overspent your budget. You may even start wondering if I talked you into making this investment just so that I could earn a commission. Probably your brother-in-law will tell you you've made a mistake. However, none of these is true. The truth of the matter is, you've worked hard all your lives, and you deserve a little luxury on your vacations. Isn't that right?"

At one time share project I researched, I was introduced to a kindly old man who was tending roses on the grounds. I thought, "What's a nice old man like this doing, working at a place that makes the Chicago Commodities Center look like a preschool?" It turned out that he was the owner of the project.

"Could I ask you something?" I said to the sales manager. "Does he have any idea what's going on in that closing room?"

"Good lord, no," he replied. "If he had any idea he'd go slit his wrists."

Naturally, you won't want to use the kind of high-pressure tactics used by a few unethical time share salespeople. However, you should be aware that under time pressure, people become more flexible. Your chances of persuading them are much greater if they feel even the subtle effect of time pressure.

The faster you can get people to decide, the more chance you have of getting what you want. The longer you give them to think about it, the less chance you have of getting what you want.

■ KEY POINTS IN THIS CHAPTER

1. The faster you can persuade the other person to decide, the more likely you are to get what you want.

2. The longer you give them to think about it, the less chance you have of getting what you want.

3. If you give the other person time to think of a change to your proposal, it will probably be a change that benefits them, not you.

4. Learn from your children. They ask you for things at the very last moment, because they instinctively know that under time pressure, you become more flexible.

5. Let people know that the opportunity you're offering won't be around for very long.

6. Put teeth into it. If you say that a special price is available today only, you must mean it. The moment they suspect that they could still get the same price tomorrow, you have neutralized

the effect of time pressure. You may lose some sales as you put this policy into effect, but in the long run, you'll win.

7. Learn how to "bring people back from the mountain." They may regret the decision later and want to rescind the transaction. When you do get them to make a decision under time pressure, you must have them affirm their decision in a less emotional atmosphere.

CHAPTER SIX

THE ZEN-LIKE ART OF SHARING SECRETS

■ THE MAGICAL THREE-STEP FORMULA FOR GETTING COOPERATION FROM THE OTHER PERSON

The next Power Persuasion technique is the art of sharing secrets, and it's something that will really fascinate you. It's Zen-like in its ability to influence people.

Interrogators use it to break people's resistance to sharing information, and you can also use it as a remarkable persuasion tool. It's a three-step process that is magical:

1. Tell a secret.
2. Make a confession.
3. Ask a favor.

It developed from a technique taught to our spies in World War II, that would help them if captured. A spy who completely denies any wrongdoing antagonizes the interrogator and causes him to try even harder to get a confession. Instead, the prisoner tells a secret by making a confession. For example, he confesses that he's been visiting a married girlfriend or transporting merchandise stolen from his friends. Then he asks the interrogator the favor of keeping it secret. It draws the other person into a conspiracy, and this makes it harder for the questioner to abuse the prisoner.

Here's how it works in business. Harry sells luxury yachts. He says, "Mr. Buyer, I think we know each other well enough that I can share a little secret with you. This model has been outfitted with an upgraded radio by mistake, and the owner of the boat yard didn't notice it yet. If you promise not to tell a soul, I'll let you have it for the base price."

Charlie is a manager who has just had one of his key people hand in his resignation. He uses the tell-a-secret, make-a-confession, and ask-a-favor technique.

He says, "Fred, I can understand exactly how you feel right now. If you promise to keep it a secret, I'll tell you why I know exactly how you feel. Fair enough? Do I have your word that you won't repeat what I'm about to tell you?"

Fred leans forward like a conspirator. "Sure, Charlie," he says, "just because I'm leaving, it doesn't mean you can't trust me."

"I quit this company once. I've never told anybody about this before, but just like you I was the top salesperson in the region. A competitor offered me a higher commission split and a new Cadillac if I'd go with them. I thought I was so well liked by my customers that they'd follow me whichever company I went with. Boy, did I make a mistake! Sure they liked me, but I found out they liked what I'd been selling them even better. No way would they change suppliers. That was back in the days when this company was willing to bend the rules about rehiring people. When I came crawling back, they were good enough to give me a second chance. That wouldn't happen today. Do me a favor, Fred, don't make the same mistake that I did, please."

What's the key to this technique? It's the fact that secret information always seems more valid. If you want to convince people of something you doubt they'll believe, start by saying, "I shouldn't be telling you this, but . . ." or "I'm telling you this in strictest confidence."

People who have mastered the art of large corporation politics have used this to engineer their own promotions. They corner the company's biggest gossip in the lunchroom, and they lean toward him and whisper confidentially, "Bob, can I trust you to keep a secret?"

Bob, blissfully unaware that David singled him out solely because he could be trusted *not* to keep a secret, whispers back, "Of course you can, David, you know me."

Then David continues, "I really shouldn't be telling you this. It was told to me in strictest confidence. No, I'm sorry, I really shouldn't."

By now Bob is drooling at the thought of some new juicy piece of gossip. "Go ahead," he encourages, "you know I won't tell a soul."

"You're right," David says, "I can trust you, can't I? Actually I was going to ask you a favor. Somebody told me in strictest confidence that I was up for promotion to vice president. Have you heard anything about it?"

Bob's eyes widen in amazement, "No, I haven't David, but I'll ask around and see what I can find out."

"No, no, Bob, you mustn't do that. Don't mention a word of this to anyone. You have to promise."

In fact, there never was a rumor about a promotion. However, there will be, and by the end of the day, it'll be a big one. Everyone will be talking about David's impending promotion. Eventually, somebody in top management is going to say, "I've been hearing a lot lately about David Smith getting a vice presidency. What have you heard about this?"

The other person will say, "I haven't heard anything official, but everyone's talking about it, so there must be something to it. He's doing a good job for us. I guess he's due." Soon, David's name has come to the top of the list for people getting promoted to vice president.

■ WHY FORBIDDING AGGRAVATES FAMILY PROBLEMS

So what's the magic in telling secrets? Every parent knows that if children are denied something, it makes them want it more.

Once, a lady I was dating banned her 15-year-old daughter from going to the shopping center with a certain boy. If the daughter hadn't been so sure her mother would object, she probably wouldn't have wanted to go out with the boy in the first place.

My experience in raising three children is that you should focus on the true objective of parenthood, which is to make your children independent. So when they're about 14 years old, you should be through telling them what to do. Of course they still need guidance, but it needs to be done through persuasion, not instruction.

Let's say you're the father of an 18-year-old daughter who's just informed you that she plans to spend the upcoming three-day weekend in the mountains with her boyfriend. Probably it's totally innocent, but your experience of this relates back to when *you* were dating 18-year-olds! That thought causes you to freak out! You yell at her, "Does three days also include two nights?"

"Oh, Daddy, you don't trust me at all, do you?" she replies. "I'm an adult, and I can do exactly what I want."

"Not as long as I'm paying the bills," you reply. "As long as you live in this house, you'll follow my rules." Neither of you meant for the situation to escalate like that, but now you've taken positions, and you're both obsessed with defending those positions.

Problems like this arise because the father doesn't understand the power of secrecy: that forbidden fruit always tastes sweeter.

A better approach is to use the technique of "painting a picture of the future." You tell her, "I'm glad you want to discuss it with me first, though you're an adult and can make your own decision. Honey, who knows what lies in your future? Maybe one day you'll be running for president, or vice president, or U.S. senator. And there you are at a press conference having to answer questions from reporters about this weekend. Don't you think it would be smart to be more discreet? Why don't you both come up to the lake with us instead?"

■ WHY CENSORED INFORMATION SEEMS MORE VALUABLE

I think our Founding Fathers were blessed with extreme insight when they wrote such strong guarantees of freedom of speech into the Constitution. Censoring anyone from doing anything clearly makes them want to do it more.

Judges face a peculiar problem when it comes to what juries see as secret information. Very often, during a trial, attorneys introduce information that shouldn't be considered by the jury. The judge can do two things: declare a mistrial, which would be extreme, or instruct the jury to disregard the evidence. The problem with an instruction to disregard is that it has the opposite effect on the jury. Information given in secret tends to be especially believable.

An extensive study at the University of Chicago Law School proved this. The professor impaneled juries to decide the amount of damages in an injury lawsuit. When he introduced evidence that the defendant was insured against the loss, the average award went up 13 percent. Yet, when the judge told the jury they must disregard this piece of information, the average award shot up 40 percent.

Clearly, there's persuasive value in letting people in on confidential information. Try drawing people into your confidence by sharing a secret with them. If you want them to really pay attention to what you're saying, tell them how much trouble you'd be in if you got caught telling them.

■ KEY POINTS IN THIS CHAPTER

1. The magical three-step formula for getting cooperation from the other person is (a) tell a secret, (b) make a confession, and (c) ask a favor.

2. Sharing a secret draws the other person into a conspiracy and makes it harder for them to oppose you.

3. Forbidden fruit always tastes sweeter. When you use your authority to try to stop someone from doing something, it makes them want to do it more.

4. Censored information always seems more valuable. If you want people to really take notice of what you're saying, explain that you shouldn't be telling them, and you'd be in trouble if you got caught.

THE POWER OF ASSOCIATION: TYING YOUR PERSUASION TO SOMETHING GOOD

Wouldn't it be interesting if, as we tried to persuade someone, we were able to conjure up in his or her mind thoughts that were very pleasant and warm? Wouldn't it make them very receptive to what we were saying? Of course it would! Power Persuaders do it all the time, taking advantage of this error in human thinking: once we associate one thing with another, it's very hard for our mind to break that association. I call it the power of association, and it's a critical persuasion technique.

Singer Robert Goulet points out that early in his career, Ed Sullivan got it in his head that Goulet was from Canada, despite strong denials from the performer. "Ed Sullivan introduced me on national television so often as being from Canada, I began to wonder if it wasn't true," Goulet would quip.

> Casey Stengel: "Robert Goulet has effeminate appeal, just like me."

Business genius Harold Geneen has a similar obsession with numbers. A president of one of his companies told me that when Geneen first bought that company, management was intimidated by his reputation and didn't know how to handle him. "He shot a question at me, and I didn't know the answer. Rather than having the courage to tell him I didn't know the number, I made an educated guess. When I researched it, I found that I was way off. On his next visit I told him what had happened, and gave him the correct figure. That was fine with him, except that I could never budge him from the original figure he'd set in his mind." Once he'd heard that number associated with that statistic, he wasn't able to break the association.

How can we use the power of association to influence other people? We don't have to search far for examples. Look at the celebrity ads on television. It's no coincidence that your teenager wears the same tennis shoes as Michael Jackson and drinks the same soft drink. Texaco gas stations still make us think of friendly service, years after they quit giving it, because of the long association with Bob Hope. We think of AT&T in friendly terms, largely because of the warm and friendly voice of spokesperson Cliff Robertson.

Manufacturers don't pay fortunes to celebrity spokespeople because they're credible experts on the qualities of the product. They pay because we have trouble disassociating their product from the celebrity. The product itself becomes warm and friendly, or sexy, or desirable, or supermasculine, or whatever other traits we see that celebrity as having.

Another example is the way that sports fans associate with their teams when they're winning. "We're number one! We're number one!" is the chant. I'm sure the players must be thinking, "What's this 'we' stuff, buddy. Where were you last year when we were in the cellar?"

When a football or baseball team fights its way to the Super Bowl or the World Series, and then loses, we're treated to the spectacle of fans screaming at the television cameras, "*We* had a chance to win the championship, and *they* blew it!"

Listen to your local radio station. The call signals come right after the most popular hits. The program director wants to hit you with their identification signal when you're feeling good, in order to create a positive association.

Persuaders can use these kinds of association techniques. For example, people react more favorably to a proposal when they're doing something they enjoy, such as golfing, skiing, or sailing.

I remember a salesperson who tried to apply this principle with me, but didn't think it through. He invited me to play golf at the beautiful Coto de Caza Golf Club in Orange County, California. A golf course is a good place to build association power with a potential customer. With luck I would always associate him and his company with the fine feeling I would get from that round of golf. The problem was that this course was a killer! Rated one of the toughest courses in the country, it was far beyond my playing capability. I lost two balls and took a 10 on the first hole, and it went downhill from there!

> Chi Chi Rodriguez: "Golf is the most fun you can have without taking your clothes off."

As hard as I tell myself it was all my fault, not his, I'm well aware that when I think of that salesperson and his company, I associate them with that miserable day on the golf course. Why on earth would any salesperson do that? Unless you're sure you've got a par golfer on your hands, take him to a course where he can have a good time and shoot the lowest score of his life!

Very often salespeople offer to buy their clients lunch, but they do it for the wrong reason. It's true that buying something for the client creates an obligation—we talked about that in Chapter Three—but that's not the reason you buy someone lunch. Chances are, the client is perfectly capable of buying her own lunch. You do it because you want her to associate you and your product with the pleasurable experience of a fine lunch. That's why astute businesspeople spend a fortune on business lunches, not because it creates an obligation, but because the pleasurable act of eating will be linked with the proposal in the customer's mind.

It's amazing to me that psychological researchers misunderstood this principle for decades. Any salesperson will tell you that it's easier to sell a customer over lunch. "A well-fed customer is one who will buy" is a salesperson's standard belief. Nobody bothered very much to find out why this works so well.

Then curious researchers conducted studies and came to the conclusion that when people are distracted by something, they are more likely to be persuaded than if you have their total concentration. Studies as far back as 1964 by Leon Festinger and Nathan Maccoby seemed to prove it. However, subsequent studies finessed this by researching exactly what distraction worked best. Guess what? They found that food and sex are the two best distractors. Stick a plate of good food in front of someone while you're trying to persuade him, and you'll do better than if you have his undivided attention. Show a man pictures of naked women, and you can sway his opinion more easily than you can if there is no distraction. Conversely, if the distraction is an unpleasant one, your persuasive ability goes down.

It seems clear to me: the theory that a mild level of distraction enhances your ability to persuade is sheer bunk. What's really going on is that people associate your presentation with the distraction. If it's a pleasant distraction, such as a fine lunch, they associate your presentation with that pleasure and are more likely to buy.

Power Persuaders know how to finesse the business lunch experience even further. Let's imagine you're taking a key client to lunch. However carefully you plan, there will be high points and low points to the meal. There may be an unexpected wait for the table—a low point. Once seated, the waiter comes promptly, and quickly serves generous drinks—a high point. A chosen item on the menu is sold out—a low point. And so on.

Power Persuaders are careful to pace the mention of their company's name, or talk about their product, to the high points. Don't magnify the problem by shutting up during the low points, but be careful to avoid mention of you, your company, or your product. You'll be amazed at how subliminally associating your message with other pleasurable moments will build a positive base for your persuasive abilities.

Watch how auto manufacturers use this technique in their TV commercials. Have you ever seen a car ad that shows how well the car does in gridlock traffic during the evening rush hour? No! It's always zooming around on a beautiful mountain road, free as a bird, with a beautiful woman at the driver's side.

Smart salespeople know how to paint mental pictures of the pleasurable feeling that comes from using the product. People don't buy a thousand dollars' worth of new ski equipment because of the latest technical advances. They buy them for the sheer joy of zooming down a mountainside on a crystal-clear morning.

People don't buy travel trailers because of the money they'll save. They buy them for the sheer joy of waking up completely alone in a meadow by the side of a pristine alpine lake.

Power Persuaders know how to associate their message with pleasurable images in the other person's mind.

■ KEY POINTS IN THIS CHAPTER

1. Once we associate one thing with another, it's very hard for our mind to break that association.

2. Manufacturers don't pay fortunes to celebrity spokespeople because they're credible experts on the qualities of the product. They pay because we have trouble disassociating their product from the celebrity.

3. People react more favorably to a proposal when they're doing something they enjoy, such as golfing, skiing, or sailing.

4. Pace the mention of your company and product to the high points of a business lunch.

5. Learn how to paint pictures of your product or service that visually tie it in to pleasurable experiences.

■ CHAPTER EIGHT

■ CHAPTER EIGHT

THE POWER OF CONSISTENCY: IT'S MORE IMPORTANT TO DO IT OFTEN THAN TO DO IT RIGHT

In this chapter I'll teach you the most incredibly powerful persuasion technique of all: consistency. People are drawn to you if you act consistently and are repelled if you act inconsistently. It's a concept that takes only seconds to learn, but it may take a lifetime to appreciate fully its power.

Why do we admire this characteristic so much? Our need for consistency comes from the tremendous need we have to develop a predictable world in which to exist. You know, don't you, that your most basic and intense need is the desire to survive. This is a key reason why humans, above all other species, have survived and prospered on earth. When our backs are against the wall, we will adapt, change, or do almost anything to assure our survival.

Our next strongest instinct is the need for security in our lives. Security is the assurance that we can continue to survive.

Think of being shipwrecked on a desert island. Your first concern would be to figure out if you could survive on the island. Is there enough food and fresh water? Having established that you can survive

78

on a short-term basis, your next concern would be to assure the continuance of your survival. You might develop a system to store rainwater so you wouldn't run out of drinking water. You might build a compound in which you could store supplies of food, protecting it from the elements and any rodents or animals that might be in the area.

The same basic need for survival and security, which would be obvious to us on a desert island, still drives us in modern civilization. We surround ourselves with an environment that is consistent and predictable. Instead of foraging for food on a day-to-day basis to assure our survival, we store it in huge freezers. Instead of daily looking for ways to make money, we prefer an association with an organization that consistently offers us predictable rewards.

So in our minds, we equate consistency with our two most basic needs: survival and security. If there is consistency in our world, we feel secure. When faced with inconsistent people and circumstances, we feel insecure. So, in our relationships, we admire people who act in consistent patterns of behavior. Thus we are much more likely to be persuaded by someone whom we see as consistent.

Abraham Maslow came to see this need for consistency in our lives as the very highest of human needs. Maslow is famous for his pyramid of human needs, which showed our needs as

1. Survival
2. Security—the need to assure our continued survival
3. Social—the need to interact with other humans
4. Self-esteem—the need to be respected by others
5. Self-actualization—the need to feel fulfilled

After he'd developed this pyramid, he came up with two needs higher than those:

6. Cognitive needs—the need to know
7. Aesthetic needs—the need for beauty and consistency

Our cognitive needs are clear. Human beings have a tremendous need to know what's going on: we can't stand a mystery. Human beings will spend a billion and a half dollars to put a Hubble telescope up in space, because we've just got to know what's going on, but a cow in a field will stay in that field all its life and never wonder what's on the other side of the hill.

Our aesthetic needs are also obvious: we are attracted to beauty and order. We can't stand a painting that isn't hanging straight—we have an inborn need to straighten it.

The need for consistency in our lives is a powerful force because it bonds the sophisticated need for an aesthetic environment—for beauty in our lives—with the most basic of needs—the need for survival.

This need for consistency is an awesome force, and Power Persuaders can ride that force to get what they want from other people.

■ USING THE POWER OF CONSISTENCY

Remember the movie *The Bridge on the River Kwai*? It was David Lean's superb adaptation of Pierre Boulle's book about prisoners of war in the Asian jungles during World War II and a brilliant portrayal of the power of consistency! You may recall that Alec Guinness played the role of a British officer, persuaded by the Japanese to build a bridge over the River Kwai. He determines that it will be the finest bridge he and his men can possibly build. (Boulle based his book on a true incident, when the Japanese crossed the border into neutral Thailand to construct a supply line built with prisoner-of-war labor.)

The fascinating thing to me is that David Lean made the movie in 1957, some 15 years after the incident. And today, over 35 years since the movie was released, the actual location of the bridge is still a major tourist attraction. Even the place where Lean filmed the movie, a thousand miles away in Sri Lanka, is a must-see location for tourists visiting that country.

Why this extraordinary fascination? Because the movie vividly portrayed one of the most important traits about which a Power Persuader can learn: consistency.

The British colonel suffered incredible torture because of his initial refusal to let his men work on the Japanese bridge, which was vital to the Japanese war effort. He finally agreed with the justification that it would be good therapy for the men. The men under him assumed that this was some kind of trick, and he wanted them to sabotage the bridge with poor workmanship. They obviously didn't understand the mind-set of the British army officer. Having spent a lifetime standing for pride in his country, in his regiment, and in his service to his king, he simply found it inconsistent to do less than his best in building the bridge. Although it would aid the enemy, he urged his men to show the Japanese just how fine a British bridge could be.

So here we have the irony of British prisoners of war laboring to build a bridge that would help the combat efforts of their mortal enemies. When escaped prisoner William Holden returned to blow up the bridge, did Guinness cheer him on? Not at all! He did everything he could to stop Holden from blowing up "his" bridge.

Here's the fascinating thing for persuaders: who was the hero of the movie? The American who was risking his life to destroy the bridge? or the Englishman who was aiding and abetting the enemy? The British officer, played by Alec Guinness, was clearly the hero.

Why? Because we revere people who have consistent behavior. We despise and fear people who are erratic. Power Persuaders understand that exhibiting consistency in behavior is an incredibly potent force, because it conditions the other person to trust you.

■ WHY IT'S BETTER TO BE A TYRANT THAN A WIMP

In our minds a high degree of consistency is synonymous with intellectual and personal strength. We'll overlook almost anything if a person is reliable in their behavior. Winston Churchill was a bellicose, belligerent person. His desire to impose total control on the British Empire beyond the end of World War II was hopelessly archaic and could have led to anarchy. However, we love and respect him for his strength of convictions. Similarly we've come to love Harry Truman and forgive him for his salty language and outbursts of temper.

John F. Kennedy spoke in grand terms of the new frontier, of the mantle of power passing to a new generation born in this century. He projected a consistent set of standards. He did it very well. Bobby Kennedy in his last years as a presidential candidate also learned to do it well.

One of the most beloved presidents of this century, Ronald Reagan, was brilliant at projecting the power of consistency. He could get away with some outrageous acts because of it. We have a law in this country stopping our government officials from ordering the assassination of another government leader. However, Reagan got away with ordering our Air Force to drop a load of 6,000-pound bombs on Muammar al-Qaddafi's tent, and we loved him for it. Why? Because he was acting consistently. He told us he was that kind of person, and he lived up to his image. Conversely, the low point of Reagan's popularity was when he appeared to have been negotiating with the Iranians for the release of the hostages held in Lebanon, when he'd told us he'd never do that.

The Senate spent $50 million on the IranGate hearings and couldn't prove any presidential wrongdoing. Yet, public opinion reacted in completely the opposite manner. We loved him for the apparent show of strength in trying to send Qaddafi into the next world as a war hero, and we maligned him for his apparent inconsistency in trying to trade arms for hostages.

■ WHY WE'RE SUSPICIOUS OF INCONSISTENT BEHAVIOR

Conversely, to illustrate how suspicious we are of inconsistent behavior, let's look at this scenario.

Let's say you're on a camping trip. Perhaps you've backpacked into a remote area of the Grand Teton National Park. You appear to be the only person for miles around, until a man comes into the clearing and starts to set up his tent. The stranger may make you a little nervous. Could this be the serial killer that you read about in the Jackson newspaper? Will he steal from you, or threaten you in some way? You watch him closely, and you trust him only when he's established a consistent pattern of behavior.

■ USING CONSISTENCY TO MOVE THE MERCHANDISE

Here's how all this applies to the power of persuasion.

We like and admire consistent behavior in other people. They like and admire it in us. If we're willing to take a stand for our principles, especially if it appears we're risking financial loss, it builds trust in the other person, and he or she loves us for it.

For example, you might sell computers, and you've got the courage to say to your customers, "Of course you'd like to save money. And I'd favor it too, if it were the right thing for you to do—but it isn't. I know that you won't be completely happy unless you get the model with the 100-megabyte hard drive. So, I'm sorry, but I won't sell you anything less."

They love you for that! Of course it'll raise a few eyebrows, but if you've done your homework and you're right, you'll have power with that customer. If you back down, how are they going to respect you?

Suppose your doctor told you that you needed triple bypass heart surgery, and you said, "I think I can get by with a double bypass."

If he said, "OK, let's try a double and see how it works out," how would you feel about him then? You'd probably want a second opinion, wouldn't you?

■ WHY CARTER'S DOWNFALL WAS REAGAN'S WINDFALL

Inconsistency was President Carter's downfall. He was one of the nicest, most moral and ethical presidents we've ever had. He was also one of the hardest-working men who ever occupied the White House and probably among the most intelligent—he majored in nuclear physics. However, he lost his ability to persuade because he appeared to vacillate on issues. We never knew if he felt strongly enough to follow through if the going got tough.

Take, for example, his handling of the visa for the shah of Iran. The shah was living in his beautiful villa on Acapulco Bay. He became seriously ill and requested a visa to come to this country for medical treatment. At first Carter said no, fearing repercussions in Iran. Then he changed his mind and approved the visa so that the shah could get cancer treatment in New York. When this created a surge of anti-American protests in Iran, he changed his mind again—and made him move to Panama, to take the pressure off the situation.

Lillian Carter: "Sometimes when I look at my children I say to myself, 'Lillian, you should have stayed a virgin.'"

I don't think Ronald Reagan would've done that. Reagan would've made a decision, one way or the other, and stuck with it.

Now take Reagan's decision to deny Yasir Arafat a visa he needed so that he could address the general assembly of the United Nations in New York. How would you react if you got voted down 150 to 2 in the United Nations—and one of the two was your vote— then have the United Nations decide to move its assembly to Geneva to go around your decision? Wouldn't you think that you'd want to take another look at it? Wouldn't you tend to think, "Maybe I goofed on that one"? No! You make a decision and you stick with it, because projecting that you're consistent in your behavior is the most powerful persuasion factor you have going for you.

During George Bush's first few years as president, he was all over the board on his level of consistency, and you could see his popularity ratings move in direct relationship to it. At first he was very consistent in his opposition to new taxes. "They're going to come down from Capitol Hill," he told us, "and tell me we've got to have new taxes. And I'm going to tell them, 'Read my lips, no new taxes.' So they'll go back and talk about it, and they'll come back and say, 'Mr. President, we've got to have new taxes.' And I'll say, 'Read my lips, no new taxes.'"

We loved him for it! Then he had to back down on that issue, and we hated him for it—his popularity dropped from 80 percent to 45 percent almost overnight.

Then along came the Persian Gulf War. How would you rate him for consistency on his handling of the war? A perfect score, right? Nobody could have been more consistent in handling Saddam Hussein. And we loved him for it! His popularity soared from the forties up to the nineties.

Then he was faced with the problem of the Kurdish refugees. One day he was saying, "I will not send American troops into the middle of a civil war that's been going on forever." That's great; take a stand, but stick with the stand you've taken. The very next day, he changed his mind and sent troops into northern Iraq. His approval rating immediately dropped from the nineties down to the fifties.

What clearer proof could we have? People want to follow, they want to be led, by someone they see as consistent in his behavior.

If you're a manager or employer, I can tell you one thing with absolute certainty about your people. They'd rather you got them together and said, "Hey gang, this is what we stand for around here. These are our moral and ethical standards, and you can count on it that we'll never deviate from them." They'd rather you say that than have you vacillate on every little issue that came along.

We don't want to be influenced by people with inconsistent standards. Power Persuaders understand that consistency is an awesome force. If we act consistently, people will be persuaded to follow us. If we understand how strongly people need consistency in their lives, we can use that to mold their behavior.

■ KEY POINTS IN THIS CHAPTER

1. People are drawn to you if you act consistently and are repelled if you act inconsistently.

2. Our need for consistency comes from our tremendous need to develop a predictable world in which to exist.

3. In our minds, we equate consistency with our two most basic needs: survival and security.

4. This need for consistency is an awesome force, and as a Power Persuader, you can ride that force to get what you want from other people.

5. Exhibiting consistency in behavior is an incredibly potent force, because it conditions the other person to trust you.

6. We trust strangers only when they've established a consistent pattern of behavior.

7. Make a decision and stick with it, because projecting that you're consistent in your behavior is the most powerful persuasion factor you have going for you.

8. People want to follow, they want to be led, by someone they see as consistent in their behavior.

■ CHAPTER NINE

WHY CONSISTENT BEHAVIOR KICKS YOUR PERFORMANCE INTO HIGH GEAR

There's a tremendous personal benefit to developing consistent behavior. It frees up your energy for more important things. Do you sometimes feel that you lack energy, even when you're healthy and rested?

Look and see if a lack of consistency in your behavior isn't draining your vigor. Stay with me, though it may seem that we're drifting away from the topic of persuasion. Far from it! A set of value blueprints can be the most powerful weapon in your persuasion arsenal. This can lead to a perception that you and your business have a consistent set of values by which you operate.

Roy Disney, the financial genius behind Walt Disney Enterprises, used to say that "decision making is easy when values are clear." Very early, the Disney brothers established a clear-cut doctrine. Part of it was the policy to produce only movies suitable for all the family to watch. Over the years outsiders presented Walt Disney with many projects that would've made him another fortune. During times of financial crisis it would've been an infusion of desperately needed capital. However, he never wasted any energy considering these projects, agonizing over whether to take them on or not, because these projects would've violated his preestablished values.

■ THE PERSONAL VALUE BLUEPRINT

If we all had a value blueprint with which to work, a life plan against which we applied our decision making, we could free up vast stores of energy for the really important things.

Let's take the simple act of driving the car to the store. It's only a mile away—should we bother to put on the seat belt? If our value blueprint says that we always drive with a seat belt, there's no wasted energy making a decision. We slip it on almost without realizing it.

On the way to the store, the traffic signal turns yellow. A surge of adrenaline occurs. Should we go for it or hit the brakes? If our value blueprint is that we always stop for yellow lights, we stop calmly, without wasted energy.

A car is standing in a driveway, waiting for an opening to pull into traffic. Should we wave it ahead of us or let it wait? With a value blueprint in place, there's no hesitation.

Now please understand that I'm not telling you how to drive, although I do care about your safety. If your blueprint tells you to gun it for yellow lights, or never wear a seat belt, and never let a jerk pull in front of you, that—I suppose—is your business. The point here is that if you don't have a value blueprint by which you run your days, you're operating an inefficient, energy-wasting life.

If you waste that much nervous energy just driving to the store, imagine how much waste there is in an *organization* that doesn't have a value blueprint! I've been in organizations like that. The leader has everybody on such a tight rein that people at all levels agonize over decisions, wondering whether the boss will agree with what they're about to do. Because the game plan changes every week, people can never be sure that what was the right decision last week will still be the way to go this week. Organizations that do have a value blueprint are a joy in which to work. As Roy Disney said, when values are clear, decision making is easy.

■ LIFE IS SWEETER WITH A VALUE BLUEPRINT

If you want to be a more persuasive manager, salesperson, business owner, or parent, start with your personal value blueprint.

Let's say that part of your personal value blueprint is that you won't take anything that isn't yours. Does that seem like a lofty goal? I hope not. Moses carried it down from Mount Sinai on stone tablets. Thou shalt not steal. For clarification, let's also say that we've decided that stealing means taking something that's not ours.

Fair enough; no problem, that shouldn't be hard to live with. Simply don't take anything that's not ours. But what about on the golf course. There's not another golfer in sight, and there, nestled in the rough, is a brand new Top Flight XL? Another golfer obviously abandoned it. Surely, it's OK to take that, isn't it? No! If your value blueprint says that you won't take anything that's not yours, you leave it where it is. Let someone else pick it up, but not you.

I've been at prestigious private golf clubs and seen members being screamed at because they picked up somebody else's ball. It's not because they needed the ball—they could afford to stand there hitting new balls off into the sunset for the rest of their lives, if they chose.

Suppose that you're walking along a deserted beach, and there, half buried in the sand, is a Rolex watch. Clearly it was lost at sea and drifted in with the tide. It would be OK to take that, wouldn't it. No! Turn it in to lost and found, or leave it there and let someone else take it, but not you.

OK, now let's try a tougher one. What if you were walking down Wall Street and found a pouch full of negotiable bearer certificates worth over $37 million. Then couldn't you . . .? No! That's exactly what 44-year-old assistant cashier Jim Priceman found and returned to the owners, the A. G. Becker Company. He got a $250 reward from them. A measly $250 for returning $37 million! Oh, well, nobody said it was going to be easy!

■ TRYING TO LIVE WITH THE GOLDEN RULE

I challenge you simply to apply the oldest of personal value blue-prints, the golden rule, and see if you can live with it for 48 hours.

Let me warn you, it isn't going to be easy. On my father's 85th birthday, I rented a 50-foot yacht for his birthday party. It cost $150 per hour, and we could have it for only three hours, because it was booked later in the day. I alerted the whole family and told them exactly at which berth in the San Pedro marina to meet us.

Everyone was there on time except my daughter. The meter was running on the boat, and she was nowhere to be seen. Half an hour went by, and still no word. Everybody was beginning to tear their hair out. It looked as though a carefully planned day was going to be ruined. The two other children were petitioning me to leave without her.

"Not yet," I said calmly. Forty-five minutes went by, still nothing. "Come on dad," the boys said, "if she's this late, she doesn't deserve to go."

"Wait a minute," I said. "There's no big decision to be made here. We operate by the golden rule, don't we? We won't leave until we're sure that she'd want us to leave without her. That time will come, but it isn't here yet."

Exactly one hour late, we saw Julia coming down the dock. She'd been at Elizabeth Arden on Rodeo Drive having her hair done. Were we entitled to be upset? Of course! But anybody can live with the golden rule when it's easy. It takes character in situations like this. My parents, who taught me about the golden rule, were calm, but the boys couldn't wait to start giving her a bad time.

"Remember the golden rule," I said to them out of the corner of my mouth, "if you were her, how would you like to be treated?"

Believe it or not, they went and gave her a big hug, not even mentioning her tardiness. She apologized profusely, and my father said later, with tears in his eyes, that it was the finest day of his entire life.

Straight up. It's a way to climb a mountain, a way to pour a drink, and a really fine way to live a life.

■ KEY POINTS IN THIS CHAPTER

1. A key part of Power Persuasion is having the courage to persuade yourself to live by a set of personal standards.

2. Develop a personal value blueprint—it frees up your energy for more important things.

3. Decision making is easy when values are clear.

4. If you don't have a value blueprint by which you run your days, you're operating an inefficient, energy-wasting life.

5. If we accept the definition of stealing as taking something that's not ours, most of us don't even live by that basic rule.

6. I challenge you simply to apply the oldest of personal value blueprints, the golden rule, and see if you can live with it for 48 hours.

7. Straight up. It's a way to climb a mountain, a way to pour a drink, and a really fine way to live a life.

■ C H A P T E R T E N

BONDING—THE MAGIC KEY TO PERSUASION

In this chapter, I'll teach you a magic key to persuasion, the ability to get the other person to bond to a position.

What do I mean by bonding? Bonding is a term that psychologists use to describe the change that takes place when a mother touches her new baby for the first time. A bond forms between them that lasts into eternity.

Power Persuaders use the term to describe the movement of getting a person to commit to a position. If we can get people to commit to a position, any position, we can then build on their need to remain consistent to that commitment. We've bonded them to that behavioral pattern.

We bond to people with expressions such as, "I've always thought of you as a fair person, and you see yourself that way too, don't you?" Get them to commit to that, and you've almost prescribed their future behavior toward you. It's very hard for them to do anything unfair.

"Harry, you do believe in win-win, don't you? If I show you how you can win, you don't mind me having a win too, do you?" Get a commitment, and you've bonded Harry to that behavior.

Verbal reinforcement of a person's behavior like this is a powerful tool. Can you change the way people behave by complimenting them when they behave the way you want them to, and withholding compliments when they don't? You bet! At Hollins College 24 students in a psychology course decided to see if they could use compliments to change the way the women on campus dressed. For a while, they complimented all the female students who wore blue. It caused the wearing of blue outfits to rise from 25 percent to 38 percent. Then they switched to complimenting any woman who wore red. They caused the appearance of red on campus to double, from 11 percent to 22 percent. You're doing the same thing when you comment favorably on a person's behavior.

By bonding people slowly, layer by layer, we can persuade them to do almost anything. Of course we'd never use persuasion bonding to get somebody to do something illegal or immoral, but it's fascinating to see how powerful it is in action.

In the movie *Wall Street*, Michael Douglas used it to subvert Charlie Sheen to the illegal use of insider information. As you'll recall, Sheen played a Wall Street account executive anxious to get some of Michael Douglas's business. He tells Douglas of an airline company that's about to be exonerated by the FAA in a crash investigation. He helps him make a killing investing in the company's stock. He doesn't tell Douglas that he got this inside information from his father, who works for the airline. However, Douglas finds out, and reminds Sheen that he's committed a criminal act—which bonds Sheen to that new self-image. Douglas's next step is to get Sheen to follow another investor to find out which company he's about to take over. This is objectionable to Sheen, but Douglas has skillfully pushed him into thinking of himself as someone who's capable of breaking the law.

Had Douglas come right out at the start and tried to persuade Sheen to become an overt inside trader, he wouldn't have been successful. But by bonding him one step at a time to this new behavior, he could subvert him.

■ HOW TO SELL UP A STORM USING THE PRINCIPLE OF BONDING

The principle of bonding tells you that you shouldn't be too concerned if you can't get full compliance in the early stages of the persuasion process.

If you can get the other person to agree to even a watered-down request, you'll have more success later. While getting the person to agree to the reduced request, you bond them to a new self-image.

Perhaps you sell office equipment, and a big profit item for you is a service contract that extends the warranty. You may initially have trouble getting the customer to agree to this. The customer says, "We know you make profit on those service warranties. We're a big enough company to take the risk ourselves." If you'll go back to this after you've reached initial agreement, you may find that their attitude has changed completely.

Before you leave, have the courage to say, "Mr. Buyer, could we take another look at this extended warranty? I really believe it's the way for you to go. The issue isn't cash flow, it's preventive maintenance. If your equipment is covered, your employees will call us much sooner, because the call doesn't cost you anything. We'll spot problems before they get worse, and your equipment will last longer."

The customer had just made a big commitment to you, and what you stand for, by agreeing to purchase your equipment. You've got a good chance of them responding with, "Well OK, if you think it's really that important, let's go ahead."

Any time a person bonds to a behavior pattern, she has a mental momentum to reinforce that decision. While she may have rejected the idea out of hand before, it may be a completely different story now. All over America, salespeople are walking away with half a piece of pie when they could have it all. Always make a second effort once the other person has bonded by agreeing to part of your proposal.

■ HOW PEOPLE BOND TO THEIR MENTAL INVESTMENTS

Let me give you an example of how the process of bonding causes the mind to reinforce decisions it has made earlier. Like many other states, California has lottery fever. One week the prize in the weekly "pick six" drawing was $39 million. The day of the drawing, dollar lottery tickets were selling around the state at the rate of five thousand per second! The odds of winning were 14 million to 1, but nobody seemed to care.

My golfing buddy, Michael Crowe, bought $50 worth of tickets. Just to see his reaction, I tried to buy his lottery tickets from him. He turned down $150 for his tickets, although he had plenty of time to rebuy them and pocket a $100 profit! There's far more going on here than gambler's superstition. Before he bought the tickets, I'm sure that Michael was reluctant to invest $50 on a 14 million-to-1 shot even though he'd reduced it to 280,000 to 1 by buying fifty tickets. However, having made the decision to go ahead, he now had mentally bonded to that decision. Because he turned down $150, you could conclude he was now three times more sure of his investment than he was when he bought the tickets.

Think of that the next time you're using your powers of persuasion. Whether you're a salesperson marketing a product or a manager persuading an employee, after you reach initial agreement, say this to yourself: "This person is now three times more sure of the decision he's made than he was when we met. Now I can nibble for the extra items that really put the icing on the cake."

If you work for a large corporation, look at its annual statement, and compare net earnings to gross revenues. Probably, your company is lucky to be bringing 5 percent down to the bottom line. With profit margins so slim, you lose money on the first item you sell a customer, because you have to amortize all your development costs, fixed production overhead, and marketing costs against that first item. It's only on the add-on items and the repeat purchases that your company really makes any profit.

In the shoe business, they say that when you buy a dozen pairs of shoes from the manufacturer, you lose money when you sell the first eleven pairs. It's only when you sell the twelfth pair without having to mark them down that you make any money. In the supermarket business, if you buy $50 worth of groceries and tip the box boy $1 for carrying them out to your car, the box boy made more profit from the transaction than did the store.

In light of this, let's take another look at the person selling office equipment. The add-ons, such as the service contract or supplies, may be the only thing on which they're making any money! Having the courage to go back for more after you reach that initial agreement is one of the most profitable things that you can do.

■ EXPERIMENTING WITH BONDING IN YOUR PERSONAL LIFE

To see how effective this persuasion technique can be, experiment in your personal life. Perhaps you have a spouse who handles the family budget for you, and it's tough to get her to spend money frivolously.

If you were to suggest that you take a weekend, rent a luxury car, and get a suite at the resort hotel up in the mountains, she'd have a fit. Try getting an initial bonding to the idea of a weekend in the mountains, and then build on it, rather than making all your demands up front. You might start out with, "Why don't we spend a weekend up at the lake next month. It wouldn't cost very much. We could get a room at the Happy Hollow Motel for about $49, and we could pack a picnic so we wouldn't be spending much money on food."

> Mae West: "Marriage is a great institution, but I'm not ready for an institution."

Having reached agreement on that, wait a few days, and say, "Do you know the resort hotel at the lake has reduced rates at this time of year? I bet it wouldn't cost that much more to stay there. Shall I give them a call and check it out?"

Then a couple of days later, "I called the resort hotel, honey, and they had a weekend package available, so I booked it. We get two nights with breakfasts and a round of golf for only $198."

A week before the trip you point out a rental car ad in the newspaper. "I'm concerned about our old car overheating on the way up there. Why take a chance when for only $80 we can rent a Cadillac and go in style?"

Pretty soon you'll have your luxury weekend, and you didn't even have to put up a fight!

■ HOW INTERROGATORS USE THE POWER OF COMMITMENT

Here's how interrogators of prisoners of war use bonding to persuade their captives to betray their country.

Chinese interrogators during the Korean conflict had remarkable success in getting the prisoners to cooperate with their demands. Faced with determined troops drilled to give nothing more than name, rank, and serial number, they developed a deceptively simple program—start small and build—in other words, the law of bonding. If you can get someone to take even the smallest stand on something, you can build on his desire to remain consistent with the previous position.

So a prisoner might be asked in a friendly manner to agree that not everything in the Western world was perfect and to concur that unemployment was lower in communist countries. Apparently harmless and accurate comments that subtly commit the prisoner to a procommunist point of view.

Later he might be asked to elaborate on his comment that things were not perfect in the West. Would he mind listing a few of the things that caused him to say that? And why did he state that unemployment wasn't a problem in communist countries? Where had he heard this?

Building on these seemingly inconsequential bondings, the Chinese got many prisoners to sign petitions condemning the war and had them record statements for broadcast that seemed blatantly procommunist.

Dr. Edgar Schein, who spent years investigating the Chinese interrogation methods, stated that nearly all prisoners of war in the Korean conflict collaborated in one form or another with the enemy— a remarkable change from World War II, when very few did so.

■ THE ESSAY CONTEST PHENOMENON

Have you ever wondered about those manufacturers' contests where your entry requires an essay of twenty-five words, describing why you like a particular brand of ketchup or potato chips? Who cares? Surely they don't expect you to come up with some brilliant piece of prose that their advertising agency overlooked? Not at all. They're using the power of bonding. If hundreds of thousands of consumers go on record as liking the product, they're bonding to a position. In all likelihood, those customers will reinforce that position by continuing to like, and buy, the product.

Although it happened over thirty years ago, I vividly remember a day when I was attending the London School of Photography. A group of us was stopped by a fellow student who was running for student body president. He made a brief pitch, and then asked us to vote for him the following day. As we walked on, I told my friends I liked what I'd heard and would vote for him. My friends said they wanted to hear the other candidates before they decided. Later in the day, another candidate made a presentation to our class, and I liked what he had to say much better. I wanted to vote for the second candidate, but was uncomfortable going back on my previously announced intention to vote for the first student. So in a secret ballot what's wrong with revising your vote in line with current information? I agonized over this, and finally decided the lesser of two evils was not to vote at all rather than act inconsistently with my earlier statement.

It's interesting to note that the key ingredient here was that I made my decision known. If I had kept the decision to myself, I would have readily changed my vote. An experiment conducted by Hobart and Hovland, and published in the *American Psychologist*, clearly shows this. They took 100 high school students and exposed them to a speech in favor of reducing the voting age. They then asked them to write an essay expressing their point of view. Half the students were told that their essays might be published in the school newspaper; the other half was told that their essays would be confidential. Then they had all the students listen to a very convincing speech that the voting age should not be lowered. It changed very few of the minds of students who had written for publication. But most of the students who thought their articles were confidential changed their mind. It was one of many experiments that have shown conclusively that if you can get a person to commit publicly to a position, he will rarely change from that position.

■ MAKING COMMITMENTS TO YOURSELF

Now that we understand the power of bonding, we can use it not only to persuade others, but we can use it to persuade ourselves. If that sounds strange to you, consider this. Have you ever made a New Year's resolution and not been able to keep it? Perhaps you had determined to lose weight, or quit smoking or drinking, and could stick with your commitment for only a few days. Are you too hot tempered? Do you wish you could devote more time to your spouse and children?

You can change almost any habit or trait with the personal commitment exercise that I'm going to share with you now. I've been using it for ten years, and I find it remarkably effective.

Look at the box on the next page. Then think of something about yourself that you'd like to change. It will work for the accomplishment of any goal, but let's see how it would work for losing weight. I lost 40 very stubborn pounds doing this.

The last step, listing the problems you know you'll encounter, is powerful! Then, when they come up, you can think of your list and say to yourself, "Oh, sure, I knew this would come up. I can handle it." Let's say that part of your goal is to go jogging three times a week.

HABIT OR TRAIT I WISH TO CHANGE

"Lose forty pounds"

BENEFITS TO ME OF DOING THIS

1. "I'll feel more energetic."
2. "I'll look better."
3. "My friends will all admire me."

LIST AT LEAST THREE THINGS I MUST DO

1. Quit drinking alcohol.
2. Eat only fruit before twelve noon.
3. Lift weights at the gym three times a week.
4. Ride my LifeCycle three times a week for 24 minutes at level 6.

DATE BY WHICH I WILL HAVE ACCOMPLISHED THIS

November 1

THREE POSITIVE STEPS I WILL TAKE THIS WEEK

1. Buy and read *Fit for Life* by Friday.
2. Renew my membership at the gym on Thursday.
3. Lock up all the booze in the garage by tonight.

LIST THREE THINGS THAT WOULD STOP ME FROM SUCCESS

1. At dinner with friends, they'll encourage me to drink.
2. I won't want to exercise if I've been out late the night before.
3. I'll step on the scales and get discouraged because it doesn't seem to be working.

Some of the excuses that might come up are "I won't want to if I was out late the night before," or "I need to be at work early today," or "it's been raining and I might slip and twist my ankle. "

Erma Bombeck: "The only reason I would take up jogging is so I could hear heavy breathing again."

The minute those thoughts pop into your mind, you can greet them like an old friend. "Oh, hi, you again? Sorry, can't stop now, I'm going jogging. Care to come along?"

Having completed the form, tape a copy over your bathroom mirror. And carry one with you, to look at during moments when you begin to weaken. If you really want to assure your success, mail copies to six friends or business associates. Make your commitment public.

If you'd like a copy of the form I use, just send me a note and a stamped addressed envelope. Mail them to my company, Roger Dawson Productions, P.O. Box 3326, La Habra, CA 90632. The telephone number is (310) 691-6306.

■ KEY POINTS IN THIS CHAPTER

1. If we can get people to commit to a position, any position, we can then build on their need to remain consistent to that commitment. We've bonded them to that behavioral pattern.

2. By bonding people slowly, layer by layer, we can persuade them to do almost anything.

3. Any time a person bonds to a behavior pattern, he has a mental momentum to reinforce that decision. That's why you should always make a second effort once the other person has bonded by agreeing to part of your proposal.

4. Having the courage to go back for more, after you reach that initial agreement, is one of the most profitable things you can do.

5. It's so powerful that Chinese interrogators could use it to get American troops to write statements condemning the war.

6. Write to me for a free copy of my personal commitment form.

■ CHAPTER ELEVEN

PERSUASIVE SPEECHES

For the past ten years, I've been a full-time professional speaker. I started out speaking for nothing, just to learn how to do it. I think I must have spoken free to every Rotary, Lions, and Kiwanis club in the Greater Los Angeles area. Sometimes three times a day, a breakfast meeting, a lunch meeting, and a dinner meeting. I must have put on twenty pounds, but it taught me the fundamentals of persuading an audience. It thrilled me to get my first speaking fee of $100, and now I charge several thousands of dollars. If you'd like to find out more about this, contact Roger Dawson Productions, P.O. Box 3326, La Habra, California 90632. Telephone 800-YDAWSON (932-9766).

Along the way I found that if you do a good job, the audience wants to buy your books and cassette tapes. At first I measured my sales in hundreds of dollars, and now it isn't unusual to sell $10,000 worth from a single talk. One day I sold $28,000 worth of tapes. The purpose of the talk is never to sell tapes, and I take only a minute or so to mention that they're available. But when people want to buy that much, you know you've done a good job of persuading them!

So in this chapter, I'll teach you all I've learned, from personal experience and research, about how to persuade from the platform.

Whether you're speaking to a handful of people in a committee meeting or thousands at a national convention, it will teach you what you need to know to make persuasive speeches.

■ KNOWING WHAT CAUSED YOUR AUDIENCE TO BE THERE

The first point to consider in persuading an audience is: How did they get there? Are they there because they were told to be there, or did they choose to be there? For example, at a corporation, management may have told the employees they must attend. They may even be hostile toward you because they don't want to be there. On the other hand, you might be conducting an evening seminar and they choose to come and hear you. Or you're the speaker at a break-out session at a convention, so they selected your talk from among several other choices.

What's the significance of this? Obviously, you stand a better chance of having a friendly audience if they choose to be there. Yet there's something even more important to you as a persuader. If your audience chooses to be there, you can almost count on it that they're already sold on what you have to say.

Who do you think attends speeches when the speaker is a Democrat running for office? It's Democrats, who are already sold on what the speaker has to say anyway. Republicans, who are the ones the speaker really wants to talk to, rarely come.

Who do you think attends PTA meetings? It isn't the parents of problem students, who are the ones who could really benefit from the meeting. It's the parents of good students, the ones who aren't having trouble anyway.

Researchers call this the selective exposure syndrome. Guess who are the largest readers of ads for any particular model of car. It's people who already own that car, not the people whom the advertising is paying money to reach. It's a reason why television is such a powerful advertising medium—you reach everybody, not just the people who have an interest in your product.

This happens because people like to stay in their comfort zone. Given a choice of listening to a speaker who will say things that they already believe, or someone who will challenge their existing views, they nearly always pick the one with whom they'll be comfortable.

So the first thought of the persuasive speaker should be: Did this audience choose to be here? If they did, you can almost assume they already support what you have to say. You don't have to present opposing points of view, and you don't have to worry about converting them. All your persuasive power can be concentrated on your call to action. Be clear and strong in telling them what you want them to do.

■ KNOWING WHETHER TO PUT YOUR STRONGEST ARGUMENT AT THE BEGINNING OR AT THE END

Researchers call this the primacy-recency issue. Are you better off to make your strong argument up front and then follow up with supporting evidence, or should you save your big guns for last?

You're on the right track here. There's no question that people remember best what they hear first, or what they hear last. So your strongest argument should be either at the beginning or the end, just as the first and last paragraphs of a letter should be the strongest. And the first and last chapters of a book should be memorable. However, if you have 20 minutes to persuade an audience, are you better off to hit them between the eyes with your best argument first? Or are you better off to finish with a rousing call to act by putting your strongest points last?

It depends on the audience. It's a reason why you need to know whether your audience chose to be there or whether they were required to be there.

If the audience is friendly, and already believes in what you have to say, save the strongest argument for last. They'll be supportive enough to listen to what you have to say. You can then save your big gun for the call to action at the end. You might end with, "I know you see the importance of this issue. I'm sure that you all want to do something to support it. Here's what I want you to do. Please take out your pen and a business card—whether you're going to follow through or not—would everybody please do that now . . . ."

If the audience isn't already sold on the issue you're presenting, if they're either passive or hostile, put your big argument up front. You need a strong attention getter, so they'll listen to what you have to say. You need to shock them into realizing the size of the problem or opportunity. You might start out, "You might not like what I have to say this evening, but somebody has to have the courage to say it. If we don't take action tonight, there's a danger that this organization won't be in existence next year. Ladies and gentlemen, we are an endangered species . . . ."

■ IF SEVERAL SPEAKERS WILL PRESENT, KNOWING WHETHER TO GO FIRST OR LAST

The right way may surprise you. I always thought that I'd be better off to be last. Be the person who presents their argument last, just before the audience votes. However, research in this area proved me wrong. You're better off to go first. (Because of primacy-recency, if you can't go first, go last.)

Researchers have done extensive studies on this topic. They very carefully created an environment where arguments of equal persuasive strength were presented in different sequences to perfectly balanced audiences. They proved conclusively that you're better off to go first. You'll be more successful if you present your argument first, and then let the other speakers shoot you down. Sure, you have the disadvantage of not knowing what the other speakers will say. Sure, another speaker could run down your argument, but you're better off to have first shot at the hearts and minds of your audience.

■ HOW TO POSE THE QUESTION WHEN ASKING THE AUDIENCE TO VOTE

The key here is that people like to vote with the majority and are reluctant to oppose it. Let me illustrate how you can use this with an easy example.

Let's say that you want to get a prohibition on smoking in the room during your speech. You know that 50 percent of the people strongly oppose smoking, 20 percent don't mind others smoking, and 30 percent strongly favor smoking. If you take the vote democratically, the smokers will lose, but you'll have much of the audience who felt they lost, and they'll be hostile to your speech. A Power Persuader knows how to make the vote unanimous and avoid hard feelings.

Say to the audience, "Let's handle the smoking issue democratically. It doesn't matter to me either way, so let's vote, and the majority rules, fair enough? Raise your hand if you don't want to permit smoking during the meeting." At this, the 50 percent opposed to smoking will raise their hands, along with a few sympathizers. It will look like a clear majority. The smokers, seeing that they're going to lose anyway, will very seldom raise their hands. It will appear that nearly everyone is opposed to smoking, and it prevents you from having to take sides.

■ A SIMPLE AND EFFECTIVE WAY TO GET THE AUDIENCE ON YOUR SIDE

It's really easy: start by supporting an issue about which you know the audience is enthusiastic.

Researcher W. Weiss, reporting in the *Journal of Abnormal and Social Psychology*, showed why this works. He took a group of 120 college students and split them into two groups. His persuasion topic was the government fluoridation of water, which he knew by conducting a previous questionnaire the students favored, but not by a strong majority. Before the talk on fluoridation, the speaker told one group of students how strongly he supported student freedom, which was clearly an issue they enthusiastically supported. He didn't tell the other group of students this. He asked both groups of students to support a ban on fluoridation. Remember that the students actually supported fluoridation, so the speaker was asking them to change their minds. He could persuade the first group who had heard him speak out for student freedom. He couldn't persuade the second group.

It's important to understand what was going on here. Further research told him that speaking in favor of a popular issue didn't get the audience to support the other issue. But it did diffuse many potential critics and, therefore, gave him the majority.

The lesson to be learned is: if you want to minimize opposition to your argument, start by supporting an issue that you know the audience is enthusiastically behind.

■ KNOWING WHETHER TO USE EMOTION OR LOGIC TO PERSUADE

Most salespeople will tell you that people buy with emotion. If this is true it follows that a speaker would be more persuasive when she presents an emotional, rather than a logical, appeal.

The problem is that there is no credible research showing that people are more easily swayed by emotion than logic.

The truth is that it depends on the audience to whom you're speaking. Some people are very emotional, and are swayed by emotional appeals. Just as many others think so logically that emotional appeals seem phony and turn them off.

Research has shown that the intelligence level of the audience makes a big difference also. Logic sways highly intelligent people who are turned off by emotion. Logic baffles low-intelligence people, who are vulnerable to emotional appeals.

Research was also done on what's called integrative complexity, which compares how hard it is to persuade people who think concretely versus those who think abstractly. Concrete thinkers are more rigid in their attitudes and have trouble using information in new and meaningful ways. Abstract thinkers, the creative people in our society, are much more open to new ideas. From this you'd conclude that it's easier to persuade creative people like artists and writers than it is to persuade noncreative people like accountants and engineers. In reality, the opposite is true. While the creative person is more likely to seek out new opinions and listen to your arguments, he is harder to persuade. The accountant or engineer may be very reluctant to hear your message, because her mind is made up. However, she'll very quickly change her mind if you can prove her wrong because she has no emotional attachment to preconceived ideas.

A Power Persuader knows how to read the audience. It's a reason why I always like to shake the hands of the people coming into the room. It helps me to know them better.

■ IMPROVING YOUR ABILITY TO PERSUADE AN AUDIENCE

Get your audience involved. Having a question and answer session, conducting role plays, or breaking them up into workshop groups dramatically improves your ability to persuade, particularly if the involvement requires the audience to take a position supporting your point of view. Even if it's only game playing, people will support an issue of which they've spoken in favor.

There are four ways to get an audience involved:

1. *Question and answer sessions.* I prefer to permit questions throughout my talks. If anybody raises his or her hand, I'll stop and take the question. I don't like question and answer sessions at the end because I want to finish on a high note, and a question and answer session is not the way to do it. You lose the attention of the audience, partly because they're not all interested in the question you're being asked and partly because they can't hear the question being asked. If I find that the audience isn't asking questions as we go along, I stop every half hour or so and ask for questions on anything I've covered up to that point.

    Always be supportive of people who have the courage to ask questions. You don't have to agree with them, but tell them it was a good question, and treat them warmly.

    If you're uncomfortable throwing the meeting open to questions, you probably don't know your topic well enough. Don't be afraid that you'll get a hostile questioner who will make you look like a fool. Unless you've been hostile toward your audience, they're not going to pick on you like that.

    If you get a question you can't answer, do what all good speakers do. Simply say, "That's a terrific question! Let's throw that one open for discussion. Who wants to comment on that?"

2. *Workshop sessions.* There are many ways to break the audience into groups and have them discuss your topic. Here's the one that helps you persuade them the most. Let's say that you want to get the group behind buying some land and turning it into a public park. After presenting part of your argument, you might say, "Of course, this will cost a lot of money. So let's explore ways we could raise the money if we decided to go ahead." Then break your audience into groups of from six to fifteen people. Each group is to appoint a group reporter. Tell them that you expect each group to come up with six ways to raise the money. After 20 minutes, the reporter from each group is to present the group's best idea. The point is that you now have everyone in the room focused on supporting your proposal. People tend to

continue to support things of which they've spoken in favor, even when it's just game playing.

3. *Role playing.* Here you have members of the audience act out a scenario in front of the audience. Have the meeting planner help you to pick out some extroverts, whom the audience holds in high regard, to be the role players. You can either script the entire scenario or give them some close guidelines and let them ad lib. You might appoint two high-powered audience members to be in favor of the park. Choose a less articulate person to present the arguments against the park. They role play the debate in front of the rest of the group. Either way you have some of your highest-profile members speaking out in favor of your motion.

4. *See one, do one, teach one groups.* This is my favorite, and I've used it for years in my "Secrets of Power Negotiating" seminars. I developed it from the way that hospitals teach physicians to do surgery. They watch the instructor suture a wound, then they do one themselves, and then they have to teach someone else to do it. Guess when you learn the most? When you're teaching someone else. If you really want to learn something, go out and teach it.

I break the audience into pairs. One partner becomes the teacher and the other, the student. First, I ask the teacher to coach her partner on the importance of something I covered earlier in the seminar. I tell the student to pretend he hasn't heard this before, and encourage him to challenge the teacher. The teacher must prove that the technique she's teaching is a valuable one. Then I move onto another point, and have them reverse roles. Now the student becomes the teacher. Rotating roles, we may do this for 15 minutes several times during the day. It's an excellent way for the audience to learn. It's also a valuable persuasion tool, because I have all the audience arguing in favor of the value of the ideas I teach.

Research shows that not only are people much more easily persuaded when you've actively involved them, but they also remain convinced for much longer. People quickly forget what they hear, but long remember what they've done.

Power Persuaders understand the importance of getting their audiences actively involved.

■ USING CONSTRUCTIVE DISTRACTIONS TO IMPROVE YOUR ABILITY TO PERSUADE

Don't be too concerned about distractions. People are more easily persuaded when they're moderately distracted.

Sounds strange, doesn't it? But it's true. People are more easily persuaded when they're being distracted than when they're being forced to concentrate on the matter at hand. However, to work, the distraction must be moderate, and it must be pleasant. A business lunch is a perfect example of pleasant but moderate distraction—it's an ideal setting in which to persuade someone. In Chapter Seven, on the power of association, I told you the prime reason business lunches are effective, but the fact that it's a pleasant distraction helps also.

When you think about it, the reason a pleasant distraction helps you to persuade is obvious. When people are forced to concentrate on making a decision, it seems like hard work. Pleasant, but moderate, distractions create a warm, friendly environment where the other person is much more receptive to your message.

Humor is a good way to distract an audience, and interesting visual aids is another one. In my seminars, I use color cartoon overheads to illustrate the point I'm making. It stops the audience from being bored and provides a pleasant but moderate distraction.

■ USING HUMOR AS A PERSUADER

Humor by itself is not a good persuader. Satire, for example, can cause people to think about the problems of society, but it seldom causes real change.

Humor, as an adjunct to your persuasive message, can be very valuable. It helps for several reasons:

1. It acts as a pleasant but moderate distraction, which, as I told you, is an aid to persuasion.
2. It stops the audience from becoming bored.
3. It stops their minds from wandering.
4. It puts the audience in a friendly, receptive state of mind.

Humor stops becoming an aid to persuasion when the message itself becomes the humor. I've seen novice speakers fall into this trap a lot. Because they enjoy having the audience laugh at their jokes, they use more and more humor in their talks. Just because an audience is having a good time, and listening carefully to every word, doesn't mean that they're being persuaded.

Power Persuaders know how to use humor, but not to let humor become the message.

■ WHEN TO PRESENT BOTH SIDES OF THE ARGUMENT, OR ONLY ONE

I could bore you with scads of research on this topic, but let's just cut to the chase, and give you the rules:

You need only present one side of the argument if

1. The audience is friendly.

2. Your argument is the only one to be presented.

3. When you're looking for fast approval rather than long-term support.

You should present both sides of the argument if

1. The audience is hostile.

2. They'll subsequently hear opposing speakers.

■ AVOIDING THE OVERSTATEMENT TRAP

A little may be all right, but don't overdo it. In persuasion there's a clear case of diminishing returns when you do this.

Let's examine just two of the motivating factors (I talked about these, and others, in Chapter One—Eight Magic Keys to Influencing People). Your ability to persuade increases as you increase the perception of reward for agreeing with your proposition. On the other side of the coin, it also increases with your ability to project greater penalties for disagreeing. However, more important than the amount of the reward or punishment is the audience's belief that the pluses and minuses are real.

The moment you push it to the point where the audience no longer believes you, your ability to persuade with reward and punishment drops off dramatically.

For example, the size of the penalty doesn't deter us when we break the law. We're deterred more by the likelihood of getting caught. For example you could raise the cost of speeding tickets to $500, but it still won't be a deterrent, if only one motorist in a thousand is stopped. You can reinstate the death penalty, but it still won't be a very good deterrent to murder, unless the chance of getting caught is high.

For example, you've probably heard of the research that listed our biggest fears. Jumping out of a plane came first, giving a speech came second, and the fear of dying came in third. The first one is a natural, because it relates to one of only two fears that are inborn in human beings—the fear of falling. (The other is the fear of loud noises.) In looking at the next two, giving a speech or dying, many people concluded that we're more scared of giving a speech than we are of dying. Obviously, that's not true. Given a choice of giving a speech or dying, everyone would give the speech! The reason people listed speaking as a greater fear than dying, was that they saw a greater possibility of themselves having to give a speech, than of dying.

That's why life insurance agents have such difficulty selling a policy to a 30-year-old. Someone that young doesn't believe that he's going to die. When the agent runs into sales resistance, he tries to persuade by increasing the size of the penalty: "If you die, your children won't be able to go to college, your wife will become a bag lady." However, the young man isn't persuaded by the size of the penalty, if he sees little chance of his dying. The persuasion method the life insurance agent should be using is to increase the perception of probability. He might say: "I wish Charlie's wife were here to tell you what happened to her. Charlie was the same age as you, and in perfect health. He went out jogging one morning, and never came back. Killed instantly by a heart attack. It happens a lot more often than you'd think possible."

Fear is a persuader only up to the point where the audience feels the threat is genuine. Reward is a persuader only up to the point where the audience believes it to be true. Power Persuaders know how to push their claims up to that point, but not beyond.

■ THE ART OF GETTING THE MOST EFFECTIVE INTRODUCTION

Getting the right introduction can be very important, depending on the audience.

The easiest audience to persuade is one accustomed to authority. This would include schoolchildren, members of the military, and employees. However, to be persuaded, they must see the speaker as an authority. The authority may come from the speaker's title, credentials, or expertise in the topic. Whichever it is, it's obvious the quality of the introduction is very important with an audience that's accustomed to authority.

What can you do if you don't have strong credentials that can be brought out in your introduction? If that's the case, you're better off to have the audience told who you are after your talk. Research has proven that if the audience listens to your introduction and sees your credentials as weak, it almost eliminates your chance of persuading them. However, the opposite also applies. If you speak without an introduction, and they like what you have to say, finding out later that you have few credentials has almost no negative effect.

Research has also shown people very quickly forget who said something, even if they can remember what was said. Doesn't that ring true? You frequently hear people saying, "I heard that so and so did this and that." They remember what they heard, but they can't remember who said it. What does this have to do with your introduction? It means that the credibility given you by a good introduction is very important in short-term persuasion, such as when you want them to buy something or vote for something. However, as time passes, the credibility of the speaker becomes less and less important. Researchers call this the sleeper effect.

Let's say you're running a political campaign. In the early stages, you'd do well to have as many people as possible getting out your message. The credibility of the speaker isn't that important. What you want is a large number of people who have heard your message. You want the public out there saying, "I heard that John Doe has a great program for solving our health care crisis." They won't remember who said it, or where they heard it, but they know they heard it somewhere. As the election approaches, and you want them to take specific action by voting for you, the credibility of the people speaking for you becomes much more important. So a good introduction is very important if you intend to ask for immediate action. It's less important if you are after long-term change in attitude.

I always have my introducer use a prepared introduction that I've given them. Most professional speakers do it this way. The reason isn't to assure we get a flattering introduction, but to be sure the introducer doesn't get too carried away. Given free rein, an introducer will usually get carried away. They'll tell the audience you're the greatest speaker on the face of the earth and how lucky the audience is to have the privilege of listening to you. This damages your ability to persuade because it builds a wall between you and the audience. When you eventually get your hands on the microphone, the audience is sitting there thinking, "I can't believe he's that good. He's going to have to prove it to me." So you have a wall between you and the audience that has to be torn down before you can start.

■ THE NUMBER ONE THING YOU CAN DO TO PERSUADE FROM THE PLATFORM

The most important things to do are draw conclusions, ask for the sale, and tell them what you want them to do.

Presenting information alone doesn't change minds. You must draw conclusions, and ask the audience to do something, even if it's only to change their minds about something. Researchers have spent much time over the years, analyzing the effect of the news media on public opinion. Their findings may surprise you. The news media have almost no effect on public opinion. Because they only present information, and don't ask people to change their minds, the news media only serve to reinforce existing opinions. They don't change minds.

If you want to persuade from the platform, or one on one for that matter, it isn't good enough to present the information and hope it causes a change in the audience. You must draw conclusions, ask them to change, and tell them what you expect them to do. And when I say tell them what you expect them to do, I mean exactly that. Many times I've seen speakers do a brilliant job of bringing the audience to the brink of a decision. Then they lose it, because they don't take the final step of telling the audience what they want them to do. They don't say, "I want you to take out your credit card, and . . . " or "I want you to become a member of this organization before you leave the room tonight. And the way you do that is to . . . ."

I recently attended a service at the Crystal Cathedral, where my son Dwight was inducted as a church member. I'm a Religious Scientist and we're not big on collecting money in church. There's nothing wrong with it, but we don't think it's necessary. As metaphysicians we believe that our thoughts control the universe anyway, so if we need money we can make it appear. However, I was aware that Christians collect money at their church services, and I was prepared to contribute when the offering was taken. In the middle of the service, the minister started telling us that it was time to put a special message in an envelope, and bless the work of the church, and so on. While I was still trying to figure out what this meant, huge plastic salad bowls appeared from nowhere and were passed along the pews at lightning speed. It flashed across my mind that this might be the collection, but I didn't see much money going into the bowls, mostly envelopes. Less than 5 seconds after the bowls first appeared, one came to me, and I simply passed it on. All this may have had some spiritual significance that escaped me, but from a persuasion point of view, it wasn't smart. The minister should have done a better job of telling us what was expected. "Now is the time that we get money out and put it into the plastic bowls" would have done nicely.

Power Persuaders know that it isn't enough to ask for the sale. You've also got to tell people what you want them to do.

■ KEY POINTS IN THIS CHAPTER

1. Know what caused your audience to be there. If your audience chose to be there, they're probably already sold on what you have to say. All your persuasive power can then be concentrated on your call to action. Be clear and strong in telling them what you want them to do.

2. Your strongest argument should be either at the beginning or the end.

3. If the audience is friendly, and already believes in what you have to say, save the strongest argument for last.

4. If the audience isn't already sold on the issue you're presenting, if they're either passive or hostile, put your big argument up front.

5. You'll be more successful if you present your argument first, and then let the other speakers shoot you down.

6. People like to vote with the majority and are reluctant to oppose it. A power persuader knows how to make the vote unanimous and avoid hard feelings.

7. Start by supporting an issue about which you know the audience is enthusiastic.

8. There is no credible research that people are more easily swayed by emotion than logic. It depends on the audience.

9. Logic sways highly intelligent people, who are turned off by emotion. Logic baffles low-intelligence people, who are vulnerable to emotional appeals.

10. While the creative person is more likely to seek out new opinions, and listen to your arguments, they are harder to persuade.

11. The logical thinker may be reluctant to hear your message, because his mind is made up. However, he'll quickly change his mind if you present a convincing logical argument.

12. Get your audience involved. Having a question and answer session, conducting role plays, or breaking them up into workshop groups dramatically improves your ability to persuade.

13. People are more easily persuaded when they're distracted. However, to work, the distraction must be moderate, and it must be pleasant.

14. Humor by itself is not a good persuader. Humor as an adjunct to your persuasive message can be very valuable.

15. Learn whether to present both sides of the argument or only one.

16. More important than the amount of the reward or punishment is the audience's belief that the pluses and minuses are real.

17. The quality of the introduction is very important with an audience that's accustomed to authority.

18. If you don't have strong credentials for your introduction, you're better off to have the audience told who you are after your talk.

19. Use a prepared introduction to be sure the introducer doesn't get too carried away.

20. Most important, draw conclusions, ask for the sale, tell them what you want them to do.

CHAPTER TWELVE

EIGHT VERBAL PERSUASION PLOYS TO CONTROL THE OTHER PERSON

Now let's move into some really nitty-gritty ways of getting people to see things your way. In this chapter I'll teach you verbal persuasion ploys, specific things you can say that will persuade the other person to your point of view.

Some of them may sound very sneaky to you. Also, you may be upset because you recognize that they've been used on you. However you feel about them it's essential that you're familiar with them, and understand why they're effective persuasion tools.

VERBAL PERSUASION PLOY NUMBER ONE
Diffusion

Let's start with the skill of diffusion, which is one of the simplest methods of bringing people to your way of thinking.

When someone has taken an opposing position to you, make the case that there isn't any conflict, and that you're really out for the same thing. Here's how it works.

On a political level, let's imagine two candidates involved in a debate that has turned acrimonious. They're in a virtual screaming match about whether taxes should be raised to reduce the federal deficit. Positions have polarized, and they've made unfounded assumptions in the bitterness of the argument. For example, would raising taxes really decrease the deficit?

The smart candidate will defuse the conflict by putting on her most sincere expression and saying to the other, "But isn't it true, Joe, that we're both after the same thing? Aren't we both after what's best for our great country? We really don't have a disagreement here. Isn't that true?"

This really takes the wind out of the opposition's sails. Note that the point upon which you're claiming you both agree, must be high minded enough to be unarguable. If he were to have said, "We both agree the deficit needs to be reduced," he may have walked into a trap.

The other person could then respond with, "If you claim the deficit must be reduced, why has your party done so many things to increase the deficit?" And the argument heats up again.

How can we use diffusion in our business lives?

Here's a situation every executive has faced, at one time or another. Two of the people who work for him have stormed into his office and said, "OK, you're going to have to decide which one of us is right and which one of us is wrong. We've been arguing all morning, and we can't agree."

The Power Persuader diffuses the friction by first getting them to agree that their purpose is identical, even if they can't agree on the method. He listens to both sides and then says, "Wait a minute, fellas. First, I don't see you being so far apart on this thing. As I see it, you both want to do the same thing. You want to see the company increase its market share, and do it profitably, right? That's what we're all here for, right? Now, Joe, you're the sales manager. I want you to keep coming up with these great ideas for pumping the business. Hank, you're the controller. I want you to work with Joe to be sure that it's going to be profitable, and we don't bite off more than we can chew. That's what Joe wants too, Hank. Now let's get our heads together and see how we can put this thing together and still minimize the downside risk. Fair enough?"

Or it's the manager who has the challenging assignment of persuading one of his people to accept a transfer.

"Bob," he says, "I really don't understand why you appear to be upset about this. We're all after the same thing, aren't we? Don't forget the strength of this company is with its people. It isn't the factories and the warehouses and the office buildings that make this company great, it's the people. Believe me, we want what's best for you, just as much as you do. We're really in total agreement. Bob, I wish you could see this from my perspective. You'll look back on this move to El Paso as the greatest thing that ever happened to you."

Here's how a salesperson would use diffusion. Mary is trying to sell the top-of-the-line photo copier to a car rental company that is strongly opposed to spending that much money. "Mr. Jones, you're acting as if we're on different sides on this matter. Really, we're not. We're both out for the same thing. We both want what's best for your company. I can only grow and prosper if you grow and prosper. Mr. Jones, I'm absolutely convinced that this is the right thing for you to do. If I let you do anything less, I'd be letting you down."

Nothing works like sincerity! The next time you're faced with a persuasion task that's beginning to turn into conflict, try diffusion—"We're really both out for the same thing, aren't we?"

VERBAL PERSUASION PLOY NUMBER TWO
"Yes, I Take It Personally."

This is a powerful ploy. Someone who's trying to persuade us to do something we don't want to do, will very often start with the expression, "I don't want you to take this personally."

Whenever I hear that, I can't help thinking of the Woody Allen movie, *Play It Again, Sam.* In one of the opening scenes, his wife is leaving him. She's calmly packing all her stuff into her old Volkswagen bug, as he desperately tries to talk her out of it. As she gets into the car, she says, "Now I don't want you to take this personally!" How else are you supposed to take it when your wife walks out on you?

Whenever someone tries to lay bad news on you like that, be sure to challenge them. Power Persuaders know that you don't give up your hold on that very critical Power Persuasion point, the warm emotion that exists between you.

A key employee comes to you and says, "Don't take this personally, but I'm going to work for the competition."

You say, "Charlie, there's nobody in this company I care for more than you. And if it's the best thing for you, I'm happy for you." This is diffusion, isn't it? Positioning both people on the same side of the disagreement. "But don't ask me not to take it personally. After all we've meant to each other, of course I take it personally that you wouldn't talk it over with me first." Then you go on to bonding, which we talked about previously. "Charlie, you have an open mind, don't you. If I could show you why you should stay with us, you'd be open minded enough to listen to me, wouldn't you, Charlie?"

Incidentally, I'm always amazed when I hear a manager tell me that they wouldn't take the time to talk an employee out of quitting, however good they were. "Just as a principle, if they want to leave, I let 'em," they proudly tell me. Let me tell you something. You can ride those principles into oblivion in today's business world. I can understand a principle that you won't increase their pay to keep them, or make any other concessions under that kind of pressure. Still, a Power Persuader knows how to make them want to stay, without making any concessions.

VERBAL PERSUASION PLOY NUMBER THREE
Being Nixonesque.

The next rule of verbal persuasion is to be Nixonesque in your statements. That means don't ever make a statement that's so specific you can get nailed for it. I call it being Nixonesque because it really came to the fore during the Watergate hearings. All the defendants were very careful not to make specific statements. If you examine the testimony, you'll see that it was full of responses like, "I can't recall ever saying that." Or "I don't think that it's possible that we could have discussed that." Or "To the best of my knowledge, I didn't approve that."

That's a whole lot different than saying, "I didn't say that." Or "We didn't discuss that." Or "I didn't approve that." When you make a statement that specific, the attorney may have been setting a trap for you. The attorney could have been up front and said, "In his deposition, Mr. Jones says that you approved the action. Did you?" Instead, the attorney says, "Did you approve the action?"

You now fall into the trap of assuming that he's asking a question to which he doesn't know the answer. And you respond, "Absolutely not."

The attorney can nail you! "But we have a sworn deposition from Mr. Jones that you did approve this, on April the fourteenth, at 3:12 in the afternoon. Are you saying that Mr. Jones was lying under oath?"

Norm Crosby: "In court you're putting your fate in the hands of twelve people who weren't smart enough to get out of jury duty."

One of my first bosses drilled into me the value of being deliberately vague, when I was only 20. I'd taken a summer job at a resort hotel in Southern England. They asked me to box up and ship a piece of equipment, and then a week later the boss called me into his office. "Roger," he said, "it doesn't look as if you did a very good job of boxing up that piece of equipment. It was damaged when it arrived."

I was new on the job, and I wasn't particularly anxious to get fired over this. Since he didn't seem clear on his facts, I decided to try to bluff my way out of it, feeling I had a good chance of getting away with blaming the freight company.

"Well, sir," I said, looking him straight in the eye and holding his gaze, "I can assure you it wasn't my fault. Nobody could have done a better job of packing it. It must have been the freight company's fault."

"Really," he responded casually, "I'm surprised to hear you say that. Look at this."

From his desk drawer he pulled out an 8" by 10" glossy picture of the shipment as it had arrived at its destination, clearly showing that I'd done a sloppy job of packaging it. An 8" by 10"! Was that overkill, or what?

If I'd have been more Nixonesque, I would've said, "I can't recall exactly how I packed it for shipment, but if my memory serves me correctly, I did it well."

Salespeople and managers get caught up in this all the time, for example, the salesperson who rashly says to the buyer, "But nobody in the industry will give you sixty-day terms!"

The buyer calmly reaches into his desk drawer and says, "Oh, really? Your major competitor will. Look at this proposal from them." The salesperson suddenly knows he's lost all his credibility.

Consider the manager faced with the tricky problem of getting his people to take a cutback in expense per diem, and he makes the rash statement that everybody is having to take the same cut. Specifics can nail you! The salespeople may know perfectly well that when the top salesperson in the company threatened to quit over this, you made an exception and swore him to secrecy.

Why leave yourself vulnerable by making absolute statements, when a little Nixonesquequisity can protect you?

VERBAL PERSUASION PLOY NUMBER FOUR
"I'm Not Offended."

Here's an interesting little verbal ploy. How do you let people know that you're upset with them, without actually having to come out and say it? I call it the "I'm not offended" ploy.

Let's say that one of your employees is upset with the company. She's blowing off a little steam and she says something like, "It seems like every time we turn around, the company is sticking it to the employees!" Let's assume this is a good employee who's always been loyal and is a good worker. She just happens to be upset right now. So you don't want to make a confrontation out of it; on the other hand, you don't want to let it go by either. How do you avoid confrontation, which might lead to her quitting or getting so out of line that you'll have to threaten to fire her, while still letting her know you're not going to put up with that kind of thing?

You use the "I'm not offended" ploy. "Helen," you say, "many people would be really offended by that, but I want you to know that I'm not. Because I know that deep down you don't mean it. You've always been a loyal employee, and I refuse to believe you're doing a complete about-face over a little matter like this."

Perhaps it's the salesperson faced with the unpleasant job of facing a customer who's been overbilled for a shipment. It was a mistake caused by an oversight on the salesperson's part. He forgot to let the billing office know of the special deal he'd cut. Even so, the buyer is making a mountain out of a molehill. He screams, "You're trying to cheat me! I never should have trusted you in the first place!"

The salesperson doesn't want to raise the level of confrontation, but also he wants to tell the buyer he's not going to put up with that kind of treatment anymore.

He uses "I'm not offended." "Mr. Buyer," he says, "I want you to know that I'm not offended by your anger, or by your use of profanity. You've got a right to be upset—I would be too. However, is it fair to accuse us of a lack of integrity when in reality what happened here was a clerical error?"

The beauty of "I'm not offended" is that it enables you to say one thing, while making it clear to the other person that you mean exactly the opposite!

VERBAL PERSUASION PLOY NUMBER FIVE
"Easy to Deny."

Here's a cute little verbal ploy that would have saved many public figures a great deal of embarrassment if they'd have known about it. I hope you never have to use it, but just in case you do, here it is. I call it the "Easy to Deny" ploy. It's for those times when they catch you doing something you shouldn't be doing. You don't want to lie by denying it, on the other hand, you don't want to admit it either. It's time for the "easy to deny" ploy. "It would be easy for me to deny the accusations, and simply put the matter to rest. That would obviously be the easy thing for me to do. Still, sometimes the easy way isn't the best way. Because there's a larger question at stake here. That question is, Does my opponent have the right to make me answer to every rumor that might come his way, regardless of who might start that rumor?"

VERBAL PERSUASION PLOY NUMBER SIX
"I'm Not Suggesting."

Then he'd move into the "I'm not suggesting" ploy. "Of course I'm not suggesting for one moment that my opponent in this campaign would be party to starting such a malicious rumor, but there's a principle here to which we should both adhere."

"I'm not suggesting" is when you know perfectly well you caught the other person with his hand in the cookie jar. However, you don't want to cause a confrontation by accusing him, you want to make him aware you know what he was up to. "Joe, I'm not suggesting for one minute that you put earning a commission ahead of the best interests of the company."

Or "Harry, I'm not suggesting for one moment that there was anything immoral about you spending the weekend in the Bahamas with your secretary. I'm just asking you to see how it might look to people who don't know you as well as I do."

Harry knows exactly what you're really saying, which is, "Harry, I know what you're like better than anybody. I'm going to look the other way this time, because I don't want to fire you over this, but do it again and you're out on the street."

VERBAL PERSUASION PLOY NUMBER SEVEN
Give the Other Person Options.

This is a ploy that I call "Giving Them Options." What would you do if you suddenly realized that you had burglars in your house? I hope you'd do what every law enforcement officer would tell you to do. Give them a way to escape. Never corner a criminal so they have no way to get out. He's liable to turn violent.

The same principle applies in persuasion. You should always let the other person have a way to go. You should always let them have options.

Because we value personal freedom so much, you can very often sour a persuasion attempt for no more reason than this. That the other person feels trapped and has no choice other than to comply with your demands. That may sound like checkmate to you, but when you force people to give in, rather than persuading them to do so, they very often do self-destructive things out of sheer frustration—things like quitting your company or buying from your competitor. Or, in the case of your children, doing something against your wishes out of a sense of rebellion.

To emphasize how important freedom is to us, realize that to many foreigners, the most obvious American characteristic is the need for personal freedom. In Tanzania, I met a German man who's a top executive with Mercedes Benz of North America. Although he's lived in America for twenty years, he still thinks of himself as German, and his company has sent him home to Germany every two years on vacation. We became good friends and ended up climbing Mount Kilimanjaro together, with his son and my daughter.

On the fourth day of the climb we were at 16,000 feet, on the great saddle of the mountain which lies between the two peaks, watching the sun set on the vast African plain. At the equator the sun sets very quickly, because it goes down vertically. (In America, the sun doesn't set straight down, it sets at about a 45 degree angle.) It's a grand experience to watch that great ball of fire dive straight down for the horizon.

"Rolf," I asked him, "after twenty years of living in America, what do you think is the strangest characteristic of the American people?"

He proceeded to tell me how wonderful he thought the country was, and how he loved living there. "Yes, I agree with you about all those things," I said. "What I'm curious about is this. Is there anything about Americans that you haven't figured out yet?"

Reluctantly he told me this, "To my way of thinking, Americans have an incredible need for personal freedom. It's the best thing about them, and yet it's the worst thing. In my country we're willing to accept gun control because it reduces crime. We're willing to accept stricter building codes because it makes our cities more beautiful for everyone. Americans want personal freedom however destructive it may be."

It's an interesting point to remember in persuasion. We have a tremendous need to feel free. We don't want to feel that someone has outmaneuvered us, and we have only one choice left. So Power Persuaders work with this and understand that you should always give the other side two options from which to choose. The essence of the option ploy is to be sure that the options you give them are both acceptable to you.

The salesperson closes by saying, "Well I don't think there's any question that you need to go with the top-of-the-line machine. The question becomes, How do we work it out so you can live comfortably with the investment? Look at these two plans, and tell me which would be best for you. One is an extended purchase plan, and the other is a lease with an option to buy."

The executive says, "There's no question that as head of our West Texas Division you should be a vice president. The question is, Should we make the announcement before you transfer to El Paso, or is it better to let you settle in there and make the announcement in ninety days? Which do you think, Bob?"

So the "Give Them Options" ploy tells us two things. Never back somebody into a corner by saying things like "Take it or leave it. We're not going to reduce the price." Or "Charlie, it's the only slot we've got open for a sales manager. Take the transfer or we're going to part company."

Remember that, in this country, we prize our freedom so much that we're likely to do dumb things when people try to deprive us of that freedom.

The second thing it tells us, is that we should always offer the other person two options, both of which we can live with. "We may be able to come off list price a little, provided you prepay the order. Would you rather do that?" Or "Charlie, the only way I can keep you in Chicago is as an assistant sales manager on straight commission. Would that be a better way for you to go?"

VERBAL PERSUASION PLOY NUMBER EIGHT
"Why Would You Want to Do That?"

Here's a very simple verbal persuasion ploy that's remarkably effective. I call it the "Innocent Question" ploy.

Let's say you're a manager and you have a key employee who's threatening to quit. The employee is all worked up about it. You've refused to give him an increase in pay, and he's saying, "If you don't give me more money, I'm going to quit!"

You lean back in your chair and thoughtfully think of your home telephone number, and mentally recite it backward, including the area code. This makes you appear to be deep in thought. You might take off your glasses, if you wear them, and put the tip of one of the ear pieces in your mouth. The body language signal that means, "I need more information." A quizzical expression comes over your face, and you finally say slowly, "But, Bob, why would you want to do that?"

Bob might say, "Because I can't afford to go on working here for the money you pay me!"

"But, Bob, wouldn't quitting without another job to go to just make your financial condition worse?"

"Well, I'll find somebody that will appreciate what I do for them!"

"But, Bob, we appreciate what you do for us! It's just that we can't afford to give you any more money right now. Let's talk about ways that you could improve your productivity so we could afford to give you more money in the future. Fair enough?"

That little expression is magical: "But why would you want to do that?" Particularly if you know the other person just blurted out a statement without giving it much thought.

Your best customer suddenly loses patience and says, "Well, I'll just give the order to your competitor, that's what I'll do!" You think of your home telephone number backward, and calmly say, "But why would you want to do that, Joe?"

"Because they care about our business. They can get the parts here next week."

"And if we weren't so fussy about quality control, we probably could get them here next week too! Joe, we've been doing business together for twelve years, right? Have you ever had to shut down an assembly line because we didn't have the parts for you? So trust me, Joe, it's gonna be OK."

The beauty of the "Innocent Question" ploy is that it forces the other person to clarify and restate his objection. Often when they're forced to do that, the strong position they're taking won't make as much sense the second time around.

■ KEY POINTS IN THIS CHAPTER

1. Diffuse the opposition by making the case that there really isn't any conflict, because you're both after the same thing.

2. Diffuse friction between people by first getting them to agree that both sides' purpose is identical, even if they can't agree on the method for solving the problem.

3. Don't agree when they ask you not to take it personally.

4. Be Nixonesque—don't make a statement that's so specific you can get nailed for it.

5. When people offend you, use the "I'm not offended" ploy.

6. When you don't want to lie by denying it, it's time for the "easy to deny" ploy.

7. Use "I'm not suggesting," when you know perfectly well you caught the other person with her hand in the cookie jar.

8. Always let the other person have a way to go. You should always let him or her have options, because we all have a tremendous need to feel free.

9. When people are threatening to do something rash, think of your home telephone number backward, and calmly say, "But why would you want to do that?"

CHAPTER THIRTEEN

EXPOSING AND DESTROYING THEIR NEGATIVE EMOTIONS

In this chapter I'll teach you how to exorcise negative emotions, because it's a powerful verbal persuasion technique. To exorcise means to draw out, to expose and to banish. When people have bad feelings about you, or what you're doing, you're always better off to get those feelings out on the table. Then have them acknowledge the bad feelings and agree that they should be banished. An unexpressed emotion is like a festering wound. Unless exposed and treated, it always gets worse.

Let's take the four negative emotions one at a time.

NEGATIVE EMOTION NUMBER ONE
Suspicion
They don't appear to trust you.

How would you identify suspicion? A good clue is when people want to hide something from you. Perhaps you're dealing with two or more people and they ask for privacy to discuss something or one passes a note to the other.

Another clue is when a person doesn't feel comfortable answering your questions. Perhaps you've asked a question and the person hasn't wanted to answer it yet. You ask, "How much business does your company do a year?"

She comes back with, "We wouldn't feel comfortable sharing that information with you." Which is a polite way of saying, "None of your business, Charlie."

"Trust in Allah, but tie up your camel."

However it is that you detect suspicion, confront it—don't overlook it, or you'll make it worse. "Forgive me, but apparently, you don't trust me yet. Perhaps I haven't given you any reason to trust me. However, if we're to work together, it's important that we trust each other completely. So let's talk about it. What's bothering you?"

Now you may say, "Wait a minute, Roger. I might not want to know about this. If they start unloading on me, it could sour the relationship completely."

Trust me. You're always better off knowing. Ignorance is never bliss. Ignorance is poverty and disease.

During all of 1988 Emperor Hirohito of Japan lay dying of cancer. Yet his doctors never told him, because in Japan they think that a dying person is better off not knowing that all hope is gone. In this country we don't think like that. We say you're always better off knowing. Some husbands say, "If my wife's cheating on me, I don't want to know about it." Believe me, you're always better off knowing.

NEGATIVE EMOTION NUMBER TWO
Anger
They're upset with something that happened.

Let's consider anger. The other person hasn't come out and said she's angry with you, but it's obvious she is. You say, "Helen, it's clear to see you're angry about this. And believe me, I agree with you.

You've got every right to be angry. And maybe I've got a right to be angry with your people too. However, staying angry with each other isn't going to solve the problem. Why don't we both put that behind us and look at ways we can rebuild our relationship, fair enough?" Incidentally, in Chapter Twenty-five, I'll share six more ways to persuade the angry person.

NEGATIVE EMOTION NUMBER THREE
Greed
You appear vulnerable, and they want to take advantage of it.

The third emotion, greed, takes a little more finesse. Here we'll have to use a combination of exorcism and a technique I call, "Many people would feel. . . ." Let's say that you're selling something because you desperately need to raise cash. You're vulnerable and you feel the other side is taking unfair advantage of it.

You say, "Harry, could I get something out on the table here? I appreciate your need to drive a hard bargain, and I don't have a problem with that. Many people would feel you're taking advantage of a difficult situation. However, I've known you for years and I know you're not a greedy person. Let's talk about a figure that would be fair for both of us."

What have we accomplished here? We've brought the problem out into the open. We've let them know that we're on to them, but we've done it without being confrontational.

NEGATIVE EMOTION NUMBER FOUR
Hurt
They're upset and want revenge.

Hurt is probably the emotion people least like to admit. It means the other side trusted you, and now they feel let down. Hurt is a difficult emotion with which to deal because the hurt person always feels that they, too, were at fault—for trusting you. Treat it gently, but you're always better off to exorcise it. Obviously, this can happen a lot with personal relationships, but let's stick with a business example.

Let's say that your best customer caught your company giving a lower price to his competitor. You never would've approved it if you'd known about it, but you're the one he's been dealing with, and he's hurt because he trusted you and, in his eyes, you let him down. Promising that you'll never do it again just doesn't get it. The problem is that the guy doesn't trust you anymore. Why would he trust you that you're not lying to him now? You need to bring out the hurt, and treat it.

"Charlie, I can see you're hurt by this. I can see it in your eyes. And you've every right to be. You've trusted me for the eight years that we've been doing business together, and this is the first time we've ever let you down. Of course you're hurt, and you've every right to be. I don't want only to get your business back, Charlie. What's more important to me is getting your trust back. What would it take to do that, Charlie? You tell me."

So Power Persuaders know, when you encounter the negative emotions of suspicion, anger, greed, and hurt you don't learn to live with them. You learn to exorcise them instead.

■ KEY POINTS IN THIS CHAPTER

1. When people have bad feelings about you, or what you're doing, you're always better off to get those feelings out on the table. Have them acknowledge the bad feelings, and agree that they should be dealt with.

2. Suspicion on their part means they don't trust you yet. You can detect this if they avoid answering your questions or conceal things from you by passing notes or asking for privacy. However it is that you detect suspicion, confront it—don't overlook it, or you'll make it worse.

3. When the other person hasn't come out and said she's angry with you, but it's obvious she is, bring it out. Say, "Helen, it's clear to see you're angry about this. Why don't we both put that behind us and look at ways we can rebuild our relationship, fair enough?"

4. Handling greed takes a little more finesse. Use a combination of exorcism and "Many people would feel . . ." technique. It lets them know you're on to them, but without being confrontational.

5. Hurt means the other side trusted you, and now they feel let down. Hurt is a difficult emotion with which to deal because the hurt person always feels that they, too, were at fault—for trusting you.

6. When you encounter the negative emotions of suspicion, anger, greed, and hurt, don't learn to live with them—learn to exorcise them instead.

CHAPTER FOURTEEN

THE SWEET LANGUAGE OF PERSUASION

While we tend to think of language persuasion techniques as the province of modern-day salespeople or the Madison Avenue copywriters, in fact the philosophers of Ancient Greece raised the principles of language persuasion to an art form. People like Plato and Aristotle understood that the foundation of persuasion, which is the ability to change another person's beliefs, lay in three language skills: grammar, rhetoric, and logic.

Grammar provides us with the essential structure that underlies all language and thought. Rhetoric is the use of that grammar with power and grace. Logic is a system by which we prove or disprove the rhetoric that has been used. A clear understanding of the distinction between these three is essential to becoming a Power Persuader.

We use grammar to communicate a persuasion premise. We use rhetoric to reinforce the persuasion process. Remember that rhetoric isn't primarily concerned with the truth. Rhetoric may well mask or distort truth in order to make its point. Logic is the system we apply to figure out whether rhetoric used the truth or not, in its attempt to influence the other person.

And what a complicated system it is! The *Encyclopaedia Britannica*, for example, devotes fifty-six pages just to the discussion of the third stage, logic. Can you imagine that? Fifty-six pages of very fine print just to explain how we can evaluate whether what we've heard is true!

So language persuasion is a three-step process. Our grammar may be perfect, and our rhetoric may be forceful. However, it isn't until we've satisfied their need for logic, that people have been truly persuaded.

Obviously you could spend a year or more in the full-time study of just this one aspect of persuasion and still not know everything about it. What is fascinating for Power Persuaders is to take a brief look at each language of persuasion.

THE FIRST LANGUAGE OF PERSUASION
Fallacy

Fallacy is the word used to describe how rhetoric can be used apparently to prove a point, though the logic may be faulty.

You probably heard this one when you were in grade school. Three friends check into a hotel room and each pay the desk clerk $20. Later the clerk realizes that he's overcharged them, and sends the bellhop up with their $5 change. On the way up the bellhop is trying to figure out how he can split $5 three ways. He finally gives up, and decides to give them $1 each, and keep $2 for himself. So each person in the room ended up paying $19 each for his share, a total of $57. The bellhop got $2, which makes a total of $59. What happened to the extra dollar?

THE SECOND LANGUAGE OF PERSUASION
Defective Syllogisms

A classic fallacy is the defective syllogism. A syllogism is a formula by which we can arrive at a conclusion, using a given set of facts. For example, if we know that all the heads of the House Intelligence Committee have been men, and we also know that Lee

Hamilton is head of the House Intelligence Committee, we can conclude with certainty that Lee Hamilton is a man, not a woman. Fair enough?

The problem comes in if we twist the syllogism a little. We know that all heads of that committee have been men. We know that Lee Hamilton is a man. Therefore Lee Hamilton is head of the committee. That's not a proven piece of logic unless we can add another fact to the rhetoric—that all members of the committee other than its head are women. If that's true, then Lee Hamilton must be its head, because we know that Lee Hamilton is a man, and he's the only man on the committee, so he must be its head.

THE THIRD LANGUAGE OF PERSUASION
Rhetoric

Let's try another. "College graduates earn higher starting salaries than high school graduates. Bob graduated with a Bachelor's degree in business from Arizona State. Joe barely struggled through high school." Since we know that college graduates earn higher starting salaries than high school graduates, Bob must be making more than Joe. Has our rhetoric established this as logic?

In other words, have we proven it? Of course not. What was missing? We didn't establish that *all* college graduates make more money than high school graduates. If we said that up front, then pure logic enables us to deduce that Bob is making more money than Joe.

So let's try that statement again, and this time we'll appear to be saying that all college graduates make more money, without really stating it.

"There's no question that college graduates make substantially higher starting salaries than high school graduates, and the gap is widening. Whereas a study done in Phoenix, Arizona, in 1975 showed that the college graduates made 22 percent more money than high school students, a study completed last year showed the gap has widened to 34 percent.

"Consider the case of Bob Jones who graduated from Arizona State and went straight to work for IBM as a junior accountant. His high school class friend Joe Thompson got only good grades but decided not to go to college and went to work instead at a local car wash. Here the income disparity is over 300 percent."

From this, can you assume that Bob, the college graduate, makes more money than Joe? Well the rhetoric said so, but pay close attention to the logic, and it isn't necessarily so.

In fact Joe is making four times what Bob earns at IBM. While Bob was slaving away at college, Joe was learning the car wash business, lining up financial backing, and now owns six car washes throughout the Phoenix, Scottsdale, Tempe area.

While we're at it, watch those percentages. If Bob is making $100,000, and Joe is making 300 percent more, is Joe making $300,000? No, he's making $400,000. One hundred percent more would be $200,000, 200 percent more would be $300,000, and 300 percent more would be $400,000.

So the point is that to be Power Persuaders, we must separate the logic from the rhetoric. "Over 60 percent of adults suffer from the symptoms of hemorrhoidal pain," say the ads. Did we just hear that most adults suffer from hemorrhoids? Not at all. Merely that they suffer from the same symptoms as people with hemorrhoids.

"I first learned about Tylenol in the hospital when my doctor recommended it, and I've been using it for headache pain ever since." Did we just hear that the doctor recommended it for headache pain? Should we conclude that if hospital doctors suggest Tylenol, instead of aspirin, that we'd be better off using it? The rhetoric says yes, but the logic says no. Tylenol doesn't thin the blood the way that aspirin does. Wounds heal faster when you take Tylenol rather than aspirin. That's why doctors recommend it after surgery. While the commercial appears to suggest that doctors would recommend Tylenol over aspirin for headache pain, it just isn't so.

While we're on the subject of pain relievers, here's my favorite. "Anacin contains more of the pain reliever that doctors recommend most." Did we just hear that doctors recommend Anacin over aspirin? It appears so, but it's rhetoric we're listening to, not logic. In fact, the pain reliever that doctors recommend most is aspirin. There's a larger dose of aspirin in an Anacin tablet than in the standard 5-grain aspirin tablet.

Well, all right, but can we at least agree that doctors think aspirin is a better pain reliever, since we've established they recommend aspirin most? Wrong again! They may be saying to their patients, "Aspirin's almost as good as Tylenol and it's a lot cheaper, so go ahead and use it."

Power Persuaders learn to separate the rhetoric from the logic.

THE FOURTH LANGUAGE OF PERSUASION
Circular Logic

We may be buying a computer and the salesperson says to us, "Our computers are the finest made. And we have the best service technicians in the business." The first statement, that the computers are the finest, may be true. The second statement, about the quality of the service technicians, may not be true. It's an example of "circular logic," which means that when pressed as to why the salesperson feels the service technicians are the best, he can only respond with the premise that the best company would obviously employ the best technicians.

THE FIFTH LANGUAGE OF PERSUASION
Ipse Dixits

We don't have to go very far to find vague quotations foisted upon us in the guise of expert testimony. Known as ipse dixits to the people who study logic, they're all around us. Just pick up any magazine, and you'll find a slew of them. "Studies with people who had a heart attack show aspirin can help prevent a second heart attack. Bayer is recommended by more doctors for their cardiac patients than any other brand of aspirin."

While this statement appears to say that doctors are recommending aspirin for heart disease, that may not be true. The statement being made certainly doesn't prove it. Those doctors may just be recommending Bayer as a headache remedy for their cardiac patients.

THE SIXTH LANGUAGE OF PERSUASION
Ad Populems

Another form of defective syllogism is the ad populem, which is the logician's term for statements such as, "America's switching to tough Chevy trucks in a big way." And "This is the movie that everyone's talking about"—clearly a direct appeal to peer group pressure.

While it may be a fact that Chevy trucks are selling better, or that everyone's talking about the movie, it doesn't mean the truck is the best buy or the movie is a good one. Everybody talked about *The Attack of the Killer Tomatoes*. But what they were saying about it was that it was probably the worst movie of all time.

THE SEVENTH LANGUAGE OF PERSUASION
Short-circuiting Logic

There are many ways to make rhetoric persuasive, without the benefit of truth. For example, how often have you heard, "It must be true, or I wouldn't be allowed to say it"? It may be true that they'd be violating the law by saying it, but it doesn't stop the person from saying it anyway. Which is called, "begging the question."

Another form is oversimplification, for example, "Guns don't kill people." That may be true, but that's not justification for making automatic assault weapons available to the public, which have no purpose other than to kill people.

Also look out for sweeping generalizations such as, "All politicians are crooks" or "Everybody accepts that we are the leaders in the industry" or "We've built our reputation on quality." At first glance they seem convincing, but they really don't mean a thing.

■ LOGIC, NOT WORDS, SHOULD PERSUADE

So Power Persuaders understand that persuasion is always a two-way process. As we attempt to persuade, the other side is usually attempting to persuade us.

For example, as the salesperson tries to persuade the buyer to make a purchase, the buyer is trying to persuade the salesperson to make a better offer, or to simply go away. A mother is trying to persuade the child to quit watching television, as the child persuades the mother to let him stay for "just a few more minutes." A boss tries to persuade the secretary to work overtime, as the secretary works to persuade the boss to get someone else to do it.

As a Power Persuader, you need to know not only the verbal techniques necessary to persuade the other person, but also the tactics being used on you. When you become aware that someone is using rhetoric, rather than logic, you build a strong wall against his persuading you to give in to him.

■ KEY POINTS IN THIS CHAPTER

1. The foundation of the ability to change another person's beliefs lays in three language skills: grammar, rhetoric, and logic.

2. Grammar provides us with the essential structure that underlies all language and thought. Rhetoric is the use of that grammar with power and grace. Logic is a system by which we prove or disprove the rhetoric that has been used.

3. Fallacy is rhetoric used apparently to prove a point, though the logic may be faulty. A classic fallacy is the defective syllogism, where people appear to arrive at a conclusion using a twisted set of facts.

4. Power Persuaders learn to separate the rhetoric from the logic.

5. Look out for circular logic, where each half of a statement is only proven by the truth of the other half.

6. Ipse dixits are vague quotations foisted upon us in the guise of expert testimony.

7. Beware of ad populems, expressions such as, "America's switching to tough Chevy trucks in a big way." Even though many people may be doing something, it doesn't mean it's the right thing for them or you.

8. Look out for people using short-circuited logic such as, "It must be true, or I wouldn't be allowed to say it."

9. Also look out for sweeping generalizations that clearly can't be proven such as, "All politicians are crooks" or "Everybody accepts that we are the leaders in the industry."

10. For self-defense, you need to know not only the verbal techniques necessary to persuade the other person, but also the tactics being used on you. Don't listen to rhetoric and think you're hearing logic.

CHAPTER FIFTEEN

NEVER ACCEPT AN INVITATION TO ATTACK

The next rule of verbal persuasion is "Never accept an invitation to attack." If you were a general preparing a battle attack and your intelligence told you the enemy was deliberately exposing a flank to you, how would you react? You'd expect an ambush of course. Any time someone is inviting you to attack, you should be suspicious.

If the school bully says, "Go ahead and hit me," you'd be cautious, wouldn't you? If he's so anxious to have you attack him, you're liable to end up flat on your back with him sitting on your chest.

So why are we so eager to accept an invitation to attack when we're engaged in verbal combat?

I'm talking about the spouse who says, "I'm sure there are many things about me that you don't like. Go ahead and get them off your chest." Never accept an invitation to attack!

It's the boss who says, "I hear that you don't like the way I run things around here. My door is always open. Instead of talking behind my back, come on in and let me know how you feel. I'm big enough to take it." Never accept an invitation to attack!

Instead of walking into the ambush, you must go through the following four stages:

1. Determining your objective
2. Gathering information
3. Assessing your power by calculating each person's alternatives
4. Looking for concessions to make that don't detract from your position

Power Persuaders look out for ambushes and never accept an invitation to attack!

■ PART TWO

ANALYZING THE PERSUADEE

I think this part about analyzing the other person will fascinate you.

Power Persuasion would be a lot easier to learn if everybody reacted the same way, wouldn't it? We could simply learn what to say that would make our proposal irresistible and go out there and lay our story on the other person, who would then clap her hands together, jump up and down with joy, and yell, "I can't wait!" Unfortunately they don't.

Everyone reacts in a unique way. That's what makes persuasion challenging, but it's also what makes it fascinating. Let's take a look at the dimensions that affect the way you should persuade and how you can read them in the other person.

We'll look at these three aspects in this part:

1. How people react to what you tell them
2. What motivates the other person
3. How the other person decides

■ CHAPTER SIXTEEN

KNOWING HOW PEOPLE WILL REACT TO WHAT YOU TELL THEM

Every time we look at something, or hear a proposal, we evaluate it based on any experiences we've had with the topic. If you say the word "bear" to me, my mind automatically sifts through billions of pieces of information looking for a match. What it comes up with is a week-long solo backpacking trip high in the back country of Yosemite National Park. I was walking along a peaceful trail by a beautiful mountain lake when I glanced into a clearing to my left. A brown bear was nuzzling into a backpack left there by another hiker. Knowing that loud noises often scare bears, and naively wanting to help a fellow traveler, I tried to scare it away, by waving my arms and yelling at the top of my voice.

It took its nose out of the backpack and stared blindly at me. Then it evidently decided that I looked tastier than anything in the backpack and romped toward me. That was when I found out just how fast I could run in reverse!

So that's what I think about when I hear the word "bear." My memory searches for a match, and finds one, but other people's minds may tend to look for a mismatch. Say "bear" to them, and they might think, "I don't know anything about bears. I saw some in a zoo once, but I don't know anything about them."

Everyone tends to be either a matcher or mismatcher and being able to recognize which they are makes you a better persuader. Let's start by figuring out whether you're a matcher or a mismatcher. Take a look at the three bills on the following page.

In the lines below the bills, list five things that you observe about the relationship between the three pieces of paper. Be sure to do this before you read any further, or you'll miss the benefit of the exercise:

A matcher will see the similarities:

1. They're all U.S. bills.
2. They're all the same size.
3. They're all written in English.
4. They all have the value in all four corners.
5. They're all made of paper.

A mismatcher will see the differences:

1. They're all different values.
2. One is face down, two are face up.
3. There's a serial number on the front, but not the back.
4. Only the five is green in color.
5. The five has a building on it, the others have faces.

Of course, it's unlikely that you're either a pure matcher or mismatcher—there are varying degrees in between. You probably listed some similarities and some dissimilarities. But which did you list first? If you listed the similarities first, that's significant. You're a matcher, who also sees exceptions. If you listed the dissimilarities first, you're a mismatcher who sees exceptions.

Let's see how you identify this trait in people. I'm a professional speaker, traveling the country giving talks to corporations and associations. Let's say I want to discuss the industry with one of my speaker friends, so I say, "Tell me what you like about the speaking industry." Note that I've taken a position in the way I asked the

1. _____

2. _____

3. _____

4. _____

5. _____

question. I came at it from a positive point of view, "What do you like?" not, "What do you have the biggest problem with?"

Now it's up to my friend to match or mismatch that statement. He might say, "I love the applause and the freedom of being my own boss." Or he might mismatch me, by saying, "I like it so much, it's easier for me to tell you what I don't like. I could do without the airplanes and the taxis." See how easy it is to spot which one the other person is? (If you're a matcher, you're thinking, "Sure, no problem at all." If you're a mismatcher, you're probably thinking, "Yes, but what if they say . . .".)

H. G. Wells: "Go away, I'm all right."
(his final words)

Matchers like their world to stay the same. They're likely to stay on the same job for a long time and stay married to the same person for life. They vacation in the same place every year and seldom change their mind about anything. They are the "know what I like and like what I know" brigade.

Mismatchers like the excitement of change and frequently change jobs and spouses. They have a high level of discontent, which can be healthy and make them very ambitious. Or it can be negative and lead to great frustration and failure.

Gloria Steinem: "I never married because I can't mate in captivity."

I once ran into a man who must be the most extreme matcher of all time. I was getting fitted for a suit at Gieves & Hawkes on Saville Row in London, when he walked in. He was wearing a three-piece muted houndstooth suit made of very heavy wool. A country gentleman type of suit. He said to the clerk in a very strong British accent, "You chaps made this suit for me about twenty years ago, and it's beginning to show some wear. Suppose I should get a new one. Want it exactly the same as this one. Suppose you still have my measurements, don't you?"

Let me give you another example. Later on in the same trip, I was staying at the Royal Norfolk Hotel in Bognor Regis on the south coast. Until the mid-1950s, these resort towns were the place everyone went on vacation in England. Now everyone goes to the continent for their "holidays," and these towns are slowly decaying. A parallel in this country might be Atlantic City before the casinos. I went down to breakfast to enjoy some kippers, a favorite of mine that's hard to get in America. In England it's perfectly acceptable to join other diners in a restaurant, so I sat down with an elderly gentleman. There's only one way to open a conversation in England, and that's with the weather. So after a silent getting to know you period of a few minutes, I said, "Think we'll have rain today?"

"Wouldn't doubt it," he said, "wouldn't doubt it a bit."

Since he had now signaled that he wouldn't mind talking to me, I continued, "Stay at this hotel often?"

"I've spent my holiday here every other year since '32," he told me. "Except for the war years, of course. That put the kibosh on things a bit. Come here on even years and go to Bermuda on odd years." He was perfectly happy to continue with the same pattern for over fifty years, and saw no reason to change. What a contrast to me! I almost never want to go back to somewhere I've been, because I want adventure and excitement.

Dudley Moore: "England is a beautiful country, with great theater and fine museums, and wonderful people. It's really quite amazing that nobody wants to live there anymore."

Note that matchers and mismatchers don't always translate into positive and negative thinkers. At first you might think that he was the positive one, because he was happy with his pattern of doing things and didn't want to change. And that I must be negative, because I didn't like anywhere enough to keep coming back. In fact I saw myself as much more positive than he. I find everywhere I go so interesting that I always want to try new things. He was rejecting anything with which he was not familiar.

How does this help you become a Power Persuader? If you know whether people match or mismatch, you'll know how to appeal to them. Reverse psychology, for example, works only on a mismatcher. If you've had children, I'm sure you've had at least one who's a mismatcher. If you want your daughter to finish her homework before she goes to bed, you have to say to her, "Why don't you get up early and finish your homework in the morning, when you're fresh."

She'll say, "Daddy, I told you, I have to finish it tonight!"

If you want your son to ride his bike to school, you have to say, "Why don't I give you a ride to school, and you can catch the bus home?"

> "There's nothing wrong with teenagers that reasoning with them won't aggravate."

He'll say, "I don't want to ride the bus, I'll ride my bike instead." But it works only with a mismatcher. Try it with a matcher, and they'll say, "Sure, if that's what you want me to do."

My literary hero Ernest Hemingway was a classic mismatcher, known for his cantankerous outbursts against anyone he didn't like. For example, back in the 1920s, he had sold the movie rights to *A Farewell to Arms* outright. So when David O. Selznick wanted to remake it in 1959, starring his 41-year-old wife Jennifer Jones playing 24-year-old Catherine Barkley, he didn't have to pay Hemingway anything. However, he made a grand gesture and announced to the press that he would pay Hemingway $50,000 out of the profits anyway. Hemingway responded by telling Selznick to "take your $50,000, change it into nickels, and stick them up your ass until they come out of your ears."

> Fred Allen: "He writes so well he makes me feel like putting my quill back in my goose."

So when young journalist A. E. Hotchner was told by his editor at *Cosmopolitan* to find a way to get Hemingway to write an article on the future of journalism, he had a huge persuasion challenge on his hands. Hemingway wrote only what he wanted to write and had a reputation for verbally destroying any journalist with the nerve to approach him.

Hotchner flew down to Havana, where Hemingway was living, to plan strategy. He spent two days at the Nacional Hotel in what he described in his great book *Papa Hemingway* as a "semicomatose state induced by pure cowardice," trying to come up with a plan. Knowing that Hemingway, as a world-class mismatcher, was liable to oppose anything he said, he sent him a note explaining why he was there. He told Hemingway he didn't expect him to write the article, but he'd be obliged if Hemingway would let him have a note saying he'd tried, so that he wouldn't get fired from *Cosmopolitan*. The strategy worked. The next morning he got a call from the great author, who said he couldn't permit Hotchner to lose face with the Hearst organization (which owned *Cosmopolitan*) because it would be like getting bounced from a leper colony. Their meeting turned into a lifelong friendship, with Hotchner adapting many of Hemingway's stories for television.

Guindon: "Great moments in literature: In 1936, Ernest Hemingway caught a carp, and decided not to write about it."

Let's say that you sell office equipment, and you're upgrading a customer to the latest version of your equipment. The firm has been a good customer for years and is happy with the equipment you sold it last time, but it's now ready to trade the old equipment in and invest in the latest model.

Ask a matcher why she's thinking of making the investment, and she'll tell you, "This one has been such a great machine for us, we know we'll be even happier with the latest model."

Ask a mismatcher and he'll tell you, "This one's getting old, and we want to trade it in before it starts giving us trouble. And the new model can do so many things that this one can't."

So your sales approach should be different. With the matcher, you'd stress that the new machines are every bit as reliable as the old ones. That even though they do more, they are just as easy to use and maintain. And all the supplies or software that they've been using will work with the new equipment.

With the mismatcher, you'd want to stress the differences. Tell them how the machine has been completely redesigned. How it's light-years ahead of its predecessor, and once they have it, they'll wonder how on earth they ever got along without it.

Similarly if you were trying to persuade your child that your upcoming transfer from Boston to El Paso was the most wonderful thing that ever happened to her, you'd want to consider whether they were a matcher or mismatcher. With the matcher, you'd want to tell her how her new high school would be so similar to her existing one, and how lots of kids transfer from Boston to El Paso just before their senior year! With a mismatcher you'd stress the excitement of a new culture and all the new friends they'd make.

■ KEY POINTS IN THIS CHAPTER

1. Everyone tends to be either a matcher or mismatcher, and being able to recognize which a person is, helps you become a better persuader.

2. Matchers look for similarities, mismatchers look for differences. Many people are a combination of both. Some look for similarities and then see the exceptions. Others look for dissimilarities, and then look for exceptions.

3. Matchers like their world to stay the same and form lifelong attachments to things and people. Mismatchers are always discontent and frequently move on to what they hope will be greener pastures.

4. To persuade a matcher, stress the improvements over the previous service or product, but not the differences. To persuade a mismatcher, stress how different your product or service is from that which he's had in the past.

5. Reverse psychology works well with the mismatcher. Anticipate that he'll disagree with you and want to move away from your proposal.

CHAPTER SEVENTEEN

WHAT MOTIVATES THE OTHER PERSON

In this chapter, I'll teach you about the internal frames of reference that motivate the other person to do what you want them to do. In this context, there are four ways that people view their world:

1. *Possibility versus necessity.* People are motivated either by the possibility of reward as a result of acting or by feeling that they must take action out of necessity.

2. *Self-centered versus externally centered.* People see the considered change either in light of how it would affect them or by how it would affect others. This is called "internal sorting."

3. *Pleasure versus pain.* People either move primarily toward pleasure or primarily away from pain.

4. *Field dependent or field independent.* People care what others think in varying degrees. Some people are very much influenced, in conscious thought and unconscious feelings, by what others think; other people are not.

Let's take these one at a time.

■ POSSIBILITY VERSUS NECESSITY

We all tend to be motivated either by possibility or by necessity. Put yourself in the shoes of movie producer Mike Todd in October 1956. It was the night before his movie *Around the World in 80 Days* premiered. He was flat broke and millions of dollars in debt. He had high hopes for his new movie, but also knew it could bomb. In his Park Avenue apartment the phone rang. It was Otis Chandler, the publisher of the Los Angeles *Times*, offering to buy 50 percent of the movie for $15 million. Todd told Otis he wanted to take a vote among the people there: wife Elizabeth Taylor, son Mike, and friend Eddie Fisher. His son and friend both told him to jump at the money. His wife told him to gamble. He took his hand off the mouthpiece and turned down the offer, in effect gambling $15 million that his movie was worth at least $30 million. What kind of person would take a gamble like that? A possibility thinker, that's who.

The possibility versus necessity continuum

Possibility	Necessity
←————————————————————————————→	
Persuaded by what might happen	Persuaded by the need to take action

Robert Schuller coined the phrase "possibility thinker," but we are all either possibility thinkers or we are necessity thinkers. The first are motivated by what might happen; the second take action only when they have to.

I like to think of myself as a possibility thinker. One evening I was on my way to a dinner party in Beverly Hills with my daughter Julia. I said to her, "I'm really excited right now. I've got so many projects going that if only one of them hits it big, all my dreams would come true. I've got a great new audio program in production, two books coming out next year, and a television program going into production that could make me a fortune." I thought about what I'd said for a few moments, and then started to giggle. Soon I was laughing so hard, I had to pull the car over to the side of the road and stop.

"What's so funny?" she said.

"Oh, Julia, what a country!" I said, wiping away my tears of laughter. "Only in America could a man be driving his Rolls Royce to the Beverly Hills Hotel for dinner and find himself saying, 'All I need is one lucky break.'"

Possibility thinkers are not the plodders of the world. They are always taking great soaring leaps, and very often come crashing down. While the necessity thinker would never quit a job until they got fired—"I can't quit now, I've only got ten years to go until retirement"—the possibility thinker always has half a dozen pipe dreams going for him.

Where does this slant on life come from? Probably from feelings of security or insecurity that build up in us very early in life. Until I was 18 years old, I lived in nine different homes, and changed high schools four times. That gives you a completely different perspective on life over someone who lives in the same house until he leaves for college. You become more comfortable with change and feel more secure taking risks. That's why possibility thinkers are fascinated by the unknown. Their minds race ahead to all the exciting things that lay out there, beyond their present frame of reference. Necessity thinkers anchor to the world they know.

Let me give you a simple test to determine where you are on this scale. Simply answer this question: How old were you when you first started earning money outside your home? In asking this question of literally hundreds of job applicants over the years, I've found a very direct correlation. The younger you were when you first started earning your own money, the more initiative you'll have. And the more initiative you have, the more you will function on possibilities rather than necessity.

It's easy to see how Power Persuaders use this. Possibility thinkers are always looking for what they could gain by making a move. So we know that the key is to paint an exciting picture of the great things that could happen if they follow our suggestion.

Necessity-based people are more concerned about what they might lose by making a move. So we talk to them about how this move will enable them to maintain what they already have.

■ SELF-CENTERED VERSUS EXTERNALLY CENTERED

The next dimension is how people reference their world in terms of self-interests or external interests. On the extreme ends of the scale, you have a Mother Theresa, whose interests are totally external, with almost no self-interests. On the other end of the scale, you have a Donald Trump who seems capable of considering things only in terms of self-interests.

The self versus external sorting continuum

Narcissists	Martyrs
◄─────────────────────────────────────►	
Persuaded by how it affects them	Persuaded by how it affects others

Few people are that extreme—most of us are somewhere in the middle of the self-importance scale. We are neither martyrs (I am nothing compared to my cause) or narcissists (I am the center of the universe). Since we admire externally oriented people, and condemn people for being self-centered, we tend to think of ourselves as less self-centered than most. When we do act in a self-centered way, we tend to justify. For example, "the situation called for someone to make tough choices."

It's interesting how the difference between ourselves and other people pop into our minds during conversations. Once I was talking to a friend about marriage proposals she had received. She told me that she'd been proposed to several times and almost accepted one of them.

"Why didn't you?" I asked her.

"Because at the last moment, I started thinking to myself, why am I doing this? I'm not lonely, I don't want to have children, and I don't need financial support. So I thought 'what's in it for me,' and told him no."

This was so far from my thinking about marriage that, for a moment, I couldn't put it together with my frame of reference. To me, you don't marry someone because of what's in it for you. You marry someone because you love the person so much that you just want to give everything to her. In this instance, she was sorting internally, and I was sorting externally.

Jim Backus: "Many a man owes his success to his first wife and his second wife to his success."

This is a key clue in hiring the right person for the job; it's a way of knowing if the person will be successful on the job. In customer service positions, you want someone who sorts externally, who really cares about other people. Your attorney and your corporate controller should sort internally—they should care less about people than they do about getting the job done right.

Winston Churchill is a great example of an internal sorter who was the right man hired for the right job at the right time. Before you think that I'm criticizing him, let me explain that he's my hero. As a hobby, I collect books by and about him. I have several shelves full in my library, and I carry a catalog of them with me wherever I go. Whenever I'm in a new town for a speaking engagement, I try to get to the local used bookstore and see what they might have that I don't own yet. I even named my dog, an English sheepdog, Winston.

Much as I admire Winston Churchill, I don't see him as a people person. He was a self-centered, egotistical bully, the ultimate self-sorter. But he got the job done, when probably no one else could have saved England from Adolph Hitler. An historian once described it this way: "When faced with a bullying tyrant, England sent for a bullying tyrant—Winston Churchill—to face him down."

Adolph Hitler: "Winston Churchill is the most bloodthirsty strategist the world has ever known."

If you know whether people sort internally or externally, you know how to persuade them. Let's say you sell temporary help services to corporations. If a firm's human resources director sorts internally, you'd want to tell him how much work and hassle this will save him. If he sorts externally, you'd want to stress what a big help it will be to the company.

If you sell cars, you'd tell the internal sorter how good he's going to feel as he drives it. To an external, you'd stress how safe and comfortable his family will be.

Analyze the way people talk, and decide whether they sort internally or externally. If they are internal, appeal to their self-interests. If they are external, stress the benefits to the people around them.

■ MOVING TOWARD PLEASURE OR AWAY FROM PAIN

My parents followed me to California from England when they were in their late sixties. One evening I got a panicky call from my mother, who told me that Dad had gone for his evening walk and hadn't returned. I frantically drove to Los Angeles and retraced his steps as Mom had described his usual walk, with visions of his having collapsed from a heart attack. There was no sign of him anywhere. I called all the local hospitals and then drew a blank. Running out of ideas, I went to the local police station and they ran a computer check of the day's arrestees. There was no Tom Dawson, but at the central police station downtown, there was a John Doe who talked funny.

I went down to bail Dad out, and find out how he'd got himself in such a predicament. Apparently he had been crossing a street, when a motorcycle cop stopped him for jaywalking. I can only imagine his reaction to this heavily armed officer on a huge motorcycle with flashing lights and chattering CB, after a lifetime of observing unarmed British bobbies. Dad didn't understand the concept of jaywalking, because in England you can cross the street wherever you want, and it's your fault if you get hit by a car. Explaining American law to Dad wasn't high on the list of the officer's concerns. Explaining how things were done in England was very high on Dad's list of concerns. The officer got his pad out and starting writing a ticket. Dad kept saying over and over, "This wouldn't happen in England."

Brendan Behan: "I have never seen a situation so dismal that a policeman couldn't make it worse."

Then Dad refused to sign the ticket. The officer was beginning to lose his patience. "Just sign the ticket. You're not admitting guilt, but you have to sign the ticket, or I have to arrest you."

Dad looked at the motorcycle, considered it inconceivable that he'd be strapped on the back of it and taken to jail, and said, "Shan't sign it. Wouldn't have to sign anything in England."

The cop said, "That does it," called for a police car, and had him arrested. At central jail, they allowed him one phone call, but he couldn't remember his number.

Dad's trial was set for the next month, and he insisted he was going to plead innocent. I argued until I was blue in the face, but I couldn't get him to budge. I told him it would only be a small fine that I'd be happy to pay for him, but he was adamant.

However, on the day of his trial, the bailiff lined up all the defendants and gave them a stiff lecture. He said, "Some of you may be thinking of pleading innocent, just to give us trouble. Let me tell you what happens to you if you do that. You will immediately be handcuffed and taken to central jail where you'll stay for as long as it takes for you to come up with your new bail, which will be about $2,000."

Dad promptly marched up, pleaded guilty, and paid a $5 fine. I said, "Dad, I've been trying to get you to plead guilty for weeks. How come that bailiff could convince you in 10 seconds?"

"Son, I suppose you'd say the bailiff just explained it a bit better than you did."

I had failed because I'd been telling Dad how much easier it would be to plead guilty and pay the fine. That's appealing to his motivation for pleasure. The bailiff was telling him all the nasty things that would happen to him if he pleaded innocent. That's appealing to his need to avoid pain.

The pleasure/pain continuum

Hedonists	Cowards
←	→
Persuaded by desire for pleasure	Persuaded by the need to avoid pain

We all are somewhere on the pleasure/pain continuum. When faced with a decision, we will always decide based on where we are on that continuum. The extremes would be the hedonist (pleasure seeker) and the coward (pain avoider). But few people are that extreme. The last thing I'd call my father is a coward. I've seen him stand up to people twice his size. But he does have a strong Puritan work ethic and isn't highly motivated by the need for pleasure.

The pleasure/pain continuum is often the key to motivation. If we tend to seek pleasure rather than avoid pain, we'll move if we think it will bring us pleasure. If we tend to avoid pain, we'll be motivated to move when it will allow us to avoid pain or discomfort.

In 1990, I was climbing the Matterhorn mountain in Switzerland with my son John. My French climbing guide Guy gave me the finest motivational talk of my life. At one point, I couldn't see any way to make the next pitch. The rock was perfectly smooth. Guy was above me, belaying my rope. I could call out to him, but I couldn't see him. I yelled, "Guy, this isn't going to go. There's no way."

He called back, "Roger, you will find a way to make it go. If you don't we will 'ave to spend ze night on zis mountain." That's when I really understood motivation, as it relates to avoiding pain, for the first time. When the pain of doing nothing exceeds the pain of moving on, you will move on. I swung out onto the rock and somehow made it up.

Where we are on this continuum has a lot to do with how much discipline we have. Last Thursday I was having dinner with a date and some of her business acquaintances when one of them said, "Roger we need a fourth for golf tomorrow. We're playing at Monarch Bay, which is a beautiful course right on the ocean. Want to join us? Please come as our guest." I'm sure you've been in a situation like that, haven't you? When you're torn between the pleasure of doing something that would be really fun and the pain of all the work that will pile up while you're out goofing off. If you were in my situation, what would you have done? I'm self-employed, so I was free to take the day off. However, I was under a deadline to get this manuscript to Tom Power, my editor at Prentice Hall. If I played golf, I knew I'd have to burn some midnight oil to get caught up. What would you have done?

Perhaps the answer is clear to you. You might be thinking, "Are you crazy? Go play golf! Don't pass up a great opportunity like that." Or you may be at the other end of the scale, saying, "Roger, you'll never achieve your full potential if you goof off like that. Keep working, there'll be time for fun later." I guess I'm somewhere in the middle. I played golf with them, but I felt guilty about it!

This is an underlying key to all human behavior. Do you exercise because you enjoy it, or because you want to prevent a heart attack? Do you do what your boss tells you because you want to be on the team, or because you don't want him or her angry at you? Do you mow the lawn because of how great it's going to look or because if you don't do it this week, it'll be murder to do next week?

It's easy to see how Power Persuaders can use this to get what they want. If you see that the other person is a pleasure seeker, you paint a picture of how good it's going to make her feel. If you know she's a pain avoider, paint a picture of the penalties of not making a move.

How do you find out which someone is? Ask her, "How do you feel about that?" It's open ended, so she can't answer with a yes or no, and it goes to her feelings—which is what you're trying to uncover.

Your son says, "Dad, I've applied for a job as a box boy at the supermarket."

You ask, "How do you feel about that, son?"

If he's a pleasure seeker, he'll say, "I think it'd be great. Pay's good, and I'll get weekends off." If he's a pain avoider, he'll say, "I'm concerned that working in the evenings will make it hard for me to get my homework done. And what about if the band I play in gets a gig on a Friday night?"

In business, you might have a sales manager who says, "I'm thinking of expanding into Florida."

Instead of jumping in with your opinion about it, you say, "How do you feel about that?" If he's a pleasure seeker, he'll say, "It's a dynamite idea, and I know someone who'd die for the opportunity to run the district down there." If he's a pain avoider, he'll say, "I'm not convinced we should expand in this soft market. But if we don't, our competition will beat us to the punch."

■ FIELD DEPENDENT VERSUS FIELD INDEPENDENT

Next let's take a look at something by which we are all influenced. Some people care very deeply what other people think, and others could care less what other people think. Psychologists call this being field dependent versus field independent.

The lives of field-dependent people are constantly being affected by what's going on around them. They quickly take on the mood of the people around them. If everybody's happy and excited, they tend to be that way too. They often avoid watching the news on television, because they're so deeply affected by bad news.

Field-independent people seem oblivious to what's going on around them. They can be in Times Square at midnight on New Year's Eve and still not get caught up in the excitement. The film *Roger and Me* portrayed then General Motors chairman Roger Smith as field independent and completely oblivious to the effect plant closures were having on the people of Flint, Michigan. That wasn't accurate, but it was filmmaker Michael Moore's perception.

The field-dependent continuum

Field Dependent	Field Independent
←——————————————————————————————→	
Persuaded by what others think	Not persuaded by what others think

Both ends of the continuum have pluses and minuses. Let's first consider the person who is very field dependent, who cares very much what other people think. On the positive side, this is a person who is considerate and thoughtful of others. On the negative side, this is a person who never takes a stand on anything and is constantly being blown back and forth by the winds of change. A joiner, and never a leader.

Conversely, consider the person who is field independent, who doesn't care what others think. On the positive side, they are the leaders of society, always in the forefront of change. Also, they are what Abraham Maslow described as "self-actualizing" people, unfettered by the need to be liked or looked up to by other people. On the negative side, they might be considered as bombastic and self-centered.

Power Persuaders first need to learn how to identify the other person on this continuum. Here's an excellent way to do it. In some way find out how the other person knows she's doing a good job. Let's say you sell furniture to hotels and you're meeting with the vice president in charge of operations for a medium-sized regional chain of hotels. At some point in the conversation, you might find it appropriate to ask, "Something has always interested me about large companies like this. How do you know when you've done a good job?"

A field-dependent person will tell you, "I get an annual review just like all the other employees, and the president of the company lets me know. Usually he doesn't pull any punches!" A field-independent person will be more likely to say, "Oh, I don't need anybody to tell me, that's for sure. If I don't meet the criteria I've set for myself, I know I've failed."

You probably won't have to be as direct as that, to find out where he is on this continuum. If you're aware of it, and are listening carefully to the other person's responses, you'll quickly pick up on how much he cares about what other people think of him. Field-independent people say things like, "It's my neck which is in the noose on this one," or "I'm going to go with my gut instinct," or "They just don't know what's best for them."

Field-dependent people say things like, "I want to survey our people on this before we go ahead," or "I have to take several options to the committee," or "I don't want everybody breathing down my neck on this."

Having identified the other person as field dependent or independent, you can then plan your persuasion strategy. To the field-independent hotel furniture buyer, you'd say things like, "You can't expect your guests to be the mattress expert that you are. All they care about is if they get a good night's sleep. You are the one who has to do what's in their best interests." To the field-dependent person, you're better off to say, "It's the thing your guests care most about. You've got better things to do than listen to complaints about cheap mattresses, don't you?"

■ KEY POINTS IN THIS CHAPTER

1. People are either motivated by the possibilities of your proposal or by the perceived necessity of making a move. When talking to a possibility thinker, stress the exciting benefits of making a

move. When persuading a necessity thinker, stress the penalties of not changing.

2. People are either persuaded by self-interests (internal sorters) or by concern for others (external sorters). In some it's extreme—Donald Trump, Mother Theresa—but in most of us it's much more subtle. This is a key to hiring people, because the service sector calls for external sorting people, whereas control functions call for internal sorting. Analyze the way people talk, and decide whether they sort internally or externally. If they're internal, appeal to their self-interests. If they're external, stress the benefits to the people around them.

3. The pleasure/pain continuum is often the key to motivation. If we seek pleasure rather than avoid pain, we will move if we think it will bring us pleasure. If we avoid pain, we will be motivated to move when it will enable us to avoid pain or discomfort. If you see the other person as a pleasure seeker, paint a picture of how good your proposal is going to make them feel. If you know that they are a pain avoider, paint a picture of the penalties of not making a move.

4. Some people care very deeply what other people think, and others could care less. Psychologists call this being field dependent versus field independent. To the field-dependent person, stress how much people will appreciate his or her going along with your proposal. To the field-independent person, emphasize how he or she must take a leadership role and make bold decisions.

CHAPTER EIGHTEEN

HOW THE OTHER PERSON DECIDES

In the previous chapter I discussed the internal frames of reference that cause people to analyze your proposal in different ways. Now let's say that you have skillfully determined their internal reference points and made your presentation in such a way that it has maximum appeal to their way of thinking. Great! We're down to the actual point of the other person making a decision to go with your proposal or reject it—a decision to be persuaded or not to be persuaded. In this chapter I'll teach you some of the processes that people go through before they decide whether or not to be persuaded.

■ ASSERTIVE VERSUS UNASSERTIVE

Assertive people tend to make decisions quickly. They take a look at your proposal and either go for it or don't go for it. Less assertive people need time to make up their minds.

This is very important when you're trying to persuade someone to do something. If you don't ask the assertive person for a decision, she thinks something is wrong. Why don't you feel strongly enough to push for an approval? Conversely, if you push an unassertive person for a decision before he's ready to make it, you're creating a problem. Either he resists what he sees as a high-pressure tactic, or he thinks you're trying to get him to go along with something, before he has half the information he needs to make the right move.

So it's very important to know if the person with whom you're dealing is assertive or not. Fortunately, it's not hard to tell. An assertive person will greet you with a firm handshake and get down to business with a minimum of formalities. She needs enough information to make a decision, but not too much. If you overload her with information, she'll think, "Oh come on! Don't give me all this flimflam! Who are you trying to con? Just give me the facts."

Conversely, an unassertive person will greet you tentatively and want to spend time getting to know you before they get down to business. His approach will be more like: "Oh, hi. It's nice to see you again, come on in. Can I get you some coffee? How're the wife and children?"

So first analyze if the person you're trying to persuade is assertive or unassertive. If she's assertive, go for the close. Give her the facts and ask her to go for your proposal. If he's unassertive, take your time. Give him all the information he wants, be sure he feels comfortable with you, and then gently nudge him toward a decision.

■ EMOTIONAL VERSUS UNEMOTIONAL

The next dimension to consider is whether the person is emotional or nonemotional. You tell this by the way he greets you and the way he reacts to things. The emotional person will greet you with either warmth or excitement and react with attentive enthusiasm to your persuasion appeal. The unemotional person will greet you in a businesslike manner, which may even appear cold to you. If, for example, you're having a breakfast meeting with both an emotional and an unemotional person, you'll easily spot the differences. The emotional will be friendly toward the waitress, call her by name, and ask how she is and what she recommends. The unemotional will ignore the waitress unless he needs something, and then make brief, businesslike requests. He may not even want to see the menu. After all, bacon and eggs is just about the same thing wherever you go, so why waste time poring over a menu?

The way people react to your persuasion proposal depends on their level of emotion, combined with their level of assertiveness. Here's how the four possible combinations of these two factors will react:

Emotional/assertive. "Let's run with it, sounds like a terrific idea to me. How fast can we put it into effect?" Or "Sounds like a crazy idea to me. Too crazy for us. What else you got?"

Emotional/unassertive. "I really appreciate you bringing this to me. I like the idea, but I wouldn't feel comfortable going ahead without talking to the employees about it first. I hope you understand." Or "I just don't think this would fit in with what we do here. We don't like to rock the boat with a lot of new ideas."

Unemotional/assertive. "I'm only going to go with this if it makes us money. Show me it'll do that and I'll give you the go-ahead today." Or "We've tried that before. Sounds like a good idea, but it won't work. Trust me."

Unemotional/unassertive. "I can see you've really done your homework on this. Subject to our verifying the results of your research, I'd like to give you a tentative go-ahead." Or "I wouldn't feel comfortable jumping into something like this. We'd have to do some thorough research before we could consider it, and we're so backlogged, I don't know when we'd ever be able to get around to it."

So the emotional/assertiveness ratings of the people with whom you're dealing have a lot to do with the way you go about getting a decision. To pigeonhole them into the correct one of the four categories, be sure to evaluate their assertiveness rating first, and then their emotional rating. It's much harder to do the other way around.

Now let's move on to how the person reacts to your proposal. There are basically two steps that the person will go through as you try to persuade him. He will listen to what you have to say, and then he will process that information with either conscious or unconscious thought.

■ OPEN OR CLOSED MINDED

Let's consider the first step—listening to what you have to say. People listen with either an open or a closed mind.

Open-minded people evaluate what you have to say based on what they hear or observe. They make up their minds based on what you have to tell them or show them. Closed-minded people evaluate what you have to say as it relates to what they already know. It's the person who believes only in his or her religion and thinks that anyone from a different religion is a missionary from the Devil. It's the person who believes that Japanese cars are better made and will not listen to any evidence to the contrary. It's the buyer who is happy with his present supplier and won't take the time to listen to your proposal.

Obviously, a closed-minded person is harder to persuade. With an open-minded person, you may be able to persuade her by talking about what you or your product can do, or by letting her read about it. With a closed-minded person, your persuasion must include letting him see a demonstration or, better yet, getting him to take part in a hands-on demonstration.

So Power Persuaders know

Open minded: Show and tell.
Closed minded: See and do.

When it's not obvious, how do you tell whether they're open or closed minded? Let's say that you sell glass bottles, and you're trying to get a spaghetti sauce company to switch to you as its packing supplier. You might say to the buyer: "You tell me that your present supplier is the best in the business, but how do you know that?"

If he says, "I never hear any complaints from our production department" or "I read the quality control reports," he's probably open minded. Lucky you!

However if he says, "I personally inspect the rejects every week, and it's never more than one-tenth of 1 percent" or "I spent five days at their plant in Pacoima; nobody can touch their quality control," then you've probably got a closed-minded person on your hands. You won't be able to persuade him with show and tell. You'll have to get him to see and do.

■ CONSCIOUS OR UNCONSCIOUS THOUGHT PROCESSORS

So the first step to their decision-making process is how people listen to your proposal—with an open or closed mind. The second step is how they process the information you give them. Let's say that you've gotten past the resistance of a closed-minded person and have been able to lay your story on him. Now you have an additional factor to consider: Does he process the information you've given him with conscious or unconscious thought?

Conscious thinkers process the information with their five senses. Unconscious thinkers go with their intuitive feel about your persuasion presentation.

Let's recap the five senses, so you get an idea of the process that conscious thinkers use:

Sense		Means	For Example
Visual	=	Seeing	A painter
Auditory	=	Hearing	A musician
Tactile	=	Touch	A potter
Gustatory	=	Taste	A chef
Olfactory	=	Smell	A perfumer

Since you're not likely to run into many people whose primary sense is tactile (touch), gustatory (taste), or olfactory (smell), you will be primarily concerned with distinguishing between auditory and visual people. Here's a quick test to see which you are: close your eyes and think of the house in which you lived when you were 10 years old. Hold that thought for 15 seconds, then open your eyes and continue reading.

When you did that exercise, did you primarily *see* the house in your mind, or did you mainly *hear* things. Such as the laughter of children or your mother working in the kitchen? As I told you in the earlier chapter on credibility, most people are visual. They believe more what they see, than what they hear.

The point I'm making here is not that you should be able to analyze which of their five senses dominates. I want you to realize that some people are persuaded by what their five senses tell them, and some people are dominated by their sixth sense, intuition. However, it is interesting to note that you can tell whether people are visual or auditory by the expressions of speech they use.

Here are some comparisons:

Visuals	Auditories
I see your point.	I hear you.
Take a look at this.	Listen to this.
Do I have to paint a picture?	Do I have to spell it out?
Did I make myself clear?	Did you hear what I said?
Looks as if we should.	Sounds as though we should.

If you determine that the person you're trying to persuade is primarily using her five senses to analyze your presentation—a conscious thinker—you will know that you must be concrete in your appeal. She needs to see it, hear it, touch it, taste it, or smell it in order to be convinced. Do everything you can to let her see, hear, and touch your product or service. For food or drink, tasting and smelling will be important also.

Marilyn Monroe (after being served matzo ball soup three times in a row): "Isn't there any other part of the matzo you can eat?"

Conversely, some people don't interpret your presentation with their five senses at all. They react more by gut instinct or intuition and are called kinesthetic (feeling) people. When we add kinesthetic language to the chart, we get a new "feel" for what's going on!

Visuals	Auditories	Kinesthetics
I see your point.	I hear you.	I feel you're right.
Take a look at this.	Listen to this.	Get a sense of this.
Do I have to paint a picture?	Do I have to spell it out?	Can't you grasp it?
Did I make myself clear?	Did you hear what I said?	Understand?
Looks as if we should.	Sounds as though we should.	Feels good to me.

When dealing with kinesthetic people (unconscious thinkers) it's less important that you let them see, hear, touch, taste, or smell your product or service. The way to persuade them is to paint vivid mental pictures of how it's going to feel to be doing business with you.

What I've covered in this chapter is based on the work of famed psychologist Carl Jung, and I cover it in more detail in my tape program *Confident Decision Making*, which is available by calling my office at 800-YDAWSON.

■ KEY POINTS IN THIS CHAPTER

1. Assertive people make decisions quickly. Unassertive people are slow decision makers.

2. How quickly you push for a decision must be based on the person's level of assertiveness.

3. Next determine his or her emotional level. From this you develop four different persuasion appeals:

   Emotional/assertive. Razzle dazzle him with how exciting the project will be and how he has to jump on the opportunity before it passes him by.

   Emotional/unassertive. Warm her up slowly to the idea; tell her how good everybody's going to feel.

   Unemotional/assertive. Tell her the bottom line benefits, and push for a fast decision.

   Unemotional/unassertive. Give him lots of precise detail, because he makes a decision based on facts, but needs an overload of information.

4. Next, determine if they are open or closed minded. You can persuade the open-minded person with show and tell, but the closed-minded person must see and do.

5. Next, do they process the information you've given them with conscious or unconscious thought? Conscious thinkers process the information with their five senses. Unconscious thinkers go with their intuitive feel about your persuasion presentation. So

with conscious thinkers, you must let them see, hear, and touch your product or service. With unconscious thinkers, it's more important to romance their imaginations.

■ PART THREE

HOW TO BECOME A POWER PERSUADER

In Part Three I'll teach you how to develop the personal characteristics of a Power Persuader. While you may think that some people are naturally persuasive, this just isn't so. There are three learnable skills that will draw other people to you and make them want to please you.

First, we'll cover that hard-to-describe quality we call charisma. We simply like some people so much that if they were to ask us to do something, we would. This is definitely the case with the fan of a pop music star: ask any 16-year-old how they'd react if Michael Jackson asked a favor of them. However, it's also true for admirers of political leaders and of top people in any profession. It's a more subtle motivating factor, but it's so critical to effective persuasion.

Then, I'll teach you how to develop a sense of humor. Yes, you really can learn that. In fact there are only five things that make

171

people laugh, and everything else is a variation on those five things. What could be simpler?

Finally, I'll teach you the one thing at which everybody would like to be better, and that's how to remember names.

Personal charisma, a sense of humor, and the ability to remember anyone's name instantly: these are the three personal characteristics of a Power Persuader.

CHAPTER NINETEEN

DEVELOPING CHARISMA: HOW TO MAKE THEM LOVE YOU!

What is charisma?

> It's that rare quality that makes people like you, even when they don't know much about you.
>
> It's that intangible that makes people want to follow you, to be around you, to be influenced by you.
>
> It's that *je ne sais quoi* that causes people to see you from across a crowded room and want to be with you.

Salespeople who have it tell me, "Roger, the only reason my people do business with me, is because they like me." Celebrities who have it are at a loss to explain it. Art Linkletter gets a standing ovation whenever he walks onto a stage. "Roger," he told me, "I can tell you when it started, but I can't explain it."

We all know it when we see it, but we all have a difficult time explaining exactly what it is. John F. Kennedy had charisma. Richard Nixon did not, and it surely was the factor that cost him the 1960 presidential election. Ronald Reagan has it, but not President Bush.

Johnny Carson has it, Joan Rivers does not. And when they went into head-to-head competition with their late-night shows, laid-back charisma won out over exceptional talent.

> Pool hustler Johnny Irish: "How do you like that guy Nixon? Can't run six balls and he's president of the United States."

Robert Redford has it, oozing out of his ears. Oh, so maybe it's good looks. Maybe charisma is just our way of verbalizing the feeling we get when we meet a good-looking person. No, that's not it. Charles Bronson is as ugly as a fence post and he has it. Have you ever met a male model: one of those guys who poses for cigarette posters? They're gorgeous, but their personalities are as one-dimensional as the billboards on which their images are splattered.

■ A VERY SPECIAL QUALITY

So what is charisma? We've all heard of charismatic religions, of course. In that sense, charisma means a gift from God of a special talent. Such as the ability to heal, or to prophetise.

German sociologist Max Weber was the first person to bring the term into modern-day usage and present it as a learnable persuasion skill. He called it a form of authority. Until the turn of the century, authority was thought of as either law or tradition. Even if a mode of behavior wasn't prescribed by current law, people would still be persuaded to behave in a certain way because of tradition—a respect for the way things were done in the past. Max Weber introduced charisma as the third form of authority—that people could be persuaded simply by the personality of another person.

> THE THREE FORMS OF AUTHORITY
> 1. Law
> 2. Tradition
> 3. Charisma

In popular usage, charisma means this: a special quality that gives a person the ability to capture the imagination of another person, inspiring support and devotion.

Wouldn't it be great to walk into a room and immediately know that everyone there was aware of you? Wouldn't it be great to walk into a buyer's office and know for sure that he's going to reach out, hit that button, and say, "Hold my calls"?

How about being in a company meeting and a big argument is going on. You quietly say, "This is what I think," and the whole room goes quiet. Wouldn't it be great?

■ CHARISMA—THE NONVERBAL PERSUASION POWER

Charisma is the nonverbal form of persuasion, and Power Persuaders know that at least 80 percent of the impression they give people is nonverbal. One study, done at the University of Southern California, showed that only 8 percent of communication was the words used, 37 percent was the way the words were said, and 55 percent was entirely nonverbal. Whatever the numbers, it's indisputable that what people see and sense about you is far more important than what you say.

Someone can glare at you and spit out, "You bastard!" and it's an expression of utter contempt. Or they could laugh, punch you gently in the arm, and say, "You bastard," and it would be friendly, even complimentary.

I firmly believe that in the next century or two, human beings will evolve to the point where we can read each other's thoughts. We'll know what the other person is thinking about us! In fact, I'll go as far as saying that we can read thoughts right now. The problem is, we've trained ourselves since evolution to think in languages rather than intuitively. We just haven't learned how to interpret the data into the recognizable mental language that we, in our narrow perception of the process, understand to be thought.

If you're thinking "Da-da, da-da. Da-da, da-da," this guy's just gone into the Twilight Zone, do some research into the phenomenon called auras. An aura is the visible energy field that's given off by the human body, and scientists at UCLA and other universities are doing some very serious research in this area.

It's a scientific fact that we all give off auras to a greater or lesser degree. Also that we all can see auras to a greater or lesser degree. And when a person who has the natural ability to see them, or has trained himself to do so, meets up with a person who gives off auras, look out!

It looks like a field of static energy that surrounds a person. It can extend to as much as 12 inches all around the body, and usually appears in white, yellow, or pink. Because the aura is all around the body, the features of the person seem to fade. You're looking through the aura at their face, for example, and their face seems to turn into a glowing, formless, apparition.

Auras give off heat, too, intense heat. You can feel it across the room. To put your hand into an aura is like dipping your hand into a very warm bath. When someone who's projecting an aura lays her hands on you, a warm glow spreads throughout your body.

You don't have to be a New Age thinker to believe in this. There are some down-to-earth pragmatic scientists who can prove that our personalities do give off readable signals.

One of the remarkable things to me is that people who can naturally see auras are very matter of fact about it: they don't see it as mystical at all.

■ AURAS IN DARKEST AFRICA

I once spent some time in Central Africa with Elizabeth Sunday, a world-famous photographer and one of the most charismatic people I've ever met.

I was drawn to her as I stood on the sweltering tarmac at Nairobi airport while they fueled the eight-passenger airplane that would take my daughter and me to Zaire to track rare mountain gorillas.

I asked her, "Will you be on this flight with us?" She smiled and said, "Yes, I'm going to Northern Zaire to live with a Pygmy family for a month."

Thinking she was joking I replied, "Of course. Everybody does that at this time of year." She laughed and told me who she was and said that she was on a photographic assignment sponsored by Kodak.

Zaire is incredibly primitive. It's the second largest country in Africa, but it has almost no telephones, even in the capital, and has less than 200 kilometers of paved road in the entire nation. Outside the cities, there is almost no running water or sanitation of any kind. Most of the people live in huts woven of bamboo cane they have made themselves, packing the walls with mud. Yet here was this young woman, traveling by herself in the pursuit of her art.

We flew over vast and peaceful Lake Victoria to the tiny airport at Goma, on the far shore. We had lunch in the fine courtyard of a colonial hotel, a holdover from the days when Zaire was known as the Belgian Congo. Colonial in that part of the world refers to any building that's not falling down!

As with many talented artists, Elizabeth is incredibly sensitive to the emotions of the people around her. She could apparently read the mood of people on the other side of the courtyard. She told me that this was because of her ability to read "auras," a talent that came naturally to her as a child. "I grew up assuming that everybody saw auras, and I didn't realize I was any different."

"How did you feel when you realized that you had this special gift?" I asked her.

"I thought it was a real nuisance!" she told me. "I'd be trying to concentrate in class, and all I could see would be these weird colors shooting off the teacher's head."

As I sat there in the warm humid sunshine, listening to Elizabeth talk about auras, for the first time in my life, I suddenly understood charisma.

Ernest Holmes once said, "A flash of insight is sometimes worth a lifetime of experience." And this incredibly charismatic woman was giving me the secret to charisma in a flash of insight. Suddenly it became clear to me why some people have that aura of charisma that's such a powerful persuasion tool.

■ TO UNDERSTAND CHARISMA, IMAGINE THE OPPOSITE

To explain what I suddenly understood, let's look at the opposite of charisma. While we may have trouble defining charismatic qualities, we don't have trouble identifying the person we don't like, do we?

We don't like people who are self-centered and are concerned only with their own well-being. Take John Paul Getty, for example. He was the richest man in the world, but nobody would want to change places with him, because he was so self-centered. Aristotle Onassis once said that he could only do business with him once he understood that Getty had absolutely no sense of what was right or ethical. He would only ever act in his self-interest.

So if we accept that the least charismatic person is the one who's most self-centered, we understand that charismatic people are those who have learned to expand their center. Their mental vision of their world has expanded to include all the people with whom they come in contact. Elizabeth Sunday was just as sensitive to the emotions of the people around her as she was to her own emotions. That's what made her so charismatic.

If you were to ask Mother Theresa to tell you about herself, she'd have a tough time, because she has expanded her center to where she's now a part of the world in which she lives. Martin Luther King, Jr., had this same quality of being unable to distinguish his plight as a black man from the plight of black people throughout the world.

So to become a truly charismatic Power Persuader we must learn to expand our centers, to be just as conscious of the world around us as we are of ourselves.

However, it's not enough just to have all these wonderful feelings inside of us. To be a Power Persuader we must learn how to project that feeling to the rest of the world; that's what you'll learn in the next chapter.

■ KEY POINTS IN THIS CHAPTER

1. Charisma is the quality that makes people like you.

2. It is not related to good looks.

3. Max Weber called it the third form of authority, after law and tradition.

4. Charisma is nonverbal as is 55 percent of our ability to communicate.

5. Human beings probably have the ability to read each other's thoughts, but our obsession with languages has caused us to suppress that ability.

6. We can best understand charisma by understanding the opposite. We would least like to be with someone who is self-centered. We would most like to be with people who have expanded their center to embrace the world around them.

■ C H A P T E R   T W E N T Y

TWELVE WAYS TO PROJECT AN AWESOME CHARISMA

All right, so now we know what charisma is, but how do we project it so that people know how lovable we are? In this chapter I'll teach you twelve ways to project an awesome charisma. Without a doubt, rule number one for developing charisma, is this—"Treat everyone you meet as if he or she is the most important person you'll meet that day."

RULE ONE FOR PROJECTING CHARISMA
Treat everyone you meet as if he or she is the most important person you'll meet that day.

Easy to say, and hard to do. Obviously the people you meet in any given day have different levels of importance to you. The person who parks your car at a restaurant isn't as important to you as the waiter, and neither is as important to you as the client with whom you may be dining. However, the important thing is to leave the impression with everyone that they are important to you.

But isn't this phony? Isn't it manipulative and won't it come across as such? I don't think so, because what you'll find is that after you've adopted this habit and made it yours, these people will really become important to you.

At my seminars and speeches, I make it a habit to stand at the door and shake hands with people coming into the room. With the smaller groups I can shake everyone's hand. If somebody sneaks by me, I even make a mental note of what they're wearing, and before I start I go up to them and say, "I didn't get a chance to meet you when you came in. I'm Roger Dawson." Does this ever blow them away!

With the larger groups I can't get everybody because they're coming in through different doors. However, I can usually meet about five hundred people in a 15- to 20-minute period. The results of this are amazing.

First, the meeting planners can't believe I'm doing it. "I've been running these meetings for ten years, and I've never had a speaker meet the people at the door like that" is a typical response. Second, it dramatically improves the audience reaction to the talk. Nobody ever heckles a speaker whose hand they've shaken, because it would violate the bond we created. And, third, I can really get a fix on the mood and background of the audience when I meet them like that.

Yet far more important is the effect it has on me. I really enjoy doing it. After a while the difference between people becomes absolutely fascinating. Most people are comfortable with it. I offer my hand and say, "Hi, I'm Roger Dawson." If they look puzzled, I'll add, "Your speaker," and then they'll tell me their name and move on.

Some people are too shy to respond with their name. They'll shake my hand and smile a bit, but be too tongue-tied to speak. Others see me standing there, and will try to make a wide circle around me—so they don't have to meet this stranger! I move across and greet them anyway. Others are genuinely confused that this human being wants to meet them, but doesn't have an ulterior motive for doing so. They wait to see what kind of raffle tickets I'm selling. Still, many people will see what's going on, and be obviously glad to have the opportunity to meet someone new. When I tell them my name, they bounce right back with their name, and a friendly, "Good to meet you." Am I being manipulative? Not at all. I really do enjoy meeting them. Put it this way—how long would you want to live on this planet if you were the only person on it. Not long, right?

It's people who make life worth living. Isn't it sad that we spend so much of our time and effort to accumulate things? We've got to learn to use things and love people, not use people and love things. Don't get me wrong, I've met lots of people I don't like. Will Rogers must have led a charmed life. He evidently never met Joseph Stalin, who reportedly murdered twenty million of his fellow citizens, or Adolph Hitler, or the Ayatollah Khomeini, who put out a million-dollar contract on novelist Salman Rushdie.

There are lots of people I don't like. To this day I'll turn my back and walk away from people who make crude racial remarks or who want to run down our country.

What I'm saying is that when our life's adventure has run its course—when we're making that final review of the way things were—it will be the people we met who will give us pleasure, not the things we accumulated. So how can we project to the people we meet, even briefly, that they're the most important person we'll meet that day?

What we mustn't do is patronize people. If a person's job is to check your coat, let him do his job. Don't slow him down with tedious small talk that's a transparent attempt to show him how humble you can be.

RULE TWO FOR PROJECTING CHARISMA
Develop a sensational handshake.

If we've truly expanded our centers to include all those around us, we can get the right message across in a second or two with the right handshake, the right smile, and the right attitude.

First, the handshake. When was the last time you asked someone to evaluate your handshake? Could you be a pumper, a crusher, or a wet fish, and you don't know it? Ask both a woman and a man for an opinion.

Let me give you a great tip for eliciting responses. Don't say, "What did you think of my handshake?" Chances are they'll just say, "Great."

Try saying, "On a scale of one to ten what did you think."

They might say, "It was great—about an eight."

Then you can say, "Help me out. What would it take to make it a ten."

This is also a terrific way to probe for information in all kinds of areas. You're a salesperson and you can't get a fix on whether they're ready to place the order or not. "So where are you on investing in this equipment—on a scale of one to ten? Ten meaning you're ready to order right now, and one meaning you wouldn't take it if we gave it to you." I've never had anyone refuse to give me a number.

They might say, "Well, I guess I'm at about a six."

And you say, "Help me out, what would it take to get you to a ten."

They might respond, "I'll tell you what's bothering me. I see your figures about the projected savings, but I need something stronger than that. For me to go with this, I'd have to be guaranteed that kind of savings."

Bingo! In a few short seconds you've isolated the objection, and almost got the buyer's commitment he'll buy if you can satisfy his one concern.

Or you might be trying to hire a key executive for your company. You need to find out if the money you're offering is going to be enough to get her on board. "How do you feel about coming with us. On a scale of one to ten. Ten meaning you're ready to decide right now, and one meaning you've already ruled it out?" You'll get an instant fix on how she feels, without having to come right out and ask her if you're offering enough money to entice her.

It's one of the most powerful tools I've ever learned for finding out what's going on in a person's mind, and it seems to work every time. So get some feedback on your handshake, and practice if you have to.

RULE THREE FOR PROJECTING CHARISMA
Notice the color of their eyes as you shake hands.

Remember that you don't just shake hands with your hand, you also do it with your eyes. In the old days, when woman expected men to kiss their hands, it was almost a passionate act to place your lips on the back of the hand while gazing up into her eyes. It has just as much impact today. Here's a trick that charismatic people have learned. When you shake someone's hand and look into their eyes, make a mental note of the color of their eyes.

Making this a habit not only forces you to look into their eyes, but it also puts a twinkle into your eyes. It creates a special moment of interaction with the other person.

RULE FOUR FOR PROJECTING CHARISMA
As you shake hands, push out a positive thought.

The third part of a good handshake is the thought that you project at that moment. Remember that for a second or two, you're physically touching the other person, and you have strong eye contact. If you believe in auras, they're intertwined. I believe people can unconsciously sense what you're thinking at that point. You need to push out some powerful positive thoughts at that point. If it's a person of the opposite sex, think to yourself, "This is the person I've been looking for all my life." If they're of the same sex, think to yourself, "This is a great person, I'd really like to know him (or her) better."

Doesn't that sound silly? Yet you'll be amazed at the instant bond you create with people when you use this method.

So a charismatic handshake has a one, two, three punch: the right grip, the right eye contact, and the right thought projection.

Rose Kennedy, when reminded that son Ted lived in Virginia:
"Who's Virginia?"

Let me tell you my favorite story about shaking hands. Teddy Kennedy was campaigning for his Senate seat in 1962. He was shaking hands outside a factory early one morning. "Teddy," said a grimy worker, "I understand that you never worked a day in your life." This was something that his opponent had made a campaign issue, and Kennedy braced himself for an onslaught. "Let me tell you something," the worker continued, still warmly pumping his hand, "you ain't missed a thing."

RULE FIVE FOR PROJECTING CHARISMA
Give sincere compliments.

The next step to charisma is to develop the habit of giving sincere compliments. King George V of England said that, "Flattery is telling the other person precisely what he thinks of himself."

The reason we're reluctant to compliment people directly relates to our self-esteem. We fall into the trap of thinking, "Why would they care what I think, I'm not that important." Not exactly a self-image that's likely to draw other people to us, is it?

I remember speaking at a state association meeting of auto parts dealers in Oregon. During the lunch, with about two hundred members and their spouses in the room, the activity of the executive director of the association fascinated me. Instead of sitting up at the head table, he spent the entire time walking around the room greeting the members. He seemed to know most of them by name and appeared genuinely excited and glad to see them. He really looked like a senator or governor running for reelection, and he was sincere. He really had expanded his center to include all the people in his association.

He impressed me so much that I sent him a postcard saying that of all the association meetings I'd attended, I'd never seen anybody do a better job of working the audience. He was so good at what he was doing that he didn't need me to point it out, and I almost didn't send the card because I didn't want him to think I was trying to butter him up.

A couple of months later I happened to be talking to him on the phone, and he mentioned my postcard and told me how good it made him feel. By that time I'd completely forgotten that I'd sent it, and had to scramble to figure out what he was talking about. I was so surprised that he valued my opinion, I vowed I'd never hesitate to compliment someone again.

Sam Donaldson, the ABC News White House correspondent during the Reagan years, tells the story of casually saying to President Reagan as he was leaving the Rose Garden, "That's a nice suit you have on, Mr. President."

> Mort Sahl: "Reagan won because he ran against Jimmy
> Carter. Had he run unopposed he would have lost."

President Reagan looked a little surprised and said, "Sam, this suit is four years old," and moved on. A while later the phone rang in the ABC booth and the operator told Donaldson the president wanted to speak to him. "I just wanted to let you know, Sam, that this suit is five years old, not four."

Imagine that! Ronald Reagan, at the time the leader of the free world and the most popular president since Eisenhower, being so impressed with a small compliment that he was still thinking about it 15 minutes later.

> **RULE SIX FOR PROJECTING CHARISMA**
> Catch people doing something right.

As a manager, have you ever had an employee say to you, "You never tell me that I'm doing a good job!" We probably all have, and sometimes our reaction is callous. We think, "Oh, come on, this is a business we're running here, not a kindergarten. You're paid to do a job, and I don't have time to run around all day patting you on the back." That's a little like the husband saying to the wife, "Don't keep asking me if I love you. Of course I love you, that's my job."

Let me tell you an experience that caused me to get on the bandwagon of constantly thanking employees. Perhaps it'll change your thinking too. I was sitting in the back of the room at a convention in Las Vegas, where I'd be the windup speaker. The president of the company was thanking the employees who'd worked hard to make the convention a success and gave special thanks to his assistant for her efforts. All very routine: I'd heard it a hundred times. His assistant was sitting close to me, so I turned around to add my congratulations. Tears were streaming down her face! She was so emotionally overwhelmed by this compliment that she had to get up and leave the room.

Compliments do mean a lot to your people. If your assistants would break into tears if you paid them a compliment, maybe it's time to rethink your policy!

So let's get off this kick that people will think our compliments phony or manipulative, and play the One Minute Manager game: let's catch somebody doing something right. People really do care what you think, and they really do appreciate your mentioning it.

Jascha Heifetz, the world-famous Russian-born violinist, once told his new secretary that there was no need to compliment him after every performance. "If I play well," he said, "I know it myself. If I don't, I shall only be disappointed if you flatter me." The young man made the mistake of following these instructions. Later, after a particularly brilliant performance, an enraged Heifetz stormed up to him. "What's the matter?" he stormed, "Don't you like music?"

RULE SEVEN FOR PROJECTING CHARISMA
Looks do matter!

Every ugly kid in the world has been told by his or her parents that looks don't matter. You have to tell this to a child when he's really young, because when he's been in kindergarten for a week and a half, he'll have figured out that looks do matter, and they matter a great deal.

Since in this chapter we're talking only about nonverbal forms of persuasion, it's important that we talk about this straight from the shoulder. First, don't panic if you don't feel that you got a fair shake in the "looks" department. Charisma depends a lot more on what you do with what you've got than with what nature actually blessed you.

Franklin D. Roosevelt, confined to a wheelchair, was one of the most charismatic personalities who ever graced the Oval Office. Adolph Hitler was an ugly runt of a man, but his ability to galvanize his audiences into action was legendary; it took the combined might of the world's forces to stop him. Joseph Stalin had absolute control over the Soviet Union for twenty-nine years, and he was borderline ugly.

RULE EIGHT FOR PROJECTING CHARISMA
Smile for the magic 2 seconds longer than they do.

What's the most important thing we can wear that will improve our appearance and make us more charismatic? You've got it—a smile. I believe it's the only communication that's completely universal. At least in the eighty-six countries in which I've traveled, a smile means just one thing. I like you, I trust you, I'm glad we're together.

I remember traveling in Central China, in some of the most remote parts of a country that was for many years completely isolated from the rest of the world. A generation of people had grown up who'd never seen even a picture of a person from the outside world. However, even in the most remote areas of China, a smile was universal. Even people who had never seen a Westerner would always respond to a warm smile.

Less than a year later, I was watching television pictures of Tiananmen Square in Beijing when a million students had gathered there to demonstrate in favor of democracy. Of the four hundred truckloads of soldiers sent to quell the uprising, only a handful had made it to the square. A sea of protesters now surrounded a few dozen soldiers armed with automatic weapons. The potential for disaster was growing by the second. However, all the tension flowed away when the military commander broke into a warm, gentle smile. Perhaps that's why, when the government finally crushed the protest, they did it at night.

You know what I've found about smiling? Many of us think we're smiling when all we're doing is parting our lips a little. So let's get a little feedback on how other people see our smiles.

Let's pick three people who know us well, and ask, "On a scale of one to ten, do you think I'm a person who smiles a lot?" My guess is that the response will surprise you. While you might think you're a happy-go-lucky person who goes out of your way to be cheerful, others may see you as a very serious person who's seldom in a good mood.

If your friends give you sevens or lower on the one-to-ten scale, you need to force yourself to smile a little wider, and a little longer. Lock into the other person's eyes, making a mental note of the color of them, and smile broadly. Wait until they smile back, and hold it for 2 seconds more. Two seconds is probably longer than you think. Say slowly, "One hundred and one, one hundred and two," and that's about 2 seconds.

RULE NINE FOR PROJECTING CHARISMA
Take a check-up from the neck down.

Next I suggest a ruthless examination of your wardrobe. Spending money on clothes is a cost of doing business, just like your car, and it's a far better investment. You've got to spend money to make money, and one of the first places to start is at the dry cleaners. If you're still having shirts and blouses laundered at home, quit it right now. For about a dollar each you can get them laundered professionally. They look much nicer, and really, don't you have better things to do with your time?

Start rotating your clothes to the dry cleaner. Wear them a couple of times at most, air them out, and get them on down there for a pressing. Of course that starts to cost real money, but the look that makes you a Powerful Persuader demands that you make the investment. Don't worry about it. You're going to get it back many times over.

Next, go through your wardrobe, and throw out anything you haven't worn in the last year. You'll be amazed how many clothes you have hanging in your closet that you don't like enough to wear, but haven't thrown away.

I saw Bill Cosby do a skit on that subject in Las Vegas. He came on stage wearing an old fishing hat, explaining he didn't really like the hat, but he couldn't bear to throw it away because he had "time in" on it. He went on to point out that many of us are working at jobs that don't give us any satisfaction anymore, but we don't quit because we've got so much "time in." And many of us are in relationships that died years ago, but we hang on because of "time in" on them.

RULE TEN FOR PROJECTING CHARISMA
Push out empathy.

Another great way to develop a more charismatic personality is to work on sincerely transmitting empathy. Don't forget that there's a world of difference between empathy and sympathy. Consciously making an effort to be sympathetic can come across as condescending—like compassion or pity. Nobody wants that.

Empathy is letting our feelings and emotions flow with the other person, to identify truly with their mood and disposition. As the Native Americans say, "You don't truly know a man until you've walked a mile in his moccasins," or as the Indians in Palm Springs say, "Until you've driven a mile in his Cadillac."

Do you want a simple explanation of the difference between sympathy and empathy? Sympathy is seeing a seasick person on a boat and going over to put your arm around him. Empathy is going over and throwing up with him. Sympathy is seeing someone about to jump off a bridge and rushing over to try to talk him out of it. Empathy is saying, "I understand exactly how you feel. I'll jump with you."

Take a moment and think of somebody who has that special persuasive charisma that we've been talking about. Can you picture him in your mind? Okay, now take another moment and try to define what makes you feel comfortable when you're with him—not what impresses you about him, but why it feels good when you're around him.

Is it because he always has a big smile on his face? Because he's constantly happy, cheerful, and enthusiastic? Because he's always "up"?

No, probably not. Sure, if you're in an upbeat mood, it's fun to interact with someone who's in a similar frame of mind. But if you're under pressure—perhaps you've just been chewed out by somebody and you're struggling to meet a deadline—people like that are a pain in the neck.

The secret here is that we're drawn to someone who's in a similar emotional state. The neurolinguistic experts call this "mirroring." Some go as far as saying that you should mirror the angle of the head, or hand gestures, or the way that a person is standing or sitting. The point is, we feel more comfortable with people whom we feel are like us—and that feeling is what we call empathy.

Let's look at how empathy might work in a business situation. Joe sells office supplies and is calling on Mary Smith, one of his regular accounts. He walks into her office with his usual smile and good cheer. "Hi, Mary, how are you today?" He looks into her eyes and sees the usual sparkle is missing. She replies, "Oh, OK I guess," instead of her usual, "I'm fine, Joe. How are you today?"

If Joe centers on himself and what he wants to get out of this meeting, instead of having true empathy toward the people around him, he'd probably go right ahead and tell her the great joke about the fisherman and the mermaid he was planning to tell her. But because he's a charismatic person and has learned to center on the people around him, he immediately picks up on her flat response and says gently, "Mary, are you feeling all right?" Her answer will give him an indication of where to go from there.

She may say, "Oh, yes, I'm fine. I just have a problem with the scheduling and I was trying to figure out how to rearrange it to suit both shifts. I just hate to ask the night shift to come in early; their schedules are hard enough already. I'm glad you're here. It'll give me an excuse to think of something else for a few minutes."

Now Joe can tell his mermaid joke, set the mood, and go on with his presentation.

Still, it might go differently. She might say, "Oh, Joe, I feel awful. I had to have my dog put to sleep this morning, and I just can't put it out of my mind." Obviously not a good time to tell a joke. Instead he displays genuine empathy by mirroring Mary's emotions. "Oh, gosh, I know how terrible that can be. We had an old sheepdog for fifteen years we just loved, and we had to do the same thing. Just last year. Though you know it's better to put them out of their misery, it just makes you feel terrible, doesn't it?"

Robert Benchley: "A boy can learn a lot from a dog: obedience, loyalty, and the importance of turning around three times before lying down."

Empathy isn't only important in cases of sadness or sorrow. It also can be projected in times of joy and happiness. Let's look at a different view of Joe and Mary. Joe greets Mary with his customary smile and enthusiasm, and this time she responds with a more cheerful and happy attitude than usual. "Boy, do you look happy today? Did you win the lottery?" This shows Mary that Joe centers on her enough to notice that her smile is bigger than ever. She may or may not choose to share her joy, but the fact that Joe was interested in her feelings won't go unnoticed.

Of course the very definition of empathy, as opposed to sympathy, is that it's an involuntary expression of relating to the other person's emotions. It isn't a contrived reaction. However, many of us feel empathy, but haven't learned to express it. The charismatic Power Persuader has learned to center on the other person, not on themselves. Expressing the empathy they feel has become a natural part of who they are.

RULE ELEVEN FOR PROJECTING CHARISMA
Respond to people's emotions, not to what they say.

Have you ever wondered why some people have a remarkable ability to relate to the way you're feeling? It might be your boss. One day you lose control and go storming into her office and yell, "I've had it up to here with those people in the shipping department. They can't get anything right, why did you hire such a bunch of imbeciles in the first place?"

A bad boss will respond to what you're saying, not what you're feeling. She might say, "You can't come in here yelling at me like that!" or "I'm not going to fire the entire shipping department just because you want me to!"

A good boss will respond to what you're feeling, not to what you're saying. She might say, "Wow, you're really upset about this, aren't you? Sit down, and tell me why you feel the way you do."

You almost feel your anger melting away, and you might say, "Well, I don't mean that we have to fire them, but it really is annoying. What can we do to help them do a better job?"

I'm sure you've had a similar experience. You may not have known why your anger suddenly melted away, but it was because they responded to what you were feeling, not what you were saying.

RULE TWELVE FOR PROJECTING CHARISMA
Maintain a childlike fascination for the world in which you live.

Earlier we talked about searching for the meaning of charisma by first identifying the opposite of it and then working back from there. We said that one characteristic of a person lacking charisma is that they are self-centered. Another characteristic of a noncharismatic person is being boring, or "Borrring," as Joanne Whorley used to say on "Laugh In."

So what's the opposite of boring? Fascinating!

Have you ever taken a child to Disneyland for the first time? She's full of wide-eyed wonder. Everything is fascinating to her!

This expression of wide-eyed wonder is another aspect of charisma. It's the essence of surprise, delight, and joy that a charismatic person displays when listening to someone who's talking about their special interest.

When I first came to this country from England in 1962, I was 22 years old. I came here with a one-way air ticket and $400 to my name. I got a room at the back of a duplex in Redwood City, California, and a job as a teller at the Bank of America in Menlo Park. I used some of my precious dollars to buy a bicycle and rode the 10-mile trip to and from work every day for about two months.

> Calvin Trillin: "I'm in favor of liberalized immigration because of the effect it would have on restaurants. I'd let just about everybody in except the English."

Imagine my pride when I'd finally saved up enough money to buy my very first automobile. A 1952 Chevy I managed to get for $200. That may not sound like much, but when it's all the money you've got in the world, it means something. It was the largest purchase I'd ever made on my own, and I was proud beyond words. I worked on it day and night, cleaning it up and polishing it until it glowed.

One afternoon I was out in the driveway, putting yet another coat of wax on it, when my landlord pulled up in his shiny new Cadillac. I was afraid he'd make fun of my cheap old car, but as he approached my dream machine, his eyes widened, his smile grew. He shook his head slightly in appreciation and said, "So this is the new machine, it's absolutely beautiful. Tell me about it."

The whole time I was talking he just walked around the car slightly shaking his head and listening to my every word. When he left that day, I felt so wonderful and proud I could do something he admired. Of course the car was nothing special to him, but he wasn't reacting to the car. He was reacting to my emotions. He had expanded his center to include me. From that day on, I was never a day late on the rent!

Everyone wants to feel he or she is special in some way, that he or she does something better than anyone else, and chances are that person does. Whether it's a job, a hobby, or being a parent.

Truly charismatic Power Persuaders have expanded their centers to the point where they're just as conscious of other people's talents as they are of their own. They give the other person the opportunity to talk about her talents. They find that unique part of each person, that special interest that sets her apart from all the others.

I once met a man whose hobby was raising rare orchids. Now that's about as far from my interests as you can get. I want excitement in my life. I want to be on the go all the time. And here was a man who had the patience to work on developing a unique strain of orchid that might take fifteen years to come to full bloom! Yet, to me it was absolutely fascinating. Just spending the afternoon with him enriched my life.

In fact, the older I get, the more fascinated I become with life. The world in which we live is so complex, so varied. You could spend seventy-five years traveling around just this one planet in a vast universe and never know it all. You can live with a person for twenty-five years and suddenly realize that you never have understood him or her. You could spend an entire lifetime studying any one of a thousand subjects and never learn everything there was to be known about it.

Just imagine, if you can, that some vast cosmic force put you in charge of the creation of this planet. Would you ever, in your wildest dreams have thought to have made it so complex? To give every human being a different genetic footprint? To make every snowflake different? to make people so different that they're willing to fight wars to impose their views on other people?

Of course it's natural for us to be wide eyed in wonder at the world in which we live. And we're irresistibly drawn to people who share that wonder. It's a big part of persuasive charisma.

In the next chapter, we'll consider another aspect of charisma that will draw people to you—developing your sense of humor.

■ KEY POINTS IN THIS CHAPTER

1. Developing charisma is a powerful part of Power Persuasion. People are drawn to, and are receptive to influence by, charismatic people.

2. Charisma comes from expanding our centers, so we are just as conscious of the people around us, as we are of ourselves.

3. Be sure to treat everyone you meet as the most important person you'll meet that day.

4. When you shake a person's hand, train yourself to look into his eyes and make a mental note of the color of his eyes.

5. Learn the art of giving sincere compliments. People really do care what you think.

6. Work on your smile, and when someone smiles back, keep smiling for those magic 2 more seconds.

7. Conduct a ruthless examination of your wardrobe. Go through and throw out anything you haven't worn in the last year. Then, if you don't already, start rotating your clothes to the dry cleaner.

8. Learn to express the empathy you feel for other people.

9. Retain a wide-eyed wonder for the world in which we live, and the unique talents of the people who live in it.

■ CHAPTER TWENTY-ONE

HOW YOU CAN DEVELOP A DYNAMITE SENSE OF HUMOR

The classic Greek model of persuasion calls for ethos, pathos, logos, and a return to ethos.

In layman's language, that means start by getting them to like you, ethos; then touch their emotions in your appeal, pathos; and back it up with a little logic, logos, in case they have to justify their decision to someone else. Then use ethos again so they won't change their minds, and they'll be glad to see you the next time.

Nothing, absolutely nothing, will build ethos—liking—better than a great sense of humor. You can say all the right words and do all the right things, and still be unable to persuade unless the other person is receptive and inclined toward being persuaded. Nothing positions people as effectively as a sense of humor—even the most hostile people can be won over with the use of good humor.

Aristotle recognized the use of humor as a persuasion tool in the fourth century B.C. He said that humor is primarily concerned with man as a social being rather than as a private person, and the purpose of humor in our society is to persuade people that their behavior should be changed. Humor holds up a mirror to society to reflect its foibles and failings, in the hope that people will see the error of their ways and be persuaded to change.

> E. B. White: "Analyzing humor is like dissecting a frog. Few people are interested and the frog dies of it."

English essayist William Hazlitt pointed out, in his classic essay, *On Wit and Humor*, that "Man is the only animal that laughs and weeps; for he is the only animal that is struck with the difference between what things are, and what they ought to be." Even today, 170 years later, serious students of humor don't argue with that premise.

If Aristotle could see the nationwide proliferation of comedy clubs, and the incredible amount of humor available to us through cable television, he'd draw a very interesting conclusion. That we see more in our society that needs correcting than ever before.

So the Power Persuader sees a good sense of humor as having a twofold purpose. It makes the other person receptive to persuasion, and it is an excellent way to point out to the other person that they're wrong without causing offense.

■ HUMOR MAY BE THE ONLY THING THAT WILL STOP YOU FROM GOING CRAZY

There's an important side benefit to your sense of humor. It's going to stop you from having a nervous breakdown one day.

"What happened to Harry?" you hear at the office water cooler.

"He just couldn't take the pressure. One day he just cracked."

Ever wonder where that expression comes from? What cracks? Things that are hard and brittle. Things that are soft and warm and flexible don't crack, they bend. Many noted psychiatrists go as far as to say that the very definition of good mental health is a flexible, humor-filled attitude.

President Reagan was the only president in modern times who appeared to get younger in office: while other presidents visibly aged on the job, he appeared to thrive on it. How could he handle so much pressure, so well? One reason was that he could laugh at himself. An assassination attempt gave him a bullet wound—but he could joke with his wife Nancy about it. He told her, "Honey, I forgot to duck!" as they wheeled him in after the shooting, "I hope the doctor's a Republican."

When everyone was criticizing him for falling asleep during a cabinet meeting, he deflected it all by declaring, "I have left orders to be awakened at any time in case of national emergency, even if I'm in a cabinet meeting."

■ HOW TO DEVELOP A SENSE OF HUMOR

The problem with the need for humor as a persuasion tool is that a sense of humor is like a Rolls Royce. Everybody wants one, but very few people know how to get one. Most of us know a funny joke when we hear one, but few of us know what makes it humorous. It either seems funny, or it doesn't.

What I'll do in this chapter is to show you what it is that causes people to laugh. Knowing this will help you to remember jokes, and it will definitely help you to develop your wit—that magical recognition and expression of a humorous thought.

Our purpose isn't to turn you into a stand-up comedian. I don't want you to become a person who's known primarily for the jokes you tell. You know people like that, don't you? They're not good persuaders. As managers, they're not taken seriously, and as salespeople, they never develop the credibility of a person who takes things more seriously

However, when we understand humor better, we'll see laughter in the world around us, we'll be on our way to being seen as a person with a "great sense of humor," and we'll appreciate what a great persuasion tool humor can be.

■ THE FIVE THINGS THAT MAKE PEOPLE LAUGH

Did you know that there are only five jokes in the world? Only five things that make people laugh?

"That's crazy," you say, "I can turn on cable television and watch stand-up comedians tell jokes all evening and never hear the same joke twice."

That may be true, but in fact they're all variations on the same five original jokes. As Power Persuaders, we need to know what they are.

Unless we know why people laugh, we can't use humor as a persuasion tool. If the only way we can use humor is to hope we can remember a joke we heard somewhere else, and hope we tell it right, and hope the other person hasn't heard it, and hope he finds it funny, we'll never graduate to being a true wit. We'll simply be a poor imitation of a stand-up comedian.

Understanding and being thoroughly familiar with the five things that make people laugh is as fundamental to persuasion as learning the alphabet is to reading.

So let's talk about the five things that make people laugh, and from then on, you'll be able to identify every joke you hear with one or another of them.

EXAGGERATION
The First Type of Humor

The first thing that makes people laugh is exaggeration. Probably the first joke ever told in history was based on exaggeration. Perhaps it was in Central Europe about forty thousand years ago. A group of cave men were sitting around the fire after a busy day hunting. Thor had just stubbed his toe on a rock and was hopping around cussing up a blue storm. One of the cave dwellers was searching for a way to describe just how mad Thor was when a visual image crossed his mind.

"Thor is madder than a saber-toothed tiger with a dinosaur stuck in its throat!" he shouted.

All the others picked up on this visual image and started to laugh because it was so outrageous.

In this way the first joke was created. It was funny because he had created a visual image that vastly exaggerated the situation. When we stretch a thought to a ludicrous point, it triggers something in our minds that makes us laugh.

Johnny Carson said, "It was so cold in New York, that the Statue of Liberty was holding the torch *under* her skirt." It was the same joke, he used the same funny idea, only the situation had been changed.

Fred Allen used to talk about the scarecrow that was so scary, the crows not only stopped stealing corn, they started bringing back corn that they'd stolen two years before.

Most golfing stories are funny only because of the way players exaggerate their passion for the game.

"Why did it take so long to play? Harry had a heart attack on the seventh fairway. From then on it was: hit the ball, drag Harry! Hit the ball, drag Harry!"

I was playing golf on St. Thomas with my friend Irv Clausen. Irv's not that old, maybe in his late sixties, but he likes to joke about his age. After sinking a 30-foot putt on the first hole, he said, "Toss me my ball, would you, Roger? At my age, I don't care to get that close to a hole in the ground."

We were playing $5 greenies. When he hit the green on the first par 3, I pulled a $5 bill out of my pocket. "Why don't we just settle up at the end," he said.

"OK, but at your age, Irv," I replied, "I thought you'd like to settle hole by hole."

They're all the same joke, it's the same theme of exaggeration that triggers the laugh. Only the words have been changed.

Take a look at some famous people getting a laugh with exaggeration:

Richard Nixon: "It's the responsibility of the media to look at the president with a microscope, but they go too far when they use a proctoscope."

Tallulah Bankhead: "They used to photograph Shirley Temple through gauze. They should photograph me through linoleum."

Melvin Belli: "I'm not an ambulance chaser. I'm usually there before the ambulance."

Muhammad Ali: "My toughest fight was with my first wife."

Johnny Carson: "I know a man who gave up smoking, drinking, sex, and rich food. He was healthy right up to the time he killed himself."

Dolly Parton: "You'd be surprised how much it costs to look this cheap."

Phyllis Diller: "I was in a beauty contest once. I not only came in last, I was hit in the mouth by Miss Congeniality."

Raymond Chandler: "It was a blonde, a blonde to make a bishop kick a hole in a stained glass window."

A mother is trying to persuade her sleepy child to quit watching television and go to bed. To head off a possible conflict, she uses a little humor. As she puts her arm around the child, she says, "Come on, dear. If you watch any more television tonight, your eyeballs will turn square." The child can't resist smiling.

"Oh, Mommy, you're silly," she says. But she quietly gets up and goes with her to the bedroom.

> Robert Orben: "Never raise your hand to a child. It leaves your mid-section unprotected."

So if we take a point and stretch it to the ridiculous, it triggers a laugh. But what if we go the other way? What if we compress a point to the ridiculous? We downplay it instead of emphasizing it with exaggeration? Yes, that works too. Because the other side of exaggeration is understatement.

If the cave dweller had watched Thor hopping around and quietly observed, "He doesn't seem to like doing that," the other men probably would have laughed. It would've been the same joke, but turned inside out.

One of my favorite John F. Kennedy witticisms took place at a press conference where his support of civil rights legislation was being questioned.

"Do you mean to tell me," the reporter asked, "that if Mrs. Murphy runs a boarding house, the federal government is going to tell her who she must accept as a guest?"

Kennedy calmly replied, "That would depend on Mrs. Murphy's impact on interstate commerce." A classic piece of understatement!

Here are some other classic examples of understatement:

Muhammad Ali: "I'm retiring because there are more pleasant things to do than beat up people."

Theater manager as flames lick up the curtains behind him: "Please listen carefully to the following announcement."

Ronnie Shakes: "I like life. It's something to do."

Woody Allen: "The universe is merely a fleeting idea in God's mind—a pretty uncomfortable thought, particularly if you've just made a down payment on a house."

So the buyer leans back in his chair and says to the salesman, "Joe, we'd love to buy your product, but your prices are too high!" But Joe's a Power Persuader. Instead of taking offense at that, and creating a confrontation, he diffuses the comment by feigning surprise and saying, "Gee, Charlie. You're the first buyer who's ever mentioned price to me. I didn't know price was important to you!" Charlie sees the humor in this understatement and responds with an understatement of his own. "Well, yes, Joe, sometimes it makes a difference."

THE PUN
The Second Type of Humor

Probably the next most popular form of humor is the pun.

A pun describes any time that you use the same word, but out of context. Or substitute a word that's so similar in sound that it's almost indistinguishable.

The new oriental cookbook: *Fifty Ways to Wok Your Dog* is an example of that kind of pun.

Senator Alan Simpson of Wyoming starts his dinner speeches by saying, "I know you all want the latest dope from Washington—well here I am."

The most famous one liner of all time, Henny Youngman's "Take my wife—please!" is really a pun. Nobody ever stops to analyze it, but the humor really comes from using the word "take" out of context. He leads you to believe that when he says "take," he means "for example." The "please" added to the end of the sentence switches the meaning of the word "take" to that of "remove."

Here are some other examples of jokes that may not appear to be puns, but really are:

Robert Byrne: "Get in good physical condition before submitting to bondage. You should be fit to be tied." (Robert Byrne is the author of my favorite book of quotations: *637 Best Things Anybody Ever Said.*)

David Chambles: "Better to have loved and lost a short person than never to have loved a tall."

Dean Martin: "If you drink, don't drive. Don't even putt."

Henry Morgan: "A kleptomaniac is a person who helps himself because he can't help himself."

Jack Pomeroy: "A communist is a person who publicly airs his dirty Lenin."

Mae West: "She's the kind of girl who climbed the ladder of success wrong by wrong."

Zsa Zsa Gabor: "I am a marvelous housekeeper. Every time I leave a man I keep his house."

Andrew Mellon: "Gentlemen prefer bonds."

Of course the pun purist will take exception to my saying that all twists on words are puns. They're into the more convoluted word construction jokes, such as this one:

A salesperson is so overworked that he decides to have himself cloned. He biologically produces a replica of himself and sends him out to work half his territory. Everything's going fine, and nobody notices the difference. But suddenly the clone starts using bad language on his clients. Nothing he can do stops him. In desperation he takes him to the top of the Empire State Building and throws him off. He was arrested for making an "obscene clone fall."

The problem with pure puns like that, is that they tend to get a groan rather than a laugh, because they're cerebral. While clever, they appeal to the intellect rather than the funny bone.

We can analyze humor to figure out what can trigger a laugh, but nobody knows what really causes humans to laugh. Probably the surprise connection of two illogical thoughts causes a neural misfiring in the higher cortex—the frontal lobes of the brain—creating a unique reaction in the limbic system resulting in an intense feeling of enjoyment.

The convoluted pun can't do that.

"Take my wife—please!" can do it every time.

So Power Persuaders are always alert to the possibility of the pun to use as a tool to divert the other person's attention from a sensitive point. Remember the politician who was determined not to get dragged into the debate over abortion? He deflected attention with a clever pun. A reporter yelled, "And just what do you think that the governor should do about the abortion bill?" He replied, "I think he should pay it!"

THE PUT-DOWN
The Third Type of Humor

The third form of humor is the put-down. Perhaps the first put-down was when one of the cave dwellers pulled out a chicken he had killed that day and started to share it. Perhaps someone said, "Good old Og, he never forgets his friends!"

"Big deal," somebody else may have laughed, "he's only got two."

The cave dwellers would've looked at each other with apprehension. In the past, whenever somebody had said something unpleasant, it was usually just before a fight, and somebody got killed. However, this seemed different. The person who had said it wasn't angry, he was laughing. Suddenly the butt of the joke, Og, started to smile. Then they all started to laugh. For some reason, insulting other people makes us laugh. It's probably relief that we're not the one being put-down.

"Dan Quayle took lessons from Ronald Reagan to try and improve his image. He was always out at Reagan's ranch, chopping horses, riding wood."

It's really the same joke, only the words have been changed. For many years, nearly all American humor was based on this same joke—the put-down. Here's some examples:

David Letterman: "Fall is my favorite season in Los Angeles, watching the birds change color and fall down."

Fred Allen: "The town was so dull that when the tide went out, it refused to come back."

Bob Hope: "Ronald Reagan was not a typical politician because he didn't know how to lie, cheat, and steal. He'd always had an agent for that."

Comedy teams became popular, with one person always putting down the other. Abbott and Costello, Laurel and Hardy, Dean Martin and Jerry Lewis, Burns and Allen, Rowan and Martin, the Smothers Brothers—the list goes on and on.

Then suddenly "put-down" humor changed. It took a new twist. Comedians changed the butt of the joke from the other person to themselves. They started putting themselves down, and it was funnier, because nobody could get offended.

Jack Benny's self-imposed reputation for stinginess was legendary. The longest laugh ever recorded on radio occurred when a supposed mugger pointed a gun at Jack, and yelled, "Your money or your life!" Jack didn't say anything for a full 30 seconds. His expression didn't change. "What's the matter with you?" the furious mugger yelled, "I said 'your money or your life!'"

Finally, Jack protested, "I'm thinking, I'm thinking."

The studio audience roared with laughter, stopping the live radio show for many minutes.

Here are some other examples of self-deprecating put-downs:

Rodney Dangerfield: "My wife has cut our lovemaking down to once a month. But I know two guys she's cut out entirely."

Joan Rivers: "After we made love he took a piece of chalk and made an outline of my body."

Gary Shandling: "I have such poor vision, I can date anybody."

Of course, all racial humor is of a put-down nature. It's curious that the same jokes are told around the world, and only the nationality is changed. In America it's the Polack who threw himself to the ground and missed. In Canada, it's the Newfy—the person from Newfoundland. In England it's the Irishman, in Ireland it's the Englishman, and in Australia it's the Tassie—someone from Tasmania.

The problem with racial humor is that acceptance of a mild put-down of a national or racial characteristic can become license for vicious slander.

If it's all right for me to tease a Scot for his thriftiness, how can I protest when a South African pokes fun at a black worker in a diamond mine?

Remember what Aristotle said? That humor is primarily concerned with man as a social person, not as an individual. And that the purpose of humor is to hold a mirror to our foolish actions and hope that by revealing them, we change people's behavior. When we bear that in mind, we can quickly distinguish between the put-down that is designed to reveal a foible and bring about change and a put-down that is merely malicious. Never was this more clearly illustrated than with the hit television series, "All in the Family." We knew the purpose in Archie Bunker's racial slurs was to hold his foolish actions up to the public and in doing so change people's behavior, which the program did remarkably well.

Power Persuaders are interested in humor for bringing about change in the other person's thinking. We're not interested in malicious put-downs.

Even today, a surprising amount of humor is put-down. For example:

A real estate agent in New York calls her unemployed husband at home and says, "Honey, you can't believe what just happened! I just sold the Empire State Building. I'm getting a five-million-dollar commission! I'm on my way home—hurry up and get packed!"

So he asks her, "Shall I pack for cold weather or warm weather?"

And she says, "What does it matter, I just want you packed and out of there by the time I get home."

Power Persuaders are always aware that putting themselves down can charm even the most hostile antagonist. Both Presidents Kennedy and Reagan were masters at this. Remember when Kennedy had the challenge of getting people to quit focusing on the rumors that his father had bought his Senate seat for him? Kennedy put it to rest, and brought the house down at a 1952 Gridiron dinner, when he pulled a telegram out of his pocket and told the audience that it was from his father. "Dear Jack: Don't buy a single vote more than necessary. I'll be damned if I'll pay for a landslide."

SILLINESS
The Fourth Type of Humor.

The fourth thing that makes us laugh is silliness. Groucho Marx said, "Last night I killed a lion in my pajamas. How he got into my pajamas, I'll never know!" The mental image of a lion in his pajamas is silly. It doesn't match our established way of thinking, so it makes us laugh.

Whereas most American humor is based on the put-down, most British humor, even to this day, is based on silliness. Robin Williams says: "British policemen don't wear guns. If they're chasing someone, they yell, 'Stop! Or I'll yell stop again.'"

Probably the British like this kind of humor because it's a complete reversal of the stuffy English life-style.

The "Goon Show" was immensely popular on British radio in the 1950s. Here's a typical scene from the "Goon Show":

Henry and Minnie are recurring characters. They're an elderly couple enjoying a quiet evening at home. Suddenly there's a noise outside like an invasion of savages. Henry softly remarks, "They've come to rape and plunder, Minnie." Minnie quietly replies, "I'd better go upstairs and get ready, Henry."

Incidentally, it's amazing how humor can stay with us, and a good line can become part of the language. I remember being in Nairobi Airport, and finding an enterprising young African who had set up shop in the men's rest room. He was standing by the towel dispenser handing out paper towels and soliciting tips. Although he wasn't supposed to be there, and had no intention of cleaning the rest room or doing anything else that would deserve a tip, I knew the rule in Africa is, "If it moves, tip it. You don't have to tip it much, but tip it."

But a young Englishman hadn't heard the rule. When asked for a tip, he replied by saying, "Surely you jest." Now even in England, they don't talk like that. "Surely you jest" was a Harry Secombe line from the "Goon Show" of thirty years ago. And the way that he used it, as a Shakespearian type of response to an everyday request, always got a laugh. To make the point further that a good comic line can become a part of the language, the young Englishman who had used it had clearly not even been born when the "Goon Show" was being broadcast.

Peter Sellers was one of the Goons. Even when he became a worldwide superstar, much of his humor, such as Inspector Clouseau in the Pink Panther films, was based on incongruity or silliness. For example, "Are you going to come quietly or do I have to use earplugs?"

"Monty Python's Flying Circus" was one of the few British shows that became popular in the United States without massive rewrites. Relying heavily on men playing women's roles and totally absurd themes, the entire show is an expansion of Groucho Marx's "lion in my pajamas" comment. It's a glorious salute to silliness. Today, the *Airport* and *Naked Gun* movies have picked up the silliness banner and lurched forward with it.

It's all the same joke, only the words have been changed.

Here are some other examples of silliness:

Tallulah Bankhead: "The less I behave like Whistler's mother the night before, the more I look like her the morning after."

Yogi Berra: "Toots Shor's restaurant is so crowded nobody goes there anymore."

Groucho Marx: "I don't have a photograph to give you, but you can have my footprints. They're upstairs in my socks."

Jack Warner (about Ronald Reagan): "It's our fault. We should have given him better parts."

A national newspaper in England did a survey to find out what their readers thought was the funniest joke ever told. The winner, believe it or not, was this little gem:

At the head table at a huge banquet, one man leaned to another and said, "Pardon me, old boy, did you realize that you just wiped your face with a piece of cabbage?"

"Did I really? I'm so glad you told me. I thought it was a piece of lettuce."

To illustrate how there are no new jokes, fifty years before, Sigmund Freud had used this story in his book *Jokes and Their Relation to the Unconscious*:

A man in a restaurant dipped his hands into a mayonnaise bowl and ran them through his hair. When the waiter looked surprised, the man said, "Oh, pardon me. I thought it was spinach."

Which may have been the real reason Freud had to leave Vienna so suddenly!

Incidentally, Freud's extensive study of humor led him to believe that laughter was a coping mechanism, a way of dealing with repressed feelings and releasing them. To substantiate this, he pointed to the fact that so much humor is sexual in nature.

But then many of Freud's theories seem off the wall in today's world. Did you know that for many years Freudian analysts saw deep significance in the fact that Sigmund always sat on the right side of the couch when he was treating patients?

He was astonished when he found out that his disciples around the world would only treat patients when seated on their right. "Don't they know that my couch was arranged like that only because I'm hard of hearing in one ear?" he exclaimed.

Power Persuaders know when to use a little bit of silliness to defuse a tense situation. Many years ago I worked for a boss who needed constant reassurance that I was loyal to him, which I was. The problem was that we had different biological clocks. He was always at his desk by 6 o'clock in the morning and in bed by 9 o'clock in the evening. I prefer to work late at night and definitely see no point in confusing my day by having two 6 o'clocks in it.

One morning I wandered into my office at a little after 9 and he was waiting for me, so upset that his veins were popping out of his forehead.

"You know Roger, I don't think that you have any loyalty to me at all."

This wasn't a good way to start the day. I knew that I'd have to find some way to get across how silly this was.

"Of course I'm loyal to you," I reassured him, "Why, I'd come to work in a dress if you wanted me to."

"I don't want you to come to work in a dress," he screamed at me, "I just want you here at the same time I get to work in the morning."

I gave it a long pause, and finally said, "I really had my heart set on the dress!"

He finally burst out laughing, we went off to get some coffee, and he never questioned my work schedule again.

SURPRISE
The Fifth Type of Humor

The fifth form of humor is based on the element of surprise.

One of my favorite jokes relies on surprise:

"Did you hear that Uncle Harry wants to marry a 20-year-old girl. Can you imagine that? And he's 80 years old! I told him he's a fool. It could be fatal. And he said, 'If she dies, she dies!'"

Why is that funny? Because the ending surprises us. One moment we're talking about an old man risking his life, a very serious subject. The next moment we've completely switched gears, and we're portraying him as an adventurous old rascal.

When we're surprised by something, our fight or flight syndrome goes into instant action. Our pulse quickens, and adrenaline starts to flow. When we suddenly realize the situation isn't dangerous, laughter results. Joke writers use this to lead us down one path, and then quickly take us 180 degrees in the opposite direction. It makes those neuron explosions in your frontal lobes that much crisper.

"Me worry?" says the wife, "why he'd never cheat on me. He's too honest, too pure . . . too scared."

"You'll be glad to hear that our auditors have come up with a very workable solution to our cash flow problems . . . bankruptcy."

Woody Allen: "I have an intense desire to return to the womb. Anybody's womb."

Tallulah Bankhead: "If I had to live my life again, I'd make the same mistakes, only sooner."

Phyllis Diller: "Burt Reynolds once asked me out. I was in his room."

W. C. Fields: "Start everyday with a smile and get it over with."

Will Rogers: "Diplomacy is the art of saying 'Nice doggie' until you can find a rock."

Mark Twain: "I thoroughly disapprove of duels. If a man should challenge me, I would take him kindly and forgivingly by the hand and lead him to a quiet place and kill him."

Mae West: "Whenever I'm caught between two evils, I take the one I've never tried."

Henny Youngman: "Do you know what it means to come home at night to a woman who'll give you a little love, a little affection, a little tenderness? It means you're in the wrong house, that's what it means."

They're all the same joke, only the words have been changed.

Note that in each of these jokes, the punch line or word must come as close to the end of the joke as possible. Comedians call this the train wreck approach. You get the listener on board the train with your opening line. Then you head them off in a particular direction. Just when they're convinced they know where the train is heading, you wreck the train with the surprise punch line.

■ LEARNING WHAT MAKES IT FUNNY

So we've seen that there are really only five jokes—exaggeration, a pun, a put-down, silliness, and surprise. Let's make up an OVPA—an outrageous visual picture acronym—that will help us remember those. A good acronym should conjure up a silly visual image, so how about, "Every pickled person sounds stupid."

The initials of "every pickled person sounds stupid" will remind us of exaggeration, puns, put-downs, silliness, and surprise.

At this point you may be thinking, interesting, but so what? What's this got to do with the power of persuasion?

With a little practice, any time you hear a joke, you'll be quickly able to identify what makes it funny. This will help you remember it, if you should want to repeat it. That's because you've identified the only part of the joke worth remembering—the reason it makes people laugh. If you want to retell it and can't recollect the words, it won't matter because you'll be able to fill in the inconsequential details. The only thing that matters is keeping the point of the joke intact. If you know what makes people laugh, you won't have to rely any more on trying to remember the joke that you heard the other day to inject a lighthearted note in any proceedings.

Moreover, you'll now be able to customize the joke. Since you understand what makes it funny, you can change all the characters and circumstances, since the basic humor remains. The joke will be yours, you'll get the credit for it, and you won't have to wonder if they've heard it before.

It's a quirk of human nature that if we're the one telling the joke, it's funny to us however many times we hear ourselves telling it.

However, if someone else is telling us a joke we've heard before, it doesn't make us laugh. The surprise is gone. Those neurons in your frontal lobes won't pop because they've built up an immunity.

So the key to humor is to sneak up on people and surprise them with the punch line. Of course they'll have heard the joke before—there are, after all, only five jokes in the world—but when you customize the joke, while maintaining the reason why it's funny, they won't recognize it. So the surprise element is there and that's what makes those neurons in your frontal lobes pop crisply.

■ A PRACTICE SESSION ON IDENTIFYING THE STYLE OF HUMOR

So let's try this out and see how we do. Let's practice.

I'll tell you a series of old jokes, and you decide whether the joke is exaggeration, a pun, a put-down, silliness, or surprise. Remember the acronym, Every Pickled Person Sounds Stupid.

Let's start with a Henny Youngman classic. "They have a new thing nowadays called Nicotine Anonymous. It's for people who want to stop smoking. When you feel a craving for a cigarette, you simply call up another member and he comes over and you get drunk together." What's the joke? Is it a pun, a put-down, an exaggeration, silliness, or surprise? The formula is surprise. There are forty-two words in the joke. Forty of them take you in one direction, and the last two take you in a completely different direction.

Let's try another Henny Youngman story: Despite warnings from his guide, an American skier in Switzerland got separated from his group and fell, uninjured, into a deep crevasse.

Several hours later, a rescue party found the yawning pit, and to reassure the stranded skier, shouted down to him, "We're from the Red Cross!"

"Sorry," the imperturbable American echoed back, "I already gave at the office!"

What's the joke? Well, silliness of course. I'm surprised that Henny didn't make it an Englishman down in that crevasse! Our formula tells us that the perceived pomposity of the English would add to the silliness.

In the presence of a client he wished to impress, a high-powered executive flipped on his intercom switch, and barked to his secretary, "Miss Jones, get my broker!"

The visitor was duly impressed, until the secretary's voice floated back into the room, loud and clear: "Yes, sir, stock or pawn?"

What's the joke? Of course, it's a put-down.

Notice that a put-down is always more effective when the person being put down is pompous and full of self-importance. When the Marx Brothers threw the cream pie, it was far funnier if it hit the opera singer than if it hit the janitor.

Now let's try a Myron Cohen favorite: Irving made a lot of money one year in the garment business and decided to buy a racehorse. One day he brought all his friends to the stable as the vet was laboriously working on the horse.

"Is my horse sick?" asked Irving.

"She's not the picture of health," said the vet, "but we'll pull her through."

"Will I ever be able to race her?"

"Chances are you will—and you'll probably beat her, too!"

What makes that funny? Is it an exaggeration, a pun, a put-down, silliness, or surprise?

Well, it's a pun, isn't it? It's "take my wife—please," with the words changed. The setup was using the word "race" to mean competitively, with another horse. The punch line changed the meaning of the word "race" to mean the owner running with the horse.

This is from comedian Dick Shebelski: Tommy came home from school very dejected.

"I had an awful day," he told his mother. "I couldn't remember an answer and it was embarrassing."

"Forgetting one answer is nothing to be embarrassed about," soothed his mother. And the boy said, "During roll call?"

What's the joke? Exaggeration, of course. The thought of someone not able to remember his own name is so absurd that it's funny.

By the way, doesn't that joke sound vaguely familiar? It should. Exaggeration is a very popular comedy theme. Probably 30 percent of all the jokes you'll ever hear involve exaggeration.

WITTICISMS
The Persuader's Best Type of Humor.

The most useful form of humor for the persuader is the witticism, that spontaneous cross connection of two diverse thoughts.

There's no question the level of wit is directly related to a person's level of intelligence. You may have a different definition of intelligence, but mine is very basic. "The ability to research the memory banks and pull together two unconnected concepts."

The ape in the cage sees a banana just beyond its reach. However, there is a stick within reach, and the ape uses the stick to pull the banana to him. That's not intelligence, that's instinct or trial and error. But let's suppose the ape finds the stick too short to reach the banana. However, he uses the stick to pull toward him a longer stick that's out of his reach and uses that stick to reach the banana. That's intelligence.

Here are some examples of pure wit that required intelligent thought:

David Brenner: "A vegetarian is a person who won't eat anything that can have children."

Herb Caen: "The trouble with born-again Christians is that they are an even bigger pain the second time around."

Johnny Carson: "When turkeys mate, they think of swans."

Sam Levenson: "The reason grandparents and grandchildren get along so well is that they have a common enemy."

Dorothy Parker: "One more drink and I'll be under the host."

Helen Rowland: "It takes a woman twenty years to make a man of her son, and another woman twenty minutes to make a fool of himself."

George Bernard Shaw: "A government which robs Peter to pay Paul can always depend on the support of Paul."

Arturo Toscanini: "I kissed my first girl and smoked my first cigarette on the same day. I haven't had time for tobacco since."

See how each one of these depends on an intelligent mind making a connection between two previously dissimilar thoughts?

All good humor involves some cleverness—some display of intelligence. Let's validate that against each of our five jokes:

Exaggeration is funny only if it's clever. If Johnny Carson says, "It was so cold in New York today, the people were bundled up like Eskimos," that's exaggeration, but it isn't funny because it isn't clever. If he says, "It was so cold in New York today the attorneys on Wall Street had their hands in their own pockets," that's funny because it's a clever exaggeration (plus a put-down).

The classical-style pun relies almost exclusively on its cleverness. But also lesser puns require the rapid association of one word with a similar sounding but illogical second word. The optician is examining a Japanese businessman's eyes and says, "I see you've got a cataract."

"No, no. I've got a Rincoln Continental."

Even the bluntest of humor, the put-down, must be clever to be funny. If Joan Rivers were to say, "I went to a nude beach and a gang of Hell's Angels insulted me," that's not funny. However, "I went to a nude beach and a gang of Hell's Angels viciously gang dressed me," is one of her classic lines.

Silliness also needs to be clever. Take Dudley Moore's classic drunk act in the movie *Arthur*. On the evening he reluctantly proposes to the heiress, played by Jill Eikenberry, he gets smashed at the dinner table. She lovingly says, "A good woman could stop you from drinking, Arthur." Dudley Moore processes this piece of information through the fog of alcohol and concludes, "It would take an awful big woman."

It's interesting to see how social standards affect our sense of humor. When the first *Arthur* movie came out in 1981 it was a big hit. Seven years later, *Arthur 2* was a flop. What changed was the public's perception of drunkenness. It's no longer seen as silly: now it's seen as tragic. Drunks now conjure up visions of broken homes and mangled bodies on the highway.

Similarly, "crazy" jokes are no longer funny. Our more enlightened society sees mental problems not as an aberration but as a disease and a potentially curable one, at that.

The fifth style of joke we talked about—surprise—takes a lot of intelligence to construct.

On the borders of California, we have signs that say, "Leaving California. Please resume normal behavior." Remember that our definition of a surprise joke is one that leads you in one direction and then quickly diverts you to another train of thought. To think of a line like "resume normal behavior," you'd have to be visualizing a "resume normal speed" sign, and then search through millions of other mental images in your memory banks to come up with the surprise association "behavior."

Witticism takes that kind of mental association. Witticism is the construction of one of the same five jokes, but done instantaneously, as the situation calls for it. But it can be learned.

■ A THIRTY-DAY PROGRAM TO IMPROVE YOUR SENSE OF HUMOR

So here's a thirty-day program to improve your sense of humor and increase your ability to come up with witty comments.

First, use the one-to-ten technique to find out how people you know rate your sense of humor. Since this is a sensitive area, take two off any number they give you. Take five off if you're asking someone who works for you!

Then, get one of those joke books that lists hundreds of jokes, and go through it, quickly identifying whether the joke is exaggeration, a pun, a put-down, silliness, or surprise. Some, of course, will be a combination of two or more.

Then, get in the habit of analyzing a joke every time you hear one. Once you become thoroughly familiar with identifying the core of every joke, you're ready to start developing your own witticisms. Now that you understand that there are really only five jokes in the world, it will be a lot easier for you.

Power Persuaders understand that personal charisma is a key factor in getting the other person to see it your way. And developing a good sense of humor is a big part of charisma.

If you're not sure how important developing a sense of humor is, remember that the two most popular presidents of the last three decades have been the two with the best sense of humor—John Kennedy and Ronald Reagan.

In the next chapter, we'll work on another thing that will build your charisma—the ability to remember and use the other person's name.

■ KEY POINTS IN THIS CHAPTER

1. Nothing positions people as effectively as a sense of humor—even the most hostile people can be won over with the use of good humor.

2. The flexibility that comes with a good sense of humor will stop you from having your nervous breakdown.

3. Don't try to remember jokes; instead learn what makes people laugh. It's not hard because there are only five things that make people laugh.

   – Exaggeration and its flip side, understatement

   – A pun, which describes any time that you use a word out of context, or substitute a word that's so similar in sound that it's almost indistinguishable

- Put-downs, which are much funnier when the storyteller is putting himself or herself down
- Silliness, which can be very effective in defusing a tense situation
- Surprise, which leads us down one path, and then quickly takes us 180 degrees in the opposite direction

4. The punch line or word must come as close to the end of the joke as possible.

5. The initials of "Every pickled person sounds stupid" will remind us of exaggeration, puns, put-downs, silliness, and surprise.

6. The most useful form of humor for the persuader is the witticism, that spontaneous cross-connection of two diverse thoughts.

7. All good humor involves some cleverness—some display of intelligence.

8. Get a joke book that lists hundreds of jokes, and go through it, quickly identifying whether the joke is exaggeration, a pun, a put-down, silliness, or surprise.

■ CHAPTER TWENTY-TWO

YOU NEED NEVER FORGET ANOTHER NAME

This will be the fourth, and final, chapter on developing the charisma that makes you a Power Persuader. Would you agree with me that if you could remember people's names, you'd be much more effective in dealing with people? Of course you would! It's the number one communication ability that everyone wishes he or she could perfect. Using a person's name, especially when she doesn't expect you to remember it, sets her up to be influenced by you just as surely as the machine sets up bowling pins at a bowling alley.

Don't you just hate it when you're introduced to someone and 2 minutes later, you can't remember his name. Or worse yet think you can and get it wrong! Hey, I'm not trying to make you blush! I've been there. I've done it. I know exactly how humbling that can be. Nobody had a problem remembering names the way I had a problem remembering names. I went to all the seminars, and learned all the cute tricks, and I still found myself being introduced to someone and 2 minutes later, I couldn't remember his name for the life of me. It was as if I'd never heard it in the first place.

The problem with those seminars is that they're taught by people who are brilliant at remembering names! How about a seminar by someone who's a complete klutz at doing it, like me?

■ THE MAGIC SECRET TO REMEMBERING NAMES

Well, I finally figured out a way I could become passably good at remembering names.

I can't shake hands with two hundred people, and then pick them out of a crowd and call them by name. If you come up to me in Dallas, and say, "Remember me? I was in your negotiating seminar in San Francisco two years ago," I'm still going to draw a blank.

But at least if I were introduced to you at the start of a business meeting, I could say good-bye to you as you leave and call you by name. So here's the magic secret to remembering names:

> There is no magic key to remembering names:
> It's plain hard work!

I think that the bulk of the problem is that everyone's running around looking for a secret trick that will suddenly turn around years of bad habits.

It's like dieting. Everybody's looking for the easy way to do it. A hundred diets a year are published, every one of them promising miraculous results. Yet the only people who really lose weight and keep it off are the ones who have come to the conclusion that there is no easy way. They know that to lose weight they have to quit drinking alcohol, exercise more, and eat less fat.

Similarly, there is no easy way to remember names. As my high school teacher used to say, "Don't waste any time looking for an easier way to do this. If there were an easier way, Roger would've found it years ago."

■ A VISIT TO THE CONTROL CENTER OF THE MIND

To understand better why we have trouble remembering names, let's look at how our memory works.

Imagine you're the television director of the Super Bowl program. You're sitting in a control center in front of a bank of twelve television screens, with a thirteenth screen off to the top left. The eight screens in the middle are showing live action from cameras around the stadium.

The corner screens have special functions. The one in the top left-hand corner is the instant-replay screen. It's constantly playing back a rerun of the most recent play.

Off to the far top left is a thirteenth screen that's constantly accessing the network's film files. It's bringing up scenes from other Super Bowls, from previous games in which one of the players was involved, and clips of interviews with the participants that you'd filmed earlier. We'll call it the permanent memory screen.

At the top right is your creative screen. Your creative director is constantly feeding you interesting footage from which you can pull brief interviews with the players and reports from the bench, for example. When the action on the field slows down, this is your resource to create some interesting vignettes.

Bottom right is what you call your emotion screen. A camera is constantly focused on different segments of the audience to get their reaction to what's happening on the field. That bottom right screen is a seething pit of groans, moans, cheers, and elation.

On the bottom left is your name call-up screen. A technician is sitting in front of a computer keyboard constantly inputting the name of the participants. So that you don't have to be constantly reading this screen, he's calling out the names as he puts them up. If all goes well, as you broadcast a picture, he'll have the correct name available for your use.

Do you have all that? Instant replays and permanent memory on the top left, creativity on the top right, emotion on the bottom right, and the name call-up screen on the bottom left. The positions I've used are important because, as we'll see, they tie in with neurolinguistic programming.

■ HOW THE MIND PROCESSES INFORMATION

Your job as television director is a very complex one.

Second by second, you have to decide what's most important and what should be transmitted as part of the broadcast. You can select from any one of the live action screens, and you also can pull in from the screens in the corners.

Permanent Memory		
Instant Replay		Creativity
Name Call-up		Emotion

Clockwise from the top left they are the instant replay and permanent memory screens, the creative vignettes, the emotional reaction, and the name call-up screen.

You're also selecting the key scenes that will be permanently stored and used again during the postgame wrap-up.

Simultaneously, you're analyzing the data and anticipating what's going to happen next, directing the camera operators on what they should look for.

When you first got the chance to be the director, it was an incredibly stressful job. You were vividly aware of every decision that you were making. Now, you've done it so often that you don't consciously think about the actions you're taking. The action just flows for you: it comes naturally. Only occasionally are you aware that you're making a decision to go to instant replay, permanent memory footage, creative vignettes, emotional reaction, or name overlay.

Your mind works in much the same way. You're constantly having input fed to you. You must decide what to ignore and what goes into short-term memory—the instant replay screen. Some things are worth saving for long-term use—the permanent memory screen. At the same time, you're creating future scenes in your mind, just like the creative screen in the top right-hand corner.

You're reacting to all this input with your emotions, just as the crowd is reacting emotionally on the bottom right screen. And you're getting auditory input on the name screen in the bottom left.

The model of the television control center I gave you is the same one that neurolinguistic experts use to understand what a person is thinking by watching his eye movements. If a person's eyes move to the top left, she's replaying the past. If they move top right she's creating the future in her mind. If the eyes move bottom right she's reacting emotionally, and if they move bottom left, she's thinking something through—perhaps making an effort to recall a name.

I confess that for years, I could never remember neurolinguistic eye movements. I'd be in front of someone and I could see his eyes moving when I asked him a question, but on the spur of the moment I could never remember which eye movements meant what. Until I came up with an OVPA—an outrageous visual picture acronym—by which to remember them.

Memory = MOST		Creativity = CATS
Recall = RABBITS		Emotion = EAT

As we look at the other person, let's start in the top left and go around clockwise. Top left is memory, top right is creativity, bottom right is emotion, and bottom left is recall. Memory, creativity, emotion, recall. M, C, E, R. And the outrageous acronym I use to remember MCER is, Most cats eat rabbits. That's not true, but if I remember that I shouldn't put a cat in my back yard with a rabbit, because most cats eat rabbits, I can remember MCER. Then I can translate it into memory, creativity, emotion, and recall.

Power Persuaders know that learning to read eye movements is a valuable persuasion skill.

■ SELECTIVE MEMORY—HOW IT WORKS

Like the television director, your mind is constantly analyzing information input and deciding what to do with it.

The problem with remembering names is that we very often don't make the decision to save them to short-term memory, much less make an effort to commit them to long-term memory.

It's like the television director deciding that it isn't worth saving it for a possible instant replay, much less putting it into the network's file footage.

I found that my major problem with remembering names was that I wasn't even making an effort to commit them to short-term memory, that when I was introduced to somebody, I heard the name, but I instantly discarded it, and 5 seconds later I couldn't recall it.

The solution was to develop a system that would discipline me to commit these names to short-term memory. The system I stumbled across is remarkably effective.

■ THE TRIGGER THAT MAKES YOU REMEMBER

To avoid that unpleasant experience of being introduced to someone only to realize a few seconds later that his name didn't register with us, we first need a trigger signal.

This is a signal that, the moment we think of it, triggers our memory to note the person's name. If you've ever seen a hypnotist at work, you know what I'm talking about. He implants a trigger word in the subject's mind that causes them to react automatically whenever they hear the word.

Richard Condon beautifully illustrated this principle in his book *The Manchurian Candidate*. The premise of the book, and the subsequent movie starring Laurence Harvey and Frank Sinatra, was that the communist Chinese had captured a U.S. soldier during the Korean war and secretly brainwashed him in Manchuria. They'd deliberately chosen this soldier because he had great potential to be a political candidate when the war was over. After the war, they secretly funded his political campaigns. As the book unfolds he's running for president, and has a good chance of winning. During captivity, they'd implanted a trigger thought into his subconscious mind. The trigger thought was that any time he saw the playing card with a queen of hearts on it, he was to follow the next instruction he heard. This would enable a Chinese communist operative to flash the trigger signal, the queen of hearts, in front of the president and give him any instruction, knowing that he'd be powerless to resist.

You may remember that great scene where the political candidate, played in the movie by Laurence Harvey, is in a bar having a drink. He's watching a card game, and by chance the queen of hearts is laid down—his trigger signal. Just then an argument erupts on the far side of the bar, and someone yells, "Go jump in a lake!" The candidate quietly pays for his drink, goes outside, and jumps into the nearest lake.

■ DEVELOPING YOUR PERSONAL TRIGGER

Trigger words or thoughts have been around for a long time, and they're very effective. The trigger thought I stumbled across, and have found so very compelling, is to make the color of a person's eyes the trigger signal that reminds us to take note of their name.

Here's why it's so effective. Names don't register with us, because we've developed a bad habit over the years. We hear a name and our subconscious mind automatically reacts to tell us to ignore it. Since we haven't been trained to notice the color of a person's eyes, we don't have any bad habits about that yet.

As we notice the color of their eyes, our mind is concentrating, focused on observing their eyes. That's the trigger for us also to take note of their name.

Do you recall that when we talked about charisma, I told you how important it is to take note of the color of a person's eyes? It creates a special moment of interaction with that person, that says, "I care about you." As your eye comes into focus with their eye, there's a special twinkle that takes place.

So what we're doing here is creating an unthinking response in your mind. You shake hands. This triggers the thought to notice the color of their eyes. Now add another thing to this automatic reaction. Shake hands, color of eyes, remember name.

Invariably, whenever you meet someone whose name you need to remember, you'll be shaking hands with him. You'll need to concentrate on this technique for only a few days before you'll automatically be associating shaking hands with noticing the color of the person's eyes. And this will trigger you to pay attention to his name. Shake hands, color of eyes, remember name.

■ HOW TO TRANSPOSE FROM SHORT-TERM TO LONG-TERM MEMORY

Now the question becomes, How do we transpose that name from short-term memory to long-term memory?

Using the analogy of the Super Bowl television director, we've now got the name up on the name overlay screen in the bottom left-hand corner.

We need to decide whether to put it into the instant replay memory up on the top left or perhaps even to the permanent memory file.

Sometimes you don't need to use up your long-term memory storage banks with a person's name. You'll hear their name as you're introduced, and the only time you'll need it again is when you say, "Nice to meet you, Bob," as you say good-bye a few minutes or even seconds later.

That's the way it is when I meet people in the doorway of my larger seminars. If I can remember their name until the end of a brief conversation, that's all I have to do.

Still, as a skilled director of our minds, we'll often make the decision that this is a name we'll replay later, so we'll move it from our bottom left overlay screen, through our top left instant-replay screen and onto the permanent memory screen.

It really does help to move your eyes in those directions as you think of committing the name to long-term memory. The neurolinguistic experts can explain it better than I, but it has something to do with the optic nerve in the eye transmitting a special signal to the brain.

Moving the eyes to the bottom left is the thinking mode. Moving them to the top left is the recall mode. If we decide we must commit this name to long-term memory, there are some memory recall techniques that will be helpful to us.

Let's look at some of them.

■ SIX STEPS TO BURNING THE NAME INTO YOUR MEMORY

There are some simple steps that you should take when you first hear the name, to nudge it up from the bottom left screen, up toward the top left.

There are several ways to do this. Use one, or perhaps two, of them every time you're introduced to someone.

FIRST STEP TO REMEMBERING NAMES
Clarify the Spelling

First, clarify the spelling. Is that Kathy with a "C" or a "K"? People ask me a lot, "Is that Roger with a 'D'"? although I almost never meet anybody who spells it that way. Is that Terry with a "Y" or an "I"? Is that Vivian with an "A" or an "E"?

SECOND STEP TO REMEMBERING NAMES
Find Out How They Like to Be Addressed

Second, find out how they like to be addressed. Do you prefer Dave or David? Should I call you Julia or Julie? Is it Frederick or Fred? Do you like Tom or Thomas?

THIRD STEP TO REMEMBERING NAMES
Clarify the Pronunciation

Third, clarify the pronunciation. The best way to do this is with Cockney rhyming slang. Cockneys are the Londoners who are born within the sound of Bow Bells, the church in the working-class East End of the city. They talk in a weird language that's composed almost entirely of words that rhyme with the word they really mean. For example, a Cockney says, "I'm going up the apples and pears, with a cup of rosy lee, for me trouble and strife." What he really means is, "I'm going upstairs, with a cup of tea, for my wife." In his rhyming slang, stairs became "apples and pears." Tea became "rosy lee," and wife became "trouble and strife." Now aren't you glad you invested in this book?

So verify the pronunciation with a rhyming word. Is that Chilton, as in Hilton? Is that Sutton as in button? Is that Blair like wear?

FOURTH STEP TO REMEMBERING NAMES
Relate the Name to Something Famous

Fourth, relate the name to a famous person or place if that's possible. This is a good one because it also gives you a visual image to work with. Is that Parks as in Yosemite? Perhaps you see a waterfall pouring out of his ear. Washington like the president? Maybe you see an old-fashioned white wig gradually slipping down over his eyes. Tyson like the boxer? And you see yourself ducking as a big red boxing glove comes swinging from behind his back. Carson like the comedian? And you see him standing on a gold star, swinging an imaginary golf club.

FIFTH STEP TO REMEMBERING NAMES
Use it Quickly

The fifth way to remember a name is to use it as quickly as possible. The next time you talk to the person, you should start your conversation with, "Don't you agree, Anne?" or "Mr. Travis, isn't it true that . . . ." If you find that you've forgotten the name, don't try to bluff your way through. The only way that you'll ever fulfill your potential to remember names is to correct a mistake every time you make it. Force yourself to say, "I'm sorry, but your name slipped my mind . . . . Oh yes, Anne . . . . Well Anne, don't you agree that . . . ."

At some point a schoolchild reluctantly comes to the conclusion that she's not going to be allowed to daydream and that life will be simpler if she simply pays attention. Similarly, it doesn't take long for us to train ourselves to pay attention to names if we correct ourselves every time we forget.

Remember that you'll have to suffer a few slings and arrows in the process. People say to me, "Roger, you say you're good at remembering names, but you forgot mine and you only heard it five minutes ago!"

That's true, but I care enough to be working on it and correcting myself when I goof. Don't laugh at the fat man jogging down the street. At least he's doing something about it. Save your scorn for the fat man who gave up and is laying on the couch eating french fries.

SIXTH STEP TO REMEMBERING NAMES
Use it Again When They Leave

Finally, sixth, be sure to use the name again when they leave. "Joe, it was really good to meet you." Or "Karen, be sure to call me if you come to Los Angeles." Again, if you've forgotten by then, you must ask them again. "I want to be sure that I remember your name. Tell me again . . . that's right, Cathy with a 'C.' Thanks for helping me out."

Please don't turn me off on this last point of asking them again. I realize that you're thinking, "I'm not going to make a fool of myself doing something like that. It would be too embarrassing."

Trust me, it won't take long. If you'll do it every time for three weeks, Ivan Pavlov's magical twenty-one days, you'll have broken a bad habit that has been building up for . . . how long? Ten years, twenty, maybe thirty?

Does the name Pavlov ring a bell?

So we nudge that name from the bottom left screen, up to the top left screen of instant reply, with the trigger mechanism of handshake, eye color, and take note of name.

Then we move it onto the permanent memory screen with one or more of these six techniques. To summarize:

1. Clarify the spelling.
2. Confirm how the person likes to be addressed.
3. Use rhyming slang to confirm the pronunciation.
4. Relate the name to a famous place or person if possible, and add the visual image.
5. Use the name as quickly as possible, asking the person to repeat it if you've forgotten.

6. Use the name again when you say good-bye, once more asking for the name if you've forgotten.

■ DON'T TRY TO OUTDO THE EXPERTS

Power Persuaders know another major rule to help remember names is—don't try to outdo the experts.

You've probably decided that you can't remember names because you've been to a seminar where the speaker could remember the names of the two hundred people he met at the door. Then you tried his techniques, couldn't make them work for you, and gave up. You developed a poor self-image of your ability to remember names.

What you've overlooked is that the speaker probably had a tremendous natural aptitude for remembering names. He had also been working and training with the techniques on a full-time basis for several years. And, finally, he probably spent an hour or so before the seminar, mentally preparing himself to do a brilliant job.

Now we, as rank amateurs, come along and expect to emulate this professional. It isn't going to happen.

If he has this tremendous aptitude, and we don't, we're going to have to work much harder at it than he, if we're going to make it happen.

We all fall into this trap. I know I do with playing golf. I'll play once a week at most, and then I rush out to the course, and go straight to the first tee. Then I take a couple of practice swings and start flailing away at the ball. No wonder I can't hit the stupid thing!

Meanwhile the professional golfer, who has ten times the natural aptitude I have, has put himself on a rigid exercise program to develop his or her muscles and mental coordination. Professionals invest a lot of money in exactly the right equipment. They wouldn't dream of teeing off until they've spent an hour on the practice tee, and they take more golf lessons in a month than I've taken in a lifetime. The more I think about it, it's a miracle that they're only 50 percent better at it than I.

Sometimes I'll be speaking at a corporate retreat or association meeting and I'm chatting with a business executive who's going to make a presentation before me.

"I haven't really figured out exactly what I'm going to say yet," he'll tell me.

I think, wow, this guy must be really something.

"Have you checked out the microphone?" I'll ask him.

"Oh, no, it'll be fine," he replies.

"Are you going to use the overhead projector? Did you check to see that it's set up right for you?"

"No, but it's plugged in, isn't it?"

So I think to myself, this guy must be a sensational speaker.

I've been a full-time professional speaker for over ten years, and I've spent hours preparing for my talk. I know exactly what I'm going to say. I've thought through my response to any one of the fifty things that might go wrong during my talk, from a fire alarm (it's happened three times), to the projector bulb burning out (seven times). I even have a plan for an earthquake or a woman giving birth during my talk. In spite of all this, I still get unpleasant surprises. In Freemantle, Australia, I bounded up onto the stage and found that it was beginning to separate on me, until I was almost doing the splits. In St. Paul, as I was being introduced, someone wrote "No Smoking!" on the overhead projector. Part of my planning was to set a wet napkin next to the overhead projector in case something like that happened. But I hadn't figured that anyone would be stupid enough to write on it with an indelible marker!

I was in the meeting room at 6 o'clock this morning, double-checking the physical layout and the equipment. And this corporate executive, who's an occasional speaker, is going to ad lib his talk and take all kinds of chances I'd never dream of doing.

What's the lesson to learn here?

The lesson is that if you're not brilliant at doing something, such as remembering names, you've got to give yourself every possible advantage, not disadvantage, over the people who are the top experts.

■ GIVING YOURSELF AN ACE ADVANTAGE

Power Persuaders know that giving yourself an advantage in remembering names means doing the following three things:

One way is to make a file card on each of your business associates and customers or clients. The card shows their secretary's name and the names of their spouse and children if you've been told them.

This doesn't have anything to do with remembering names, but while you're at it you might as well make a note of the town they're from and the college they attended. Also their birthday, their hobbies and sports, their political leaning, and their favorite cocktail, cigarettes, food, and restaurant.

Update the card with a few brief comments every time you meet with that person. Pay special attention to the personal things. The competition remembers the business stuff, and you will too.

Power Persuaders give themselves the advantage of being different.

How much business could you do if you could do things like this consistently? "Harry, the last time I was here you mentioned that your son was interested in going backpacking in Montana. Here's an article I clipped from my local paper I thought he might like to see."

Does all this sound excessive? Maybe so, but the objective is to give yourself an advantage that other people don't have. Harvey Mackay, in his book *How to Swim with the Sharks*, advocates maintaining a sixty-six item questionnaire on each of your business contacts. And Harvey Mackay has done right well.

The second way to give yourself an advantage in remembering names is maintain a card on your friends, also. This will be invaluable when you go to a cocktail party and can call their spouses by name. You'll be a hero.

The third way to give yourself an advantage in remembering names is maintain an overall list of people and titles for any company with which you do business. This doesn't carry all the detailed information the individual cards hold, but it lists those people you're liable to run into as you walk through the building.

■ THE KEY TO REMEMBERING FACES

Of course, remembering names is one thing. However, when you see them again, does their face conjure up the right name from your memory bank?

Remembering the name of your waiter in a restaurant is going to get you better service. He responds to your apparent caring about him, and it's a lot easier to get his attention if you know his name. But you don't need to be able to remember his face for that. Knowing that he's the tall one, short one, or skinny one is enough for that.

However, if you meet him at the gym the next day, and want to call him by name, you better have done something about remembering his face.

The key to remembering faces is the outrageous visual picture. The mind doesn't think in words, it thinks in pictures. Power Persuaders know how to use this to create pictures in the other person's mind.

Still, if we can link the person's face to their name and wrap them both up with an outrageous visual picture, it will be memorable.

We already talked about Mr. Parks with the Yosemite Falls pouring out of his ear. It's a good visual picture but it's probably not going to help you remember his name, unless his ear is the most distinctive feature he has.

If he happens to be the kind of guy about whom people think, here comes the guy with the big ears, what on earth is his name? then it will help. You'll think "big ears," big enough to pour a waterfall through, Yosemite Falls, Yosemite Park. Bingo!

So be sure that you've linked your OVP, your outrageous visual picture, to the physical feature that you'll notice first.

If you see Mr. Parks's nose coming first, then the falls comes out of his nose. If he has eyes that water, then picture them as the source of the river that ends with the falls.

We talked about Mr. Washington, with the colonial white wig that slips over his eyes. That's good if the first thing that you notice about him is his bald head. You think, I bet he gets cold, he should wear a wig, a colonial wig, like George Washington. Bingo!

However, if Mr. Washington's most prominent feature isn't his bald head, then pick somewhere else to hang his wig.

Remember that the more outrageous your OVP, the better, but it must be related to the feature that you notice first.

■ AN EXERCISE IN MEMORY DISCIPLINE

Here's an exercise that you can have fun with, and it'll cause you to take a quantum leap in your ability to remember names.

I've been using it for years now, and I've surprised myself at how well I can do it. The exercise is to see how many names you can remember consecutively, in any given day.

Here's how it works. Each day you remember the name of the first new person to whom you're introduced. Then when you're introduced to the second new person that day, you add the name to the mental list, and review the entire list each time you add a name. The objective is to see how many new names you can remember, without missing anybody.

So let's say you start the day, and the first new person you meet is the waitress at the coffee shop. Her name is Sheila. Then somebody comes over to the table and your breakfast companion introduces him as Harry.

John Kenneth Galbraith: "Breakfast is the perfect meal. Even the English can't mess it up."

As you move Harry's name into your replay memory, using the techniques we've talked about, you think to yourself, "That's two so far, Sheila the waitress and Harry the attorney."

The receptionist's name on your first call of the day is Patty. You mentally add her name to the list and then review your list of three. Sheila, Harry, and Patty.

Your business appointment is with Fred Thompson, but you've met him before, so he doesn't go on the list. But he has a new secretary, so you add Lillian to the list.

During the appointment, the controller of the company comes in and is briefly introduced. You add Susan to the list and review the list in your mind. Sheila the waitress, Harry the attorney, Patty the receptionist, Lillian the secretary, and Susan the controller.

Five so far and you're still in the game. By lunchtime, your list might look like this:

1.	Sheila	Waitress at breakfast
2.	Harry	Attorney I met at breakfast
3.	Patty	Receptionist
4.	Lillian	Fred Thompson's secretary
5.	Susan	Controller
6.	Jackson	Parking lot attendant
7.	Mark	Pumped gas for me
8.	Carla	Airline reservation clerk
9.	Jean	Rental car reservation clerk
10.	Harry	Guard at Jones Computers
11.	Sarah	New receptionist at Jones
12.	Tim	Software salesman at Jones

13.	June	Teller at bank
14.	Liz	Hostess at Denny's
15.	Dorah	Waitress at Denny's
16.	Jim	Introduced to at lunch

Note that you don't have to meet the person to have them go on the list. On this day, you called to make a plane reservation, and they answered, "United Airlines, this is Carla. How may I help you?"

You were careful to mentally note her name, and when you said your good-bye, you said, "Thank you, Carla."

When you called for the rental car, they answered, "Budget Rental Car. This is Jean. For what city, please?"

You responded, "Jean, this is for Boston on October 4. Do you have a special on a luxury car?" When you completed the conversation, you were again careful to use Jean's name when saying good-bye.

What does all this accomplish? It forces you to pay attention to names. It may not be important to remember the airline reservation clerk's name and use it when you say good-bye, but it's excellent training.

The way the game is played, if you forget a name, you're out for that day. You still work on your memory skills of course, but the game is over until tomorrow.

The enjoyable part of the game is to play with it, make it fun, and see if you can beat your previous personal best. It's a great way to hone your memory skills and have a little fun while you're doing it.

Why not have a little side bet going with your significant other? The one who has the shortest list at the end of the day has to cook or pay for dinner?

So the next time I meet you, I want to hear you say, "Hi, Roger, and you're number sixteen for the day." I'll know exactly what you're talking about!

■ HOW IMPORTANT IS IT TO REMEMBER NAMES?

Is it really worth all this effort to improve your ability to remember names? Power Persuaders know it is.

Al Tomsik, a friend of mine about whom I'll talk more in the next chapter, was the first person to show me how important remembering names is to Power Persuasion. Before he died, I asked him to tell me why calling a person by name was such a powerful tool.

He told me, "Roger, during the first six or eight months of our life, we hear our name about 8,000 times before we finally recognize it as our personal identity! In school it's the first word we learn to write. We grow up not wanting our name to be slandered or tarnished. We'll do almost anything to protect our good name. And it's one of our most valuable assets. We can borrow money 'against our name.'

"And if somebody has the nerve to forge our name, we accuse them of a felony and hope they'll be put in jail, where their name will be taken away and replaced with a number. That's how important our name is to us."

Isn't it obvious that being able to remember a person's name is a major part of Power Persuasion?

And what is your potential for remembering names? How good could you get at it, if you really worked at it? Your full potential is that you'd never forget a name, even if you didn't meet that person for twenty years. That's your potential. That's what your thirteen billion brain cells are capable of doing. If we reached 10 percent of our potential, people would call us brilliant at it.

Using these techniques may never make you brilliant with names, but isn't it worth the effort to get close? Power Persuaders know that using a person's name is a key element in personal charisma.

■ KEY POINTS IN THIS CHAPTER

1. Remembering names is the number one communication ability that everyone wishes he or she could perfect. It sets people up to be influenced by you.

2. There is no magic key to remembering names—it's just hard work!

3. Visualize the television control booth at a Super Bowl game. You're the director, and when you hear a name, you must decide whether to use it only for instant replay or to save it in the network library for long-term use.

4. Remember the OVPA for neurolinguistic eye movements, Most cats eat rabbits, which translates into memory, creativity, emotion, and recall.

5. Remember your mental trigger for remembering names—when you meet someone, observe the color of their eyes, and think of his or her name.

6. Work with the six steps of committing a name to long-term memory:
   - Clarify the spelling
   - Confirm how the person likes to be addressed
   - Use rhyming slang to confirm the pronunciation
   - Relate the name to a famous place or person if possible, and add the visual image
   - Use the name as quickly as possible, asking the person to repeat it if you've forgotten
   - Use the name again when you say good-bye, once more asking for the name if you've forgotten.

7. Don't try to emulate or outdo the memory experts, because it will only frustrate you. Give yourself every advantage, such as
   - Making a file card on each of your business associates and customers or clients
   - Updating their card with a few brief comments every time you meet with them
   - Maintaining a card on your friends also, so that you can refer to their spouse and children by names and make reference to their hobbies and interests

8. The key to remembering faces is the outrageous visual picture. This of their most prominent facial feature, so invent an OVP that leads you to their name. Such as, watery eyes, waterfall, Yosemite Falls, Mr. Parks.

9. Become aware of everybody's name and use it, even the telephone operator at a company, for example, or the airline reservations clerk.

10. Play the memory discipline exercise game. See how many consecutive names you can remember during the day.

11. Nothing is more important to us than our name. If you only developed 10 percent of your true ability to remember names, people would call you brilliant.

■ PART FOUR

LEARNING PERSUASION TECHNIQUES

In Part One, you learned how to play the persuasion game, in Part Two, you learned how to analyze the other person, and in Part Three, you learned the personal characteristics of a Power Persuader.

In Part Four, you will learn a magic technique that I learned from a former prisoner of war interrogator, which he believed could get anybody to tell him anything he wanted. Then, you'll learn the four stages of persuasion, and see how they can solve even the toughest persuasion challenges that you'll face in your business, family, or personal life.

Then, I'll show you how to persuade the two most difficult kinds of people—the angry person, and the person who won't open up.

Finally, we'll see how Power Persuaders use their skills to become great leaders.

CHAPTER TWENTY-THREE

A MAGIC PERSUASION TECHNIQUE

Let me tell you about a persuasion technique that's so simple and so effective it's amazing so few people are aware of how powerful it is.

I learned it from Al Tomsik, a friend of mine who used to interrogate Japanese prisoners of war during World War II. He told me that when he used this technique it was certain he would eventually persuade the prisoner to give him the information he wanted. He said it was so powerful, even prisoners who came into the interrogation room, willing to die rather than give any information, would break down and tell him what he wanted to know, without any physical threats.

I've used the technique consistently for several years now and find that it has remarkable effects. It will soothe an angry person, draw out a noncommunicative person, and measurably increase your percentage of positive responses.

Because it's so simple, I'm concerned that you'll dismiss it without taking the time to see how powerful it can be for you. However, Power Persuaders can develop it as a magical persuasion tool.

This simple technique is to use the person's name at the start or end of a sentence and make your request. You must tilt your head a little and smile as you say their name.

---

1. Use the other person's name at the beginning or the end of a sentence.

2. Make your request.

3. Tilt your head and smile as you say it.

Doesn't that sound incredibly simplistic? What on earth is the big deal about that? Try it and you'll see how magical it is. Experiment by leaving out one part of it, and you'll see how important it is to do it just the way I'm telling you.

Let's say that you want to get a refund on something at a store, and you don't have the receipt. You walk up to the clerk and you say, "Please refund this for me. I'm sorry, but I don't have a receipt." You're polite, but unsmiling. They're probably going to hassle you over the refund.

Now try it again. This time, note the clerk's name from their name tag, and say, "Good morning, Larry, would you mind refunding this for me. I'm sorry, but I don't have a receipt." As you finish, you flash Larry your most sincere smile, and tilt your head slightly as you hold his gaze. Larry wonders for a moment if you're honest and sincere, and then quickly grants your request.

■ WHY THE MAGIC FORMULA WORKS

What do Power Persuaders find so magical about this? Let's take each element of the technique separately.

First, the use of the other person's name. Naturally, we know that using a person's name is music to their ears. When greeting people as they come into my seminars, I've learned how to read their name badges with peripheral vision, so they can't tell I'm doing it. When I greet a stranger by name, and he's forgotten he's wearing a name badge, the effect is electrifying. I'm meeting him for the first time, but I say "Hi, Joe, how's it going?" Joe's not sure if I've met him before, or whether somebody else has pointed him out as an important person for me to meet. Yet the response is always pleasant surprise and a warm return greeting.

Second, the tilt of the head. Power Persuaders know that the tilt of the head is a basic body language skill. You can tell whether a person is hearing what you're saying, just by watching for this. If the head is straight up, it's almost certain that the person's thoughts are miles away. A slight tilt of the head means that they're paying attention. Unconsciously we know this, even if we're not aware of it. When you use this with people, they sense that you are listening and concerned about them, even if they don't know why they're getting that message. Tilting the head very slightly gives intensity to your persuasion.

Third, the use of a smile. What power there is in a smile! As Laurence Sterne wrote, "I'm firmly persuaded that every time a man smiles, it adds something to this Fragment of Life." You can make the most outrageous requests of people and get away with it as long as you keep smiling.

Put the three together and it makes a dramatic difference to the way you come across.

Let's say that your name is John. You've just come home from a busy day and you're in your favorite recliner. The *CBS Evening News* is on and you're glancing through the day's mail. Dan Rather is just finishing a story, and you hear him say, "And that's something we all need to be concerned about, wouldn't you agree, John?" At the sound of your name, you look up sharply and Dan Rather is looking at you expectantly, with a big smile on his face. Suddenly you're drawn into the scene, and he's asking for your positive response.

Sure, that's a dramatization, and the impact one-on-one is more subtle than that, but there's no question that this technique will improve your persuasion batting averages.

■ HOW TO USE THE FORMULA

Here's how you can use it.

Imagine that you sell office copy machines. You've been faithfully servicing one of your major accounts for years and regularly stopping by to see that everything is running smoothly. You've trained the client's new operators as the need arose. The company is about to move into a new, larger headquarters, and you're looking forward to writing a big new order for additional machines. Then you find out that it's already considering two proposals from your competitors, and the client didn't even ask you to bid!

You make an appointment with the vice president in charge of operations, and say, "All that I'm asking is that you listen to my proposal with an open mind, fair enough, Harry?"

A slight tilt of the head, and an open smile. Irresistible, right? Even if his mind-set was that he wouldn't even listen to what you had to say, you'll see his resistance melt.

Probably, your problem here is one of credibility. Over the years, he's come to think of you as a repairperson, not a salesperson. Your persuasion challenge is to change his perception of you.

Remember that credibility is such an important issue in persuasion, that we devoted all of Chapter Two to that one issue.

Let's say you're a sales manager and you've decided to institute a change in procedure that you know won't be popular. Perhaps the change is that you will no longer reimburse any item on an expense account, regardless of how minor, unless there is a written receipt attached.

To help persuade your people that this is a needed change, you've selected the three salespeople that have the most influence with the rest of the force. You're going to sell them on the plan before you announce it. Smart thinking, right?

There's a knock on the door, and one of the people with whom you've made an appointment, Joe, is there. "Come in, Joe," you say with a warm grin on your face. "Have a seat. I've got a new policy to implement, and I want to ask for your support."

Does that meet our criteria? No, it doesn't. While it's true that you used the name and smiled, it wasn't at the end of the key sentence.

Let's try again. Knock, knock. "Come in. Have a seat. I've got a new policy to implement, and I want to ask for your support, Joe." Now whip out a big smile as you begin to say his name.

That little shift in emphasis is what makes the magic formula work. It may be all that you need to get Joe over into your column.

Am I saying that this little technique will get Joe to support you regardless of how badly he thinks of this new policy when you explain it to him? Of course not. However, Power Persuaders know that whether you get support from a person often doesn't depend on the issue at hand. The person really doesn't feel strongly enough about it one way or the other. His or her support often depends on nothing more than his or her attitude when you first present the idea. The technique is a great one to position the person to feel receptive to your proposal.

■ CHAPTER TWENTY-FOUR

THE FOUR STAGES OF PERSUASION

There are four very distinct stages to the process of Power Persuasion. Most people get into trouble because they don't plan as they go into the persuasion situation. With work and practice we can all become such great Power Persuaders that we can wing it. Eventually we'll be able to make the right moves instinctively. Until that day comes, let's recognize that sitting down and deliberately planning a course of action is essential for successful persuasion. Do your homework!

The second reason people get into trouble in the persuasion process is that they don't understand that there are four distinct stages to go through. When we follow those four stages, we find that things start dropping into place for us.

■ STAGE 1—ESTABLISHING OBJECTIVES

The first stage is to clearly establish the objectives. You must know what it is you want, going in. How I wish I'd learned this twenty years ago! Looking back, nearly all my failures to persuade came from not clearly understanding the importance of this.

So often I'd go into a meeting with someone who was important to my future and have only a vague idea of what I planned to accomplish. Every time I did, I came away with less than I'd hoped for. Or I came away happy with the result, only to realize later that I could have done much better.

A person who has a settled purpose can stay calm and objective during the most frustrating of circumstances, coming away with what she wants, but more important, leaving the other person feeling he'd won too. Let's look at three situations where failing to clearly set an objective could really exacerbate the situation.

Case Study One: The Unhappy Employee

You're a personnel director for a company that imports and markets Japanese cameras. The president of the company has just been on the phone, screaming that you have to fire Sally, the receptionist, because she upset one of the company's best customers. Sally is, to use a personnel manager's terminology, "an adequate employee who hasn't quite come up to expectations."

The V.I.P customer showed up in the lobby, already upset because a limo hadn't been waiting for him at the airport, and he'd had to grab a cab. He saw the receptionist talking to a young man and assumed that she was wasting time with a boyfriend. In fact, it was a customer checking on a camera he had in for repair.

The already irritated customer barged in and suggested that she "take care of personal business on her own time." A more experienced receptionist would've handled it coolly, but Sally snapped back with a "who do you think you are," and the situation went downhill from there. Now you've got the president of the company on your back, all because she couldn't hold her tongue.

Sally walks into your office, and before you can open your mouth, yells, "I didn't do a darn thing wrong with that jerk, and I don't want to hear any more about it. If you fire me over it, I'm going to the Labor Relations Board!"

Case Study Two: The Problem Teenager

Your son Ben is an 18-year-old high school senior. He's never been in serious trouble, but just lately he's been involved in a series of mischievous pranks that are getting more and more out of hand.

His school principal asked you to come to the school this morning and told you that, at the school baseball game last night, Ben had figured out a way to kill all the lights in the ball park. He evidently only meant to flash them off and on for a prank, but once he got them off, he couldn't figure out how to get them back on.

To make matters worse, some clown in the crowd had yelled "Terrorist attack," and a panic had set in. When it was over there was a dislocated collar bone, a broken leg, and a thousand dollars' worth of damage to the electrical system.

The principal insists that you pay for all the damages and medical bills and is kicking Ben out of school without a diploma—although he completed all the units he needs to graduate.

What really has you hopping mad is that when Ben came in last night, he hadn't said a word about it. You'd said, "How'd the game go, Ben?" He'd responded, "Fine, Dad, but I'm tired and I'm going to bed."

Case Study Three: The Alcoholic Husband

Your husband Charlie isn't really a problem drinker, but there's no question he's been doing a lot more of it lately. The last few times you've been out, he's been in no condition to drive home, and last night really capped it off. You're a midlevel executive with an automobile manufacturer, and every year they throw a president's cocktail party at corporate headquarters. This is a key event of the social season in your town. The governor is usually there and a least one of the senators. All the leaders of your company are on their best behavior, playing host to what the society pages will call the "rich and the powerful" in your city, when they write it up in the following day's paper. Last night was the first time you'd been invited, and you really saw it as a milestone in your career with the company.

During the evening, your husband disappeared and to your horror the next time you saw him, he had cornered the chairman of the board and was clearly being loud and obnoxious. He had a big glass of bourbon in his hand and he was mopping up some that had spilled on the chairman's tuxedo. As you approached to pull him away, you could hear he was talking to the chairman about a cover story in *Forbes* magazine, where the caption had been, "Can National Motors survive this kind of management?"

Nobody talks to the chairman about that article! The last person who even brought it up was assigned to the assembly plant in Patagonia. Just as you approached, two security guards hauled Charlie off, with him yelling at them, "You can't do this, my wife will have you fired!"

The next morning your blood is still boiling, and you can hear Charlie coming downstairs. He comes into the dining room with a sheepish grin on his face, hugs you, and cheerfully says, "Wow, did I have a good time last night, or what!"

Each of these situations is a potential disaster waiting to happen. You can't wait to get a hold of the other person and tell them how upset you are. So you start yelling at them. They have no idea how to react, so they start yelling back at you. Tempers flare. Pretty soon the whole situation has gotten out of hand. Nobody meant for it to get that way, but neither side knows how to pull back from the positions they've taken.

Sally the receptionist quits, promising a lawsuit. Son Ben yells that he's getting out for good and drives off at a breakneck speed. Charlie is so humiliated that he's upstairs packing his things—all because you were emotionally distraught and went into the situation with only anger in your mind and heart.

Now let's see how a Power Persuader would approach these same three situations, with a calm confidence in their ability to get what they want.

The Power Persuader knows that the first stage is to establish the objective. The initial thought is, "What do I want to accomplish, when I meet with them?"

In the first example, the goals of the personnel director might be to:

1. Retain Sally as the company's receptionist, but to give her some training in handling volatile people.

2. Have her apologize to the customer.

3. Get some assurances the situation won't recur.

With these goals clearly in mind, he's better equipped to handle Sally's outburst when she says, "I didn't do a darn thing wrong with that jerk, and I don't want to hear any more about it. If you fire me over it, I'm going to the Labor Relations Board!"

He can respond, "Sally, nobody's going to fire you. My purpose is to discuss ways we prevent this kind of ugly scene from happening again. I've a feeling that you'd like to avoid that too, wouldn't you?"

"Well, of course I would," replies Sally, "but I'm not going to let a stuck-up jerk push me around."

"Sally, believe it or not, Mr. Jones isn't a jerk," replies the personnel director, "but he is one of the best customers this company has. There are many people around here whose jobs depend on his chain of stores buying from us. He was in a bad mood yesterday and he acted badly. However, I hired you and put my faith in you because I felt that you had the talent and the desire to become a first-class receptionist. The top-flight receptionist you're capable of becoming could've handled that kind of situation. Let's talk about people skills."

By being clear that his persuasion goal was to keep Sally on the job and to improve her skill at handling difficult people, he can stay calm at her outburst and keep moving toward his persuasion objective.

In the second example, regarding Ben's disruption of the baseball game, the father's objectives may be to:

1. Get Ben to accept professional counseling.

2. Take responsibility for the damages.

3. Come up with a plan to earn the money needed.

Still, what about Ben not letting his father know what had happened, when he came home the night before? The father is hurt because he feels they weren't close enough for the son to bring his problems to him. He probably wants to let him know how hurt he is. Yet that's not an objective. A more logical objective would be to get a commitment that, in future, Ben would talk to him about his problems.

How can that objective be reached? Not by berating Ben for failing to do so the night before. What's needed are some assurances that it's in Ben's best interests to bring his problems to his father.

So the father has three objectives:

1. Get Ben some professional counseling, which would require Ben to accept the seriousness of his irresponsible behavior.

2. Get Ben to come up with a plan to repay the money.

3. Get Ben to see why it's better for him to discuss his problems with his father.

Note that none of these objectives will be reached by yelling, screaming, and threatening, even though such action is justified under the circumstances. Getting angry is just going to take the father farther from his objective.

So Dad starts out, "Ben, we've got to come to grips with the seriousness of what happened. This may have started out as a prank, but you created a life-threatening situation. You've got to take some drastic action to turn around this behavior before it gets you into even more serious trouble. Don't you agree?"

Ben mumbles, "I guess so, Dad."

His father gently says, "Then what do you suggest?"

Note that the father never criticizes the son directly. However, he does come down hard on the son's behavior. They are two different things, and it's very important to make the distinction. It's never "you're bad," but "what you did, was bad." Accusing someone of being bad is nearly always counterproductive and leads to resentment and conflict. Criticizing the other person's behavior, on the other hand, is less confrontational and can lead to a fast commitment not to repeat what they did.

Note the father is emphasizing the seriousness of the problem, but is trying to get Ben to come up with the solution: "What do you suggest?" It's unlikely Ben is going to ask to go to a psychologist, but it may well lead to a "plea for help" kind of response, which will permit the father to suggest counseling.

Ben may well respond, "Dad, I don't know what to suggest. I just know that something's changed in my life. I'm just not happy anymore. Sometimes I feel it doesn't matter what I do, because nothing's going to turn out right anyway."

"Son, we all feel that way at times," the father responds. "Learning how to get control of your life is a part of growing up. There are doctors specially trained to help us find the way."

Note that if we've done a good job of stage 1 of Power Persuading, which is to clarify the objective of the meeting with the other person, it diffuses all the destructive anger that would otherwise control the situation.

When the auto executive confronts Charlie about his behavior at the company cocktail party, it is hoped that she has formulated clear objectives. Perhaps her goal is to

1. Get Charlie to admit he has a drinking problem.

2. Get him to decide that he wants to quit drinking.

3. Get Charlie to join Alcoholics Anonymous.

If screaming at Charlie and threatening to leave him will accomplish that objective, fine. However, it's a controlled plan of action, not senseless rage and indignation.

■ STAGE 2—FINDING OUT WHAT THEY WANT

The second stage of persuasion is to find out what the other person wants to get from the meeting.

This is critical to Power Persuasion because nobody will do anything, unless he feels it's in his best interest to do so. Let me repeat that because it's an all-encompassing statement: "Nobody will do anything, unless he feels that it's in his best interest to do so."

Many people are reluctant to accept the truth of this statement, perhaps because they're salespeople and they see their jobs as the art of getting people to buy something they don't presently want, or they're managers and they think that management is the art of getting employees to work when they don't want to. So they see persuasion as the art of getting people to do what they don't want to do.

Focus on this new definition: that successful selling, management, and persuasion involve the art of positioning people so they want to do what we want them to do. Then the answer to many problems suddenly becomes clear to us.

Suddenly we understand that great selling, management, and all other forms of persuasion aren't the product of clever verbal tricks or the manipulation of people. The art of persuasion is truly win-win. The other person wins because he sees the benefits of moving in a particular direction. We win because the move also benefits us.

"Come on, Roger," you may be thinking. "Saying that people will only do what's in their best interest is really cynical. Lots of people do things that are completely unselfish. That's what makes heroes. What about when Lee Iacocca first started collecting money for the restoration of the Statue of Liberty. A man walked into his office and said, 'Mr. Iacocca, I'm here to give you a check for $1 million, on one condition: that you agree never to reveal my name.' What about him, Roger? Surely you're not suggesting he was acting in his best interest?"

Sure I am. However, we've got to look beyond the obvious self-interest of financial gain or the respect and admiration of others. Evidently, the man had come to America as a young boy with his mother. The family got rich and he wanted to give something back to the country and also honor his mother. Donating the money was something he could afford to do, and it fulfilled those needs for him.

So in stage 2 of Power Persuasion, we figure out what it is the other person wants from the meeting. Understanding that you can persuade people to act only when they see it's in their best interest and also that they're motivated to act by the many influencing factors you learned about in Chapter One.

Of those many influencing factors the four most urgent and critical are these:

1. The need to be rewarded
2. The fear of punishment
3. A respect for other people
4. An inherent need to nourish bonded relationships

So let's apply these four to the situations about which we were talking and see how they apply.

For Sally, the receptionist, the need to be rewarded may not play a big role, but the fear of punishment—of getting chewed out or fired—would be a big factor. She may have a lot of respect for the personnel director. He plays to that respect by being honest in his appraisal of what happened. It was an ugly scene that should have been prevented. By saying, "I hired you, and put my faith in you, because I felt you had the talent and the desire to become a first-class receptionist," he's appealing to her natural need to bond the relationship.

In the scenario between Ben and his father, both reward and punishment will play a big role. However alienated they may appear at times, children usually have a deep love for their parents. There's not much you can do that will come between that.

I remember shopping for a used car many years ago and going over to look at an advertised car at the owner's home. The mother started to show me the car, but had to leave to answer the phone, so her 12-year-old son told me about it.

"My dad fixed the engine before he left," he proudly told me, "he's a terrific mechanic."

"That's great," I said, "where is your Dad?"

"He's in prison," he told me. "He'll be back in a couple of years. I think he's the best mechanic in the world."

I learned a big lesson that day, as I watched his eyes glow with genuine pride. You can get yourself thrown in jail, and your kids will still think you're the best thing that ever happened to them! So Ben's father is hopefully aware that his son is motivated just as much by need for his father's acceptance and approval as he is by his fear of punishment.

In the case of Charlie and his drinking problem, he may have become so addicted to alcohol that the need to be rewarded and the fear of punishment are no longer motivators. However much the wife threatens him, or paints a picture of a rosy future full of the rewards of sobriety, it isn't going to get through to Charlie. She's going to have to work on the other two factors: respect for other people and the need to nourish bonded relationships.

If she's a Power Persuader she'll understand this and arrange an intervention—which is a meeting of all the people in Charlie's life for whom he cares: his children, his coworkers, his friends. They confront him about the problem and its consequences for their future relationship.

So far we've covered the first two of the four stages of Power Persuasion. We've seen how stage 1, establishing our objectives, diffuses volatile emotions that may come between us and a win-win solution. Also we've seen how stage 2, determining the other side's needs, enables us to focus on the motivating factors that enable us to get them to see it our way.

■ STAGE 3—IDENTIFYING THE PRESSURE POINTS

Now, in stage 3, we need to identify the pressure points, to assess just how much power we have.

We do this with an unemotional look at the alternatives remaining for each side. We examine what faces us, if we can't persuade them to our point of view. Then we examine their alternatives, if they don't come around to our way of thinking.

Let's apply that to the three situations we posed, and see what comes out of it.

Sally the receptionist appears to have four alternatives:

1. Quit and look for another job.

2. Refuse to apologize to the customer, let them fire her, and sue for compensation through the labor commission.

3. Go over the personnel director's head and see if she can hang onto her job. (Since the president of the company wants her fired, this doesn't look like a good alternative.)

4. Make peace with the personnel director and follow his suggestions.

The personnel director appears to have three alternatives, if he fails to persuade Sally to his point of view:

1. He can fire and replace her.

2. He can "do a number" on Sally. That's a term that managers use for deliberately putting enough pressure on Sally that she'll quit.

3. He can stick up for Sally and fight for her with the president.

A lot will depend on the employment market in their area. How hard would it be for Sally to find another job, bearing in mind that she won't be leaving with a favorable reference? Assuming an average employment market—where she could find another job, but it won't be easy—the pressure points are almost evenly balanced. Neither side has very attractive alternatives. There's every possibility they'll agree, because neither side can put much pressure on the other.

The second situation, where Ben is in trouble with the school, is much less evenly balanced. Since Ben is 18, he's an adult and is solely responsible for the damages. His father is providing a place to live and probably offers Ben his only hope of going to college. The father is in a very strong position to put a great deal of pressure on his son.

The third situation, Charlie's drinking problem, isn't as clear as it might appear. Since the wife is a successful executive, her alternatives would include leaving Charlie and supporting herself. It seems she has a lot of power here, until we examine Charlie's alternative to quitting drinking and going to Alcoholics Anonymous. His other alternative is to keep on drinking. The problem is: that's exactly what he wants to do. So in this situation, his wife has very little power. Her success will depend strictly on her ability to make Charlie want to quit drinking.

In each of these situations, each side knows the other side well. In many persuasion situations, that's not so. When a salesperson is making a sale, or when a businessperson is dealing with a supplier, he very often doesn't know enough about the other person or company.

Nothing is more important to successful Power Persuasion than knowing about the other side. Knowledge is power. Knowledge enables you to structure a win-win solution, because you know better the real needs of the other side. Knowing the other side enables you to assess how much power you have, because you know their alternatives better.

■ STAGE 4—LOOKING FOR COMPROMISE

Having assessed the power of the other side, by examining their alternatives, we can now move to stage 4—looking for areas where you can make concessions to the other side.

Why would a Power Persuader be concerned about making concessions to the other side? For two reasons. First, because offering to trade concessions with the other side makes it more palatable for the other side to make concessions to you.

The personnel director says, "Sally, tell you what. If you'll apologize to that customer, we'll pay for you to go to that seminar on telephone skills that you were asking me about."

He may have planned to send her to the seminar anyway, but now he's positioned Sally to respond, "Well, all right, if you'll do that for me, I'll give him a call and smooth it over."

The father says, "Ben, do the right thing, take care of these problems. Then I'll go to bat for you with the principal so you can graduate with the other kids." This isn't a trade-off. The father would want this for Ben anyway, but he's smart enough to know that making this offer to his son, makes it easier for Ben to go with the proposal.

Charlie's wife might be smart enough to say, "Tell you what, if you'll give up drinking, I'll give up smoking, fair enough?" This enables Charlie to save face. Now instead of being forced to quit drinking, his imagination can carry him to the point where he believes that his sacrifice is saving her from dying of lung cancer.

The second reason to look for concessions to offer the other side is that Power Persuaders know the importance of "leaving something on the table." I learned a long time ago that no agreement will hold together unless cemented by the goodwill of both parties.

In hiring employees, for example, it's essential to know they're happy with the arrangement you've worked out. If it isn't a win for them too, they won't give the job everything they've got, and they'll jump at the first opportunity to leave for a better opportunity.

If the personnel director can't get Sally excited about her future with the company, his persuasion will be a short-lived victory.

If the only way Ben's father can get him to repair the damage he's done is by threatening to cut him off from going to college, his son will resent it for the rest of his life.

If Charlie's wife thinks that she can threaten him into quitting drinking, it not only won't last, but it's likely to ruin their relationship.

You know where people usually go wrong in persuasion? They're always focusing on what they want to get from the other person. It's far more productive to focus on what you can give to the other side. Understanding that when you give people what they want, they'll give you what you want.

So the Power Persuader looks for ways to make concessions to the other side, knowing it positions the other side to feel good about giving in, and it helps to make the agreement a win for both sides. An agreement that will last.

■ RECAPPING THE FOUR STAGES

So, as you approach the persuasion challenge, keep in mind the four stages. By working through them, you'll find it easier to get the other person to see it your way, and you'll create a lasting solution.

THE FOUR STAGES OF PERSUASION:

1. Know your objective precisely.
2. Gather information.
3. Assess your power by comparing alternatives.
4. Look for concessions to make to the other side.

Again, the first stage is to firm up your goals before you meet with the other person—know your objective precisely. The second stage is to gather all the information you can. The third stage is to decide how much power you have by assessing the alternatives of each side. The fourth stage is to look for concessions that you can make to them.

If you'll plan your persuasion approach to include going through each of these four stages, you'll be amazed at what an effective Power Persuader you can be.

In the next chapter we'll talk about persuading difficult people, such as the person who's so angry with you that he's not reacting logically and the person who clams up on you—who just won't talk.

■ CHAPTER TWENTY-FIVE

EIGHT WAYS TO PERSUADE THE ANGRY PERSON

Learning to be a good persuader is a little like learning warfare in military school. All the things you learn make perfectly good sense. They seem logical, and you're sure they'll work. Then you get out onto a battlefield, and the wheels come off! You're shocked into the realization that the other side hasn't gone to the same school. They're not fighting by the same rules with which you were taught to do battle.

What's the similarity between that, and learning Power Persuasion? All the things I've taught you will work fine, until you run into someone who's not playing by the same rules, the rules in this case being politeness, common courtesy, and acting in one's best interests, in other words, the difficult person.

So in this chapter I'm going to teach you to deal with the person who's so angry with you, or the world, that he or she can't see straight.

It's one thing to persuade a calm person who's thinking logically. It's another thing completely to persuade someone who's so angry that they're reacting irrationally.

The thing that separates the ordinary persuader from the Power Persuader is that we can handle even the difficult person and still

256

come away with our two basic requirements: we get what we want, and we get it by persuading them to our point of view, not with tricks or manipulation.

Running unexpectedly into a furious person is like stepping on a land mine. You're looking forward to a pleasant experience with someone with whom you've dealt in the past, and suddenly *KAPOWEE*!! you're flat on your back wondering what on earth happened.

Still, even surprise is preferable to anticipating with dread a meeting with someone you know is angry. "Mr. Johnson wants to see you in his office at three sharp," your secretary says, "and wow did he sound mad!" That kind of thing is enough to ruin anyone's day, isn't it?

Or how about this one? Your best account faxes you from Atlanta, and says "Serious problems. Be here at 9 A.M. tomorrow. Suggest you bring legal counsel."

Or what about a personal situation where the other person is angry with you? Your spouse is upset with you for some real or imagined wrong you've done him or her. He or she calls you up at work and finishes the conversation with, "I'm too upset about this to talk to you now. We'll discuss it when you get home. If you still feel like coming home!" Then he or she hangs up on you.

We've all had to deal with the angry person, so let's look at how to approach him or her. What can we do to resolve the problem, and what can we do to persuade him or her to our point of view?

■ ARE YOU THE TARGET?

The first consideration should be this: Are you the cause of the anger, or is the person upset with someone else, and it's just rubbing off on you?

Roseanne Barr: "Women complain about PMS, but I think of it as the only time of month I can be myself."

Laura Huxley, the widow of the author Aldous Huxley, wrote a book entitled *You Are Not the Target* that talks about this syndrome.

She holds that when people are rude to you, it's very seldom you with whom they're upset. It's the person they ran into before you. So first decide if you're the target of their anger, or if it's really somebody, or something, else.

Perhaps you're collecting for United Way, and, to your surprise, the personnel manager at the company on which you're calling is irritated by your request. As we discussed in Chapter Thirteen, it's important to exorcise the problem. You might come right out and say, "I can tell that you've had a bad experience with this kind of thing in the past. Why don't you tell me about it?"

My experience is that people are very willing to share their feelings with you. People who "wear their anger on their sleeve" often do so because they want to air their feelings, but don't know how.

The response you get in this situation may be, "Sure I'll tell you why I'm upset with you guys. I raised over $2,000 for you last year, and all I got for my trouble was a lousy form letter."

Psychologists will tell you that almost all depression is caused by internalized anger. It's very therapeutic for you to encourage the other person to get his anger out. If you don't do this, the person internalizes his anger even more, and becomes even more resistant to your attempt at persuasion.

I once asked a person for a contribution to United Way and he angrily told me that he wouldn't give any money if the Red Cross was going to get a share of it. Of course, a simple response to that would be to isolate the objection. It's easy to do and you avoid any confrontation.

You say, "Is that the only thing that's bothering you? You're telling me that you wouldn't have a problem with contributing to United Way if you were assured the Red Cross wouldn't get any money from you?"

"No, I don't have a problem with those others, it's only the Red Cross I won't give to."

"Fine," you say, "we can handle that. We'll just exclude Red Cross from any part of your donation. There's a place to specify your charities right here on this pledge form."

However, isolating the objection isn't the best way to handle an angry person. If you've got the time, you're better off to let them get the anger out of their system. They're anxious to do that, and after they have vented their bad feelings, they'll be much more receptive to your persuasion.

In this case I was curious. You don't often run into somebody who has anything against the Red Cross. What on earth did he have against them?

Apparently, when he was a soldier during World War II, he'd pulled into a French railroad station on a troop train, and the Red Cross was there, selling cigarettes. He felt they should have been giving them away. Almost forty years later, he was still burned up about it. Because he brought it up so eagerly, he clearly wanted to talk about it—to get it out of his system. After he'd talked about it for a few minutes, he finally answered my question. "I guess they probably had a problem with the people who had given money to them, who felt they shouldn't be giving special treatment to smokers." Then he went ahead and made a generous contribution, without asking to exclude Red Cross.

So the first rule for persuading an angry person is to decide whether they're angry at you or at somebody else.

■ A MAGIC EXPRESSION

If it really is you with whom they're upset, I've got a solution for you. It's a persuasion technique I learned at The Wilshire Country Club in Los Angeles, and I think it's pure magic. My golf partner was Maurice, a charismatic immigrant from Argentina, who'd become successful in the housing development business. One of the other players in our foursome was having a bad day. His game started off well, but then he really started flubbing shots. Maurice and I were off to the side of the fairway waiting for this man to hit. He made the mistake of "looking up" as he hit the ball, and topped it, causing it to bounce only a few yards down the fairway. His face turned purple, and he came storming over to Maurice, accusing him at the top of his voice of talking during his backswing.

How did Maurice react? Did he deny it? Did he laugh at his friend for getting so upset? Did he try to put it off by saying, "It's only a game?" Or did he yell back, "Don't take it out on me, just because you're having a bad day!"

These things just would've made the other person angrier, wouldn't they? Instead, Maurice, a master Power Persuader, pulled a magic expression out of his persuasion arsenal. He simply said with great sincerity, "David, my friend, I apologize to you, from the bottom of my heart." I watched with amazement as the anger drained out of the other man, like water draining out of a bathtub.

"Oh, that's OK," he mumbled, "it isn't your fault."

I don't know what it is that makes that expression so magical, but I've used it dozens of times since, and I've never seen anyone stay angry under the onslaught of its sincerity.

Try it the next time you're faced with a person who's angry with you. "I apologize from the bottom of my heart." You can never apologize too profusely, because the moment they feel that you've gone far enough, they'll let you know by accepting your apology.

Perhaps you've an appointment with one of your city supervisors. You're anxious to get her support for a key project that's coming up for a vote at the next city council meeting. Despite all the precautions that you take, you end up being 15 minutes late for the meeting. You squeeze her hand warmly, and look into her eyes, and lay that magic expression on her.

"I apologize to you from the bottom of my heart." Then watch her anger melt away!

■ RESTATING THE OBJECTION

Another great technique for handling a person who violently disagrees with you is to restate the objection in a question form, without agreeing.

Let's say you're selling recreational vehicles. Your prospects look at the model, but they're clearly in a rotten mood. The husband pulls out a kitchen drawer, examines it, and says, "Boy, is this thing cheap. I could do a better job than this." If you're brand new in sales, you may take that as a rejection of this model and try to soothe things over by saying, "Let's look at the next one, you may like that better."

If you're a little more experienced, you may have heard that objection before, and you're prepared to counter it. So you say, "But don't forget that weight is very important. If it were made with heavier materials, it would take more gas to run, and cost a lot more to operate."

However, if you're a Power Persuader, you simply say, "You feel that you could build better cabinets?" Don't be sarcastic. Simply restate the objection. This will quickly tell you if it's a problem about which they're really concerned, or whether it was just a passing comment.

Often, you'll find out the person was just making conversation. When you feed back the objection, "You feel that you could build better cabinets?" the person'll often reply, "Yes, I used to be a cabinet worker, and I was good too. Still, it seems like nobody can afford that kind of quality anymore."

Having found out the objection isn't going to be a deal breaker, you can move to isolating the objection. You might say, "Is the quality of the cabinets the only thing that's bothering you?" He responds, "No, the price is ridiculous too." So you counter, "If we made the price right for you, could you live with the cabinets?"

He says, "You'd practically have to give it to me." Now you can start to close them. "Let's sit down and see how far apart we are—fair enough?" Notice we never mention the other person's bad mood or in any way react to it. If we're not the target, why should it bother us?

■ THAT HASN'T BEEN MY EXPERIENCE

So we've seen how we can handle the angry person's objection by restating it, but not agreeing with it.

Another, slightly stronger way to handle the angry person is to acknowledge her problem but to disagree gently with her using the "that hasn't been my experience" technique. Communications expert Connie Merritt taught me this one.

Your boss yells at you, "This ad copy really stinks, Joe. We'd be a laughing stock if we ran it!"

"That hasn't been my experience," you quietly reply.

"We can't tell our customers the competition sells more corn flakes than we do. They'll buy from our competition."

"That hasn't been my experience."

"And what's this about an eight hundred number so they can call in and complain. The call would cost more than the corn flakes. We'd go broke."

"That hasn't been my experience."

The boss is finally beginning to run out of steam.

"Well, Joe, since you've got so much experience, why don't you tell us exactly what your experience has been!"

Now you've positioned the other person to be receptive to your ability to persuade them. Isn't that a great idea? Be careful you're not combative when you say it. Keep it very low key, almost under your breath: "That hasn't been my experience."

You shouldn't attempt to persuade an angry person before you've prepared them for persuasion by smoothing them over, any more than you should start to paint a fence before you've prepared the surface by scraping off the old flakes of paint and sanding the surface smooth.

■ HANDLING THE SHOWMAN

Some angry people are so insecure, they're heavy handed in their approach. Even though a simple suggestion would do, they feel it necessary to use threats.

You're the manager of a company-owned store that's part of a chain. The district manager storms in one day, in a foul mood.

"Harry," he screams, "this place is a disaster. Get it cleaned up, or I'll get someone in here who can."

If this is out of character for your district manager, get concerned. However, if he always comes on strong like this, there's no point in aggravating the situation.

"Don't worry, Mr. Jones. I'll get it fixed, and I'll get it fixed right now."

Mature people don't let the screamers of the world get their blood pressure up.

Though this incident happened fifteen years ago, I can remember it clearly. I was the merchandise manager of a large store in Bakersfield, California. My job was to get the sales moving, and I was willing to do what it took to accomplish that. I was in the appliance department when Jimmy Kephart, one of our top salespeople, was caught about to ring up a transaction at a sale price, the day before the event was supposed to start.

The store controller, a classic bean counter, was screaming at him, "I could get you fired for doing that! Don't you dare ring that sale up!"

Jimmy calmly said, "Oops, my mistake." Then he put the sales check away. The controller stormed off with a look of self-righteous satisfaction on his face. I moved in to salve Jimmy's wounds and give him a little pep talk.

It wasn't necessary.

When I got there, he had calmly retrieved the sales slip and was ringing it up again.

He cheerfully said to me, "Isn't life wonderful? Every day you learn something new."

"Wow, what a positive attitude," I thought.

Jimmy continued. "Today I learned not to ring these up when the controller's around."

What common sense! Why go to war with someone who's going to retreat soon anyway? When faced with a showman, learn to back off.

■ DON'T EXACERBATE THE SITUATION

When faced with an angry person, don't exacerbate the situation.

It's amazing how little situations can get completely blown out of proportion, just because somebody gets on his or her high horse and decides that he or she is not going to let the other person get away with something.

It's equally amazing how a little bit of tolerance can make even the thorniest of problems go away.

In July 1988, Attorney General Edwin Meese was in trouble. He was under investigation on several charges of impropriety, and the Democrats were holding him up as an example of corruption in the Reagan administration. Although he was never prosecuted, he was forced out of office by the problems.

In Washington, the hottest-selling tee shirt of the summer had Ed Meese's picture on it, with the slogan "Ed Meese Is a Pig." A man making a delivery to the Justice Department was wearing one of the tee shirts. They told him he couldn't come into the building wearing a shirt that contained a derogatory comment about their leader.

He said, "This is America. I can wear what I want."

Everyday he showed up in the shirt, and tempers flared. He was clearly baiting the Justice Department. An attorney who worked there, hoping to please the boss, filed a lawsuit and sought an injunction to prevent him from wearing it.

The man went to the Civil Liberties Union, and they filed a counter suit, claiming his protection under the principle of free speech. When it hit the evening news, Ed Meese heard about it for the first time. "I don't care what he wears," he said, "I've got much bigger problems to worry about."

And it was all over. The whole problem simply went away, because the attorney general chose not to be concerned by it. The man made deliveries in his tee shirt for a few more days and then quit wearing it because it wasn't fun anymore.

In August of the same year, just after the Republicans nominated Dan Quayle to be their vice presidential candidate, a woman walked into an Indiana supermarket and took a grocery checker hostage at gunpoint. What did she want? She wanted Quayle's family newspaper to print a statement on the front page.

Now I'm sure you've heard of situations like this ending in disaster. The newspaper refuses to be blackmailed, the politicians get involved, the SWAT team starts shooting, and people get killed. But not in this instance. What happened?

The Quayle family said, "We don't have any problem printing her statement." They printed a rambling statement the woman dictated to them, the content of which didn't make sense to anyone. The woman turned over her gun and went to jail. The whole problem just went away.

How much simpler does it need to be? When faced with an angry person, at least consider the possibility of ignoring the problem or simply going with their demands. Don't exacerbate the situation.

■ FIRST FIND OUT WHAT THEY WANT

The first stage of persuasion, establishing objectives, is particularly important when dealing with an angry person. First, get them to tell you what it would take to resolve the problem.

Let's say you're at home one Sunday afternoon, watching a tennis match on television. In one hand, you've got the channel changer for the commercials. In the other, you've got a glass of your favorite wine. You're having a good time! Got the picture? In the distance you hear this car coming at high speed. It's roaring down the highway. It swerves into your street on two wheels. It comes to a skidding, screeching halt in front of your garage. The car door slams open and shut. The front door of the house is flung open. Your spouse storms into the living room and yells at you, "Well, you've done it to me again!" What do you respond?

You're wrong if your response was, "Done what?" or "What are you upset about?" Power Persuaders know the correct response should be, "I'm sorry you're upset. What is it you want me to do?" First find out what the other person wants you to do. The request may be so small you're better off to go with it.

Your spouse may say, "I want you to apologize to my mother!" Then you can respond, "Fine. Hand me the phone." You can resolve this during a commercial break. You don't even have to put your wine down!

■ CHARM THEM TO DEATH

For sheer charm in dealing with angry people, you can't beat this story. British film producer and director Sir Alexander Korda once promised a part in his new movie to English actress Ann Todd. However, he reneged at the last moment and gave the part to someone else.

She was furious and let Korda know exactly how she felt about him. "I wouldn't have done it to anyone else," said Korda, "but we're such good friends, I knew you'd forgive me."

■ KEY POINTS IN THIS CHAPTER

1. Decide if you're the target. Is the person angry with you or with somebody or something else?

2. Try the magic expression "I apologize to you from the bottom of my heart."

3. Restate the objection: "You think it's too expensive?" Then, see if the person restates or backs off.

4. If this is a person who's habitually angry, consider appeasing rather than antagonizing him or her.

5. Be careful not to exacerbate the situation by needlessly taking a stand on principles when the wisest course of action may be to agree to their demands.

6. Be sure you completely understand what it would take to resolve the problem before you make any concessions.

■ CHAPTER TWENTY-SIX

EIGHT REASONS WHY PEOPLE WON'T OPEN UP

In this chapter, I'll teach you how to persuade the clam—the person who just won't talk. She won't respond to any of the suggestions or proposals you make, and you never know where you stand with her. Apart from the angry person, the next most challenging person to deal with is the clam.

That applies to a parent who can't get a child to tell why he or she's depressed. It applies to someone who can't get a spouse to say what he or she's upset about. It applies to the employer faced with the resignation of a key person—when that person won't give the real reason for quitting. And it especially applies to a salesperson who can't get the customer to raise objections. If you're not engaged in selling, you'd think the last thing a salesperson wants to hear is an objection. But salespeople love objections. Only people who have objections buy. People who just agree with everything aren't buyers, they're lookers.

My background is as a real estate broker. In real estate we knew that if we showed potential buyers a home, they weren't going to buy if they walked through it saying, "Isn't that great, don't you just love the kitchen, isn't the view fantastic?" And if you've got somebody who doesn't think the price is outrageous, you know you've got a "looky loo" on your hands.

It was the people who said, "The kitchen's on the small size. We'd have to knock that wall out. Isn't that wallpaper ugly?" They were the real buyers.

■ FIGURE OUT WHY THEY WON'T TALK

So we're faced with the challenge of persuading someone who has clammed up, who just won't talk.

Why won't they talk? The first step must be to figure out why the other person is so unresponsive. There are eight reasons they won't open up. If you guess the wrong one, you're going to make the situation worse. Either they'll become even more determined to be uncommunicative, or they'll do the opposite and you'll have an angry person problem on your hands.

Let's run down the eight reasons, with a quick action plan for each.

■ Obsession

The first reason is obsession. They can't concentrate on what you're saying because they're obsessed with another issue. Maybe the boss just told her she's being transferred to El Paso. Or the spouse just called to say they have five numbers correct on the state lottery and they'll know next week if they've won $50 million. Perhaps his daughter didn't come home last night. Or his competitor for that big promotion has just been called to the president's office.

The only way to handle the obsessed is to confront the problem. But do it gently. "What is it that's bothering you, Joe? Perhaps I can help."

In my experience, there are two ways that the exchange can go from there. Either Joe will shrug off the problem and start concentrating on your proposal, or he'll say, "It's really tough for me to concentrate right now. Could we talk about this again Monday morning? Would 10 o'clock be good for you?" Clearly this leaves you well positioned for a successful meeting Monday.

Cheerfully agree, and you've built up some obligation power that we talked about in Chapter Three. However, don't immediately jump on this—because you have another option, and it could be valuable.

You could risk going for a fast close. "Joe, I'd be happy to meet with you Monday, but it isn't that big a deal. I've determined we need a distribution center in Seattle to cover our Northwest territory. We'll cut our freight costs by $3.2 million a year. All I need is a go-ahead to spend $75,000 on a site selection study."

Since the human mind is incapable of holding two thoughts at once, Joe's going to have to force his mind off the yacht he'll buy with his $50 million lottery winnings. If your proposal doesn't sound that outrageous to him, he's going to say, "Sure, go ahead."

If the proposal freaks him out, he's going to say, "Fred, you know that kind of thing ought to go to the board. Let's talk about it Monday." Still, in going for the quick close, you usually have everything to gain and very little to lose.

■ Inhibition

The second reason for silence may be inhibition. Some people won't talk simply because they're shy. If you know the person with whom you're dealing, it's a lot easier to know what's going on. If you don't, this one can really fool you.

Often I've thought I'd been dealing with someone who was hostile or aloof. Yet, when I've mentioned it to somebody who knew the person better, they'd say, "Oh, she's just shy when she meets someone for the first time. Once she gets to know you, she's terrific to work with."

Check it out by turning the conversation to something with which they'll be comfortable. Maybe the picture of a child on the wall, or the way the office is decorated. If the person immediately turns into a chatterbox, you've found the answer.

It may take you longer to build rapport with shy people, but it's worth it. They bond well. You'll probably have a great business relationship in the future.

Salespeople know how to draw out the inhibited by asking them questions. I go as far as to say that asking questions is the very definition of selling. When you're asking questions, you're selling. When you quit asking questions, you're not selling any more. I don't know what you're doing, maybe you're giving a seminar or something, but you're not selling.

Of course, the way you ask questions makes all the difference in drawing people out. You must ask open-ended questions. That means questions that can't be answered with a yes or a no. Try this game with a friend. Ask a series of questions that start with a what, where, when, how, why, or who. Challenge the respondent to see if they can answer that question with a yes or a no.

Let me illustrate that. See if you can answer any of these questions with a yes or a no:

1. *What* country was host to the 1992 Olympic Games?

2. *Where* were the Winter Games held?

3. *When* was that?

4. *How* much did CBS pay to televise the games?

5. *Why* would they pay so much?

6. *Who* was the president of the network at that time?

It can't be done, can it? Since you're asking what, where, when, how, why, or who questions, people have to respond with something more than a yes or no.

If the inhibited person is asked an open-ended question—one that starts with one of the six words—he's forced to elaborate on his answer, and you'll be drawing him out of his shell.

■ Apathy

The third reason is apathy. Some people aren't talking because they just don't care. He's just been told he's being transferred to El Paso and intends to quit instead. Or the one true love of his life has just left for Buenos Aires with a tango dancer, and all he wants to do is survive the day without an emotional collapse. Or perhaps the board of directors has just laughed at the expansion proposal he's been working on for the last six months, the one that was going to get him a vice presidency.

You're going to have to romance the apathetic for a few minutes, until you can bring them back from the brink. Don't talk about business. Talk about snow-capped mountains, alpine meadows in springtime, and the laughter of children at the beach. Slide in a little bit about moonlight cruises to Bora Bora on barefoot windjammers. When their eyes begin to focus again, you can get back to business and how your proposal is going to make all that possible.

■ Sulking

The fourth reason for silence comes from the sulker. These folks won't talk to you because they're still upset with you for some grievous wound you inflicted upon them. Instead of getting angry, they're going to let you know how they feel by sulking.

Whether you're guilty of the offense or not doesn't have much meaning for the sulker. One of his best people quit to go to work for your company, and he's convinced that you stole the person. You sold her competitor goods at the same "once in a lifetime" special price at which you sold her. Then the competitor ran an ad for the goods on the same day at 99 cents less. Or your significant other thought you spent too much time with a coworker at the office party the other night. It doesn't take much of this to have you praying for sulkers to turn into raving lunatics and start screaming at you.

At least that would get it out of their systems, and that's what you have to do with a sulker. Like sucking poison out of a wound, you've got to bring that repressed anger to the surface and get it out.

The way to handle them is to tell a secret, make a confession, and ask a favor. It's the technique we talked about earlier. Take the IranGate crisis, for example, when members of the Reagan administration were caught selling arms to Iran and using the money to fund the Contras in Nicaragua. President Reagan should have gone on television and said, "I really shouldn't be telling you this, but I'm so concerned about what happened that I think that your right to know is more important than keeping a National Security Council secret. We made a big mistake. We never should have done it, and it will never happen again. Maybe I'm asking too much, but I'm going to ask a big favor of you. I'm not going to ask you to forgive me, but I am going to ask you to trust me that this kind of thing will never happen again."

If he'd have done that, he probably could have saved us $50 million—the cost of the Senate investigation. And he could have had his administration back on track a year sooner.

Lee Iacocca learned the same lesson when his executives were caught driving cars with the speedometers disconnected. Even when the cars were wrecked, they were being fixed and sold as new. Iacocca knew you're better off to tell a secret, make a confession, and ask a favor. Within a week he'd done away with a problem that could have done serious damage to the Chrysler Corporation. So bring the anger out of a sulker, where you can deal with it.

If it's been going on for a long time, and doesn't look as if it's going to get any better, you might risk a humorous approach. I once quit advertising on a radio station over a mistake that the station had made. I guess it says a lot that I can't even remember what the mistake was. But after the account manager made the mistake, I'd let him call on me, but I wouldn't buy.

Finally, he said, "Roger, you haven't done any business with me for a year now. I admit I made a mistake, but how long do I have to do penance. There are folks out there who have committed murder and only done nine months!"

I laughed and agreed that maybe this had gone on enough and went back to doing business with him.

■ Evaluation

The fifth type of person who's liable to clam up is the evaluator. This is the person who's not given to quick judgments. He or she needs to think things through before they make a decision.

You can spot the evaluator because she's been open and talkative earlier, but now she's clammed up on you. I'm not talking about the analytical—the accountant or engineer personality that's so hard to bring to a conclusion. I'm talking about the average person who has some concerns.

Just as a pilot won't fly a plane without going through a formal checklist, the evaluator has a mental checklist he or she needs to run through, such as:

"Who might criticize me for going ahead?"

"Have I negotiated the best price I can?"

"To which account should I charge this?"

"Is there anyone else who ought to be in on this decision?"

"Am I convinced that this is the best product or service available to me?"

If the evaluator has reached the point where she's going through her mental checklist, you've probably done everything you can to persuade them. The worst thing that you can do is talk to them, which prevents them from going through this process.

If a question comes up, answer it and shut up again. Salespeople call it the silent close. Make your proposal and *shut up!* The first person to talk loses. I once watched two salespeople do the silent close on each other. There were three of us seated at the table. One salesperson made a proposal to the other and shut up. The other salesperson realized what he was doing, the silent close, and decided to teach the first one a lesson. He wouldn't talk either.

Both sat there, staring at each other, daring each other to talk. I didn't know how it would ever get resolved. It seemed as though half an hour had passed, although it was probably only about 5 minutes.

Finally the impasse was broken when the second salesperson wrote "decizion?" on a piece of paper and slid it over to the other. But, you see, he deliberately misspelled the word "decision."

The first salesperson spotted the mistake and couldn't stop himself. He gleefully said, "You misspelled 'decision.'" And having started, he couldn't stop. He went on to say "Look, if you won't go with what I proposed, I might be willing to . . . ". He countered his own proposal, before he even found out whether the other person would accept what he had suggested!

When the evaluator starts talking again, but it isn't a question, it's time to go for the assume close: "So let's go ahead and get the paperwork out of the way." Or "You'll probably want to call your wife and tell her the good news. El Paso is wonderful in August." Or "So it's all agreed, we'll go fishing at the lake instead of going to Rio. Wait until you see those fish jumping."

■ Penuriousness

The sixth kind of clam is the penny pincher. This person is so penurious, he gets nervous about the possibility of having to spend some money. You can spot him because he's talkative, until the time you start talking about the price. Don't be fooled because you know this person has money in which to slosh around. Some really wealthy people are as tight as a wrestler's leotards.

Would you believe that some affluent people still order food in a restaurant based on the price of the dish? I know, it's hard to believe, but some people are like that! They look down the menu and say to themselves, "I'd really prefer the Eggs Benedict, but they're $8.95, and I'm not worth that much. I'll have the bacon and eggs at $6.95."

Reducing the price when you see the penny pincher is getting uptight is very dangerous. If you think they're concerned about spending money, remember that they're usually more concerned that you're going to cheat them. Special deals that you haven't told them about before can make them nervous.

Instead, keep on stressing the benefits, and the return on their investment. And it's very important to reassure the penny pincher by showing him or her everything in writing.

■ Time Pressure

The seventh type of person to clam up is the stop watch. This person is the master of time management. His entire day is broken down into 5-minute segments. He's all business, and he doesn't have time for chitchat. Be sure not to wreck his day by showing up late, and be sure to establish a time frame when you call to make the appointment. "This will take 30 minutes. Which would be better—Monday from 10 to 10:30 or from 11 to 11:30?"

Then when you get there, reconfirm the time frame. "So, Joe, you have 30 minutes that you can devote to this, right? May I close the door?"

Sometimes people who aren't necessarily time management freaks will clam up on you if they're running behind schedule. Be careful if the appointment is just before lunch or at the end of the day. Many people will avoid Fridays, and I wouldn't dream of trying to work with someone on the day before she leaves for her vacation.

Also remember that time pressure can work for you too. People become more flexible under time pressure. I've had tremendous luck getting banker loan approval on Friday afternoons. Bankers like to get their desks completely cleared off for the weekend and would rather not have any loose ends.

Whether you should avoid time pressure or try to use it in your favor depends on how good you think your chances are going in. If your request is within her normal parameters of doing business, go ahead and use time pressure. However, if your request is way out there, and will take a lot of persuading, you're better to schedule when the other person will have more time to work with you.

■ Fear

The eighth type of person to clam up is the paranoid. Some people get very talkative when they're scared, but most people clam up. If the other person is concerned you're going to take advantage of them, you can almost feel the temperature in the room drop. Look for the pupils of the eyes getting smaller and "withdrawal" body language, such as folded arms.

Quickly move to reassure the person, by telling him about your money-back guarantee and by going over the testimonial letters in your file. Perhaps you've been too pushy for their taste, so back off a little until they relax.

So while the simple answer may be that the way to get people to talk is to ask open-ended questions, you can see that there's much more to it than that. It takes a careful analysis of why the person has clammed up on you.

In this chapter, I've talked about one of the most challenging personalities with which to deal, the person who won't talk. As a Power Persuader, you'll come to relish the challenge of dealing with them.

■ KEY POINTS IN THIS CHAPTER

First, figure out why they won't talk. There are only eight reasons:

1. The first reason is obsession. People can't concentrate on what you're saying because they're obsessed with another issue. Confront the problem, but do it gently. "What is it that's bothering you, Joe? Perhaps I can help." If they're still too preoccupied to concentrate, set an appointment to discuss it later, or consider going for a fast close.

2. The second reason for silence may be inhibition. Some people won't talk simply because they're shy. Draw them out by asking open-ended questions.

3. The third reason is apathy. Some people aren't talking because they just don't care. They're probably upset about something else that has happened in their life. Romance them with talk of the good things in life, until they come back into focus.

4. The fourth type of clam is the sulker. They won't talk to you because they're still upset with you about something you did previously. Bring that repressed anger to the surface and get it out.

5. The fifth type of clam is the evaluator. This is the person who needs to think things through before they make a decision. Be quiet. Don't distract them by talking while they're thinking it over. When the evaluator starts talking again, but it isn't a question, it's time to go for the assume close.

6. The sixth kind of clam is the penny pincher. This person is so penurious, he gets nervous about having to spend money. Don't offer to reduce the price. Just keep on stressing the benefits and the return on his investment.

7. The seventh type of clam is the stop watch. This person has his entire day broken down into 5-minute segments. Be sure to establish a time frame when you call to make the appointment. Then when you get there, reconfirm the time frame. "So, Joe, you have 30 minutes that you can devote to this, right? May I close the door?"

8. The eighth type of person to clam up is the paranoid. Some people get very talkative when they're scared, but most people clam up. Quickly move to reassure the person by telling her about your money-back guarantee and by going over the testimonial letters in your file.

■ CHAPTER TWENTY-SEVEN

LEADERSHIP AND THE POWER PERSUADER

There's no greater power of persuasion than that exhibited by a great leader, the uncommon person who leads men into battle like Norman Schwarzkopf, inspires a nation like Winston Churchill, or resurrects a dying company like Lee Iacocca. How do these great leaders use Power Persuasion to get people to follow them? And how can we use those techniques to become great leaders ourselves?

If we had the skills, if we knew we couldn't fail, wouldn't it be great to lead a nation to victory or direct a great company to success—just once before we die?

■ THE LEADER'S DOCTRINE

I believe in a leader's doctrine so powerful that, if carried out fully and followed through to completion, it is sure to lead to great success.

This is the doctrine that I believe every leader should support with all their heart:

> "I care more about the success of my people than I do my future, but I care more about the organization accomplishing its mission than either one."

Great success in any enterprise comes from a balanced combination of three elements: the mission, the leadership, and the people who make it happen. By far the most important thing in this trinity is the mission. It's amazing to me how many organizations don't have a clear sense of purpose. Their people and assets are strewn around like a pile of iron filings, going in myriad different directions. Do you remember the experiment you did with iron filings when you were a kid? Just tossed in a heap on a piece of paper, the iron filings lay in a dozen different jumbled directions. Yet, when you pass a magnet under the paper, the filings are drawn to it and start lining up and moving in the same direction.

The mission is to the organization what the magnet is to the iron filings—it draws the organization together and gets its members moving in the same direction.

■ HOW TO DEVELOP THE MISSION

If you were to hire me to come into your company as a consultant, the first thing I'd do is sit with you and review your mission. That would probably tell me all I'd need to know. From that alone, I'd be able to tell you what's wrong with your business. I'd spend more time gathering data to support my conclusion, of course, but I could tell you what's wrong from the quality of your mission statement.

Harold Geneen is a legendary leader of American business. In the eighteen years that he ran ITT, he took the company from sales of $750 million a year, and struggling to make a profit, to a conglomerate with sales of $16.7 billion and annual profits of $562 million. Along the way he acquired 350 different businesses in eighty countries, so it's no exaggeration to say he knew a thing or two about building companies.

Geneen says that you build a company the way that you read a book—except that you read a book from start to finish, and you build a company in the opposite direction, from finish to start. First, you decide what the company is to become; then you research what's necessary to get the company from the start of the story—where you are now—to the conclusion—where you want to be.

So, first, you and I would sit down to discuss your mission statement. The four key elements of your mission are:

1. Do you know exactly where you want to be five years from now?
2. Is it clearly and definitively expressed in one paragraph or less?
3. Is it in language that a tenth grader could understand?
4. Is it a goal that will seem believable to everyone in your organization (not just the people of vision and self-assurance at the corporate office)?

If not, I'd suggest you go back to the drawing board and work on it more, because this one paragraph—your mission—is the key to your success as a leader.

■ THE FOUR KEY ELEMENTS OF THE MISSION

Let's look at each of these four elements:

First, do you know exactly where you want to be five years from now?

Sometimes it's less important that you make the right decision than that you make a decision, any decision. There's a tremendous release of energy that comes from the decision to move in a particular direction.

Have you ever been at a point in your life when you're frustrated and can't decide which way to go? If so, you know what I mean. The longer it takes you to decide, the lower your energy level goes. Once you pick a direction, any direction, a great release of vitality follows. Suddenly you feel better, and you can concentrate more clearly, knowing you're on the move.

Second, is your mission statement clearly and definitively expressed? Such as this: to get a 60 percent share of the widget market, with a 4.5 percent net profit before taxes, within a five-year period. Very good! It's clear, it's specific, and it has a time frame.

A specific mission statement also tends to narrow your focus. In the mid-1980s, United Airlines went into a disastrous diversification program, which included acquiring Hertz rental cars and Westin Hotels. It even dumped the name that had served the company so well over the years, and United Airlines became Allegis.

The effect on morale at the airline couldn't have been worse. While management was spending billions to acquire other companies, the flight attendants were on strike to protest a cut in wages. For several months it was hard to find a United Airlines employee who had anything good to say about his company. It took a stockholders' revolt, the firing of the president, and a well-written mission statement to get the company back on track.

Third, is your mission statement in language that a tenth grader could understand? Remember, you'll have to persuade your entire work force to follow you on this mission. Take a lesson from the carpenter from Galilee—put it in terms everyone can comprehend. When Jesus said to Peter and Simon, "Follow me, and I will make you fishers of men," it was easy for them to understand. Also, he kept bringing them back into focus, with simple statements such as, "What shall it profit a man, if he shall gain the whole world, and lose his own soul?" Thank goodness that Jesus didn't have a Harvard MBA! He'd have had his mission wrapped up in so much metaphysical mumbo jumbo, that what He accomplished in a year of preaching, would've taken decades.

And, fourth, will your mission statement be believable to everyone in the organization, not just the movers and the shakers? When Lee Iacocca made his mission statement for the salvation of Chrysler Corporation, he didn't attempt to say the company was going to sell more cars than General Motors. He didn't even say the goal was to be more profitable than General Motors. The average employee quickly dismisses that kind of hyperbole.

He simply said, "We're going to make the best cars in America." That was something that all but the most pessimistic employee could believe was possible. Also, it was in plain enough language for them to understand.

■ THE IMPORTANCE OF INFORMING THE TROOPS

Having clarified your mission statement, in an easy-to-understand paragraph, your next job is to see that everyone in the organization knows what it is.

The problem is that most executives feel the employees are too simpleminded to understand something as complicated as corporate goals. Or are too apathetic to care. So they keep the objectives of the corporation privileged information in the executive suite and attempt to get the employees in line with manipulation.

I believe that all employees can understand a well-thought-out and clearly written mission.

It's easy to spot the companies that have done this. It's the bellman who walks you to your room and says, "If there's anything at all you need, you just call me. Our goal is to have the highest occupancy rate of any hotel in the city, and we can only do it if you're happy."

It's the secretary at the real estate company who says, "We'll really work hard for you. Our objective is always to have the highest number of sold listings in our multiple listing service."

It's the service manager at the auto dealership saying, "We'll be happy to take care of it for you. We sold more pickup trucks than any other Ford dealer in the state last month and we plan to do it again every month this year. We need you out there—telling people how good we are."

All those things have happened to me, but as you know, companies like that are rare.

■ USING PERSUASION SKILLS TO SELL THE MISSION

Having clearly projected the goal to everyone in the organization, it's time to put your persuasion skills to work: to convince the people the organization is going to accomplish its mission. That's where all the things we've talked about in this book come into play.

The number one factor in leadership persuasion is the ability to project that you have a consistent set of standards by which you operate. The same persuasion factor about which we talked in Chapter Eight.

We all admire tough-minded leaders who have the courage to take a stand. However, all too often, we glorify them for all the wrong reasons. We admire Harry Truman because he "gave 'em hell." It may be true that he "gave 'em hell," but that's not the reason we admire him. We admire him because he believed in something, and he projected the belief in his philosophy with all his heart.

Do we admire Lee Iacocca because of his tough language and his streetwise willingness to fight? No, we admire him because of his unwavering commitment in his beliefs. We respect conviction, not belligerence.

Ronald Reagan became the most popular president of this century, although the vast majority of Americans didn't believe in many things he did, because we're drawn to people who fervently fight for that in which they believe.

■ BUILDING LEADERSHIP CREDIBILITY

The next most important persuasion factor for leaders is credibility. Be sure you're applying the credibility factors we talked about in Chapter Two. The first rule for credibility is, "never tell them more than they'll believe." I hope you've built that into your mission statement. If you have any doubts about the credibility of your mission to the average employee, tone it down. You might want to run it by a few people in the field, to test their reaction. A mission should be grand enough to be inspiring, but don't lose your credibility by stepping over the line into "never, never happen" land.

We talked about using precise numbers when quoting statistics. "Ivory Soap is 99 and 44/100ths pure," seems very believable, when we might not believe 100 percent pure. That's why Taster's Choice decaffeinated coffee is 99.7 percent caffeine free. If your expressed goal is a 20 percent increase in productivity, it may sound as if it's a figure dreamed up in a committee meeting. A 21.6 percent increase looks as though somebody really made an effort to come up with an accurate figure.

Minimizing the perception of personal gain was the next factor we discussed. Lee Iacocca made a brilliant move when he agreed to work for a dollar a year, as he was asking the unions to roll back pay. Because of his stock options, it wasn't a huge concession, but the symbolism of it was enormous. Later, when he started making $20 million a year, he could make a case it was justified because of the sacrifices he'd made earlier.

Also, don't forget the power of the printed word. People believe much more what they see in writing than they do when they only hear it. Don't make the plant look as if Nazi propagandist Paul Goebbels runs your P.R. department, but putting posters of your mission statement up around the plant is a powerful force. It makes the doubters believe the goal is achievable, and they love the fact that you've stuck your neck out.

Remember the "if they can do it, I can do it" syndrome we talked about in Chapter Two? As you move toward your goal, you'll want to give recognition to the top producers in your newsletters and promotional pieces. However, be aware that many people react to this with a shrug of the shoulders. They can't relate to the superstars in your business. Power Persuaders know to include some "if they can do it, I can do it" stories. Tell the story of the person who moved off the assembly line into sales and sold $10,000 the first month. It'll have a lot more impact than a piece about the superstar who sold $10 million worth.

■ BUILDING CREDIBILITY WHEN YOU'RE NEW ON THE JOB

If you're new on the job, there may be some additional things you need to do to build credibility. I've been giving this advice to new managers for twenty years: don't try to set the world on fire in the first thirty days. Unless you've been sent in to save a dying company—like Sanford Sigoloff when he took over Wickes—you're better off to lay low during the first month. You won't be able to do much good in the first thirty days, and you could harm your credibility.

It's better to go to your office, put your feet up on the desk, and sit around for a while. Let them get used to the idea of a new leader. In thirty days they'll have forgotten that there was somebody else before you, and you can start to make your moves. You might want to let the head office know what you're up to, so that they're not wondering what's going on.

Not that this first month need be unproductive. Far from it. You can do a lot of getting to know people. Reread Chapter Twenty-two on remembering names, and see how many of your employees' names you can learn. Do some management by walking around. Hold meetings with the different departments, and do more listening than you do talking.

Try this approach, "I'm new here, and I don't know enough yet to help you with the big problems. But maybe I can help you with the little problems. Who's got a little problem that's been bugging them?"

You'll be surprised at the little things the employees have given up trying to get done. You'll hear things like, "If there was a clock on the wall in the employee lunchroom, it would be a lot easier to get back to work on time." Or "How come there's never any paper towels in the rest room when we get off work?"

It's a chance to be a real hero to your people without having to play fast and loose with the company till. Be careful they don't bring up something that previous management has consistently rejected, for good reason. It's important to follow through on every commitment you make, however small it may be. It's a good idea to have a knowledgeable assistant with you who can signal you if you're about to get into trouble.

Also be aware that, if you're new, you may not be as well known as you think. Your management team may know that you've earned this promotion because of the brilliant job that you did at the Cincinnati plant, but does the rank and file know?

Michael Crichton, author of *The Andromeda Strain, The Terminal Man,* and *Sphere,* tells a story about this in his autobiographical book *Travels.* He had just completed directing the movie *Coma* and it was being released in the United States with great success. Now he had been hired to direct *The Great Train Robbery* starring Sean Connery, to be filmed in Ireland. When he showed up on location, he began to feel frustrated because he wasn't getting full cooperation from the British crew. When he proposed an idea, they'd want to discuss alternatives rather than enthusiastically carrying out the suggestion.

In the understated style of the English, one of his assistants casually said, "I think the crew would enjoy seeing one of your films." However, Michael didn't pick up on it. A few days later, the problems had worsened, and the assistant said, "I wish we could see one of your films." Michael thought about it, and then didn't do anything. *Coma* was just being released in the States, and it wouldn't be easy for him to get a copy.

Finally, the assistant said firmly, "I really do think it would be nice if the crew had a chance to view one of your films." Suddenly, Michael realized what the assistant had been trying to tell him, but had been too reserved to come out and state in plain language. The crew knew him only as an author; they had no knowledge of his abilities as a director. He called Hollywood and had a copy of *Coma* airfreighted to him, and they screened it for the entire crew. Overnight the problem went away. The crew had loved the film, gained new respect for his abilities, and never questioned his decisions again.

So be sure everyone is told about your background and experience. Obviously, you can't do this yourself, or you'll seem egotistical. However, your public relations department can handle it subtly for you, or your staff can see that the right things get said in the company newsletter.

■ LEADERSHIP AND THE ART OF CONSISTENCY

The next factor that's critical to your leadership persuasion ability is consistency. Is the mission consistent with all they know about you? People can spot a phony a mile off. You're going to have a tough time if the mission is disseminated and the people say, "Oh, oh! The boss must have been to another one of those seminars!" Top leaders are successful in large part because their actions are consistent with what people know about them.

Remember the personal value blueprint we talked about in Chapter Nine? The set of standards we use to overlay our life? If the decision you're about to make doesn't conform to your blueprint, don't do it, despite the potential gain.

A business value blueprint is essential to your success as a leader. Your people are much more concerned about what you stand for than they are about what you're claiming you can do. When they perceive that you've a set of standards by which you operate, it makes them feel more secure. They know that you won't behave erratically, acting outside the perimeters of your values. What you are overrides what you do, every time.

■ CARING MORE ABOUT THE SUCCESS OF YOUR PEOPLE

Now let's review our leadership doctrine again. "I care more about the success of my people than I do my future, but I care more about the organization accomplishing its mission than either one."

Nothing will stop a leader faster than their followers being convinced that the leader is pursuing the mission for personal gain—

whether that gain is making money, getting promoted, or becoming famous. They can live with their leader getting those things, but it must be as a by-product of the mission. It cannot be the purpose of the mission.

So the accomplished leader is skilled in projecting that he cares more about his people's success than he does about his own. If you do it well, you can get away with making $20 million in one year, as Lee Iacocca did, and still not have the peasants storming the palace gates.

■ THE MISSION IS THE MOST IMPORTANT THING

Next, you must persuade your people that the organization making its mission is more important than the individual success of any one person—including you. This is what separates the superstar leader from the merely great. That takes real Power Persuasion skills, but it can be done. It's possible to get your people so worked up about a mission that even if they personally fall by the wayside, they'll still cheer the organization on.

Nowhere is this illustrated more clearly than in the sport of mountaineering. I recently returned to climb Mount Rainier in Washington. I'd done it before in 1970, now I was returning with my daughter, who was only 6 years old when I first climbed it. I was anxious to expose her to the sport and also, frankly, to see if I could still do it.

At the 13,000-foot level, we ran into Phil Ershler, who has climbed Mount Rainier more than any other man alive, over 200 times. Phil was the central character in one of the most exciting annals of mountain climbing history. He was a member of the 1984 team that attempted to climb Everest from the North Side, from China, rather than the more popular route through Nepal. Only sixteen people had ever done this before, and ten had died attempting it.

They were led by Lou Whittaker, whose brother Jim was the first American on the summit of Everest, back in 1963. Also in the team was Lou's son, Peter, who had become an accomplished mountaineer in his own right. It was clearly Lou's dream that his son reach the top, but the team had enough confidence in Lou's leadership abilities to know that his son wouldn't get preferential treatment.

They'd attempted this climb two years before, with disastrous results. Marty Hoey and Chris Kerrebrock had fallen to their deaths in separate incidents. And this climb wasn't going well either. Bad weather pinned them down for weeks. Lou Whittaker's sun goggles failed him, and he had to retreat to base camp with snow blindness. Refusing help from his team members, who were needed to continue carrying supplies up the mountain, he descended blind and alone. It was almost a week before he would see again.

With their supplies almost exhausted, they made a last-ditch effort and sent a team of three climbers, Phil Ershler, John Roskelley, and Jim Wickwire, to the summit. Bad weather forced them to bivouac on the mountain overnight. Ershler and Wickwire were using oxygen, but Roskelley didn't believe in using it. It was against his principles to climb with the aid of oxygen, and Whittaker had reluctantly accepted this. However, now only one bottle of oxygen remained. Wickwire felt that Ershler was in better condition, and unselfishly told him to take the oxygen and go for the summit with Roskelley.

The two men got within a thousand feet of the summit and Roskelley could go no further. Without oxygen, his body was beginning to freeze from the inside. He insisted that Ershler unrope and go on alone.

They were not in visual or radio contact with Whittaker at Camp Four. But, miles away, expedition photographer Steve Marts, with a high-powered telephoto lens, could see the two men separate and Ershler start moving almost imperceptibly toward the 29,000-foot summit.

Even with oxygen it's very hard to move at that altitude, and every step takes individual effort. Raise the boot and kick the spiked crampons into the snow to form a foothold. Lock the other leg into place and rest for a second or two, allowing the oxygen in the bloodstream to reach the muscles, and then go for that next step upward. Concentrate, because it's all too easy to hallucinate when you're that high, and forget where you are.

Hours later he reached the summit ridge and crossed from China into Nepal. Inch by inch, profiled against the midnight blue sky, he moved upward until he stood on the summit. "We made it!" shouted Marts into the radio, relaying the success to the climbers down at the lower camp, who couldn't see the summit. "We made it!" Whittaker yelled at base camp, "we made it."

The fascinating thing about all this, from a management point of view, is that the leader, Lou Whittaker, didn't make it to the summit. His son didn't make it. Every person except Phil Ershler failed in what they had personally set out to do. Yet they all felt a tremendous sense of personal pride because the team had completed the mission. They didn't say that Phil Ershler made it, they said, "we made it." When I talked to Phil about it, not once did he say, "I climbed Mount Everest." He simply said, "I was on the team that climbed Mount Everest."

It's a case study in brilliant leadership. Let's examine the two key components:

1. In terms of who would make it to the summit, Lou Whittaker had put himself and his son behind the others in importance. It's the first part of the leader's doctrine: "I care more about the success of my people than I do my future."

2. He had projected to the team that the mission was more important than the personal goals of any one person on the team. That's the second part of the leader's doctrine: "I care more about the organization accomplishing its mission than either one."

With the leader's doctrine, you can build that kind of dedication and esprit de corp at your company. Then, you will be able to reach all your goals and be a hero to your people.

■ PAINTING THE PICTURE OF THE MISSION

Mountain climbing isn't the only area in which the mission becomes more important than either the leader or the followers. Look at the story of Moses leading the Israelites out of Egypt. His mission was clear: to lead them to the promised land. However, he had a unique leadership problem. His followers knew he'd never seen the promised land—no one had ever seen the promised land. His ability to sell his followers on the mission depended largely on his skill at painting pictures in the minds of his followers.

Moses never reached the promised land, and many of his followers didn't get there. However, the mission was accomplished. Moses had given more value to the accomplishment of the mission than he had to himself, or any other member of the team, making the goal.

■ THE ESSENCE OF PERSUASIVE LEADERSHIP

This, then, is the essence of persuasive leadership, the leader's doctrine:

> "I care more about the success of my people than I do my future, but I care more about the organization accomplishing its mission than either one."

■ KEY POINTS IN THIS CHAPTER

1. Great success in any enterprise comes from a balanced combination of three elements: the mission, the leadership, and the people who make it happen. The most important of these is the mission.

2. First, you decide what the company is to become; then, you find out what's necessary to get the company to that goal.

3. The four key elements of your mission are these:

   a. Knowing exactly where you want to be five years from now

   b. Clearly and definitively expressing the mission in one paragraph or less

   c. Using language that a tenth grader could understand

   d. Making the goal believable to everyone in the organization

4. Don't hide your mission in the executive suite! All employees can understand a well-thought-out and clearly written mission.

5. Project that you have a consistent set of standards by which you operate.

6. Build credibility with the tools I gave you in Chapter Two.

7. Unless you've been sent in to save a dying company, don't try to set the world on fire in the first thirty days. Build support by offering to solve the little problems.

8. If your reputation got you the job, be sure your employees know about your reputation.

9. Your people are much more concerned about what you stand for, than they are about what you're claiming you can do. Be consistent in your actions.

10. Believe in and live by the leader's doctrine: "I care more about the success of my people than I do my future, but I care more about the organization accomplishing its mission than either one."

■ E P I L O G U E

THE SECRET OF POWER PERSUASION

So what is persuasion? It's the ability to get someone else to do what you want him or her to do, whether by reasoning, urging, or inducement. That translates into the ability to make something happen. Persuaders are the motivating force in our society, whether it's a parent persuading a child to live by a set of moral and ethical standards, or a teacher in an inner-city school persuading students that they can rise above their circumstances, or a business leader persuading the employees of a company that they can reach new heights of accomplishment, or a national leader causing people to believe so strongly in their country that they're willing to die for it.

I've tried to show that Power Persuasion is a combination of factors: of personal charisma, of the ability to project personal standards that are inspiring, and of a deep understanding that the essence of Power Persuasion is that others will move in a given direction only when they feel that it's in their best interest to make that move.

So the key to effective persuasion isn't to concentrate on what you want to get from the other person. Power Persuaders know the secret of Power Persuasion is to focus on what you can give to the other person—understanding that when you give people what they want, they'll give you what you want.

■ INDEX